D1539857

COLLEGE GIRL

COLLEGE GIRL
a memoir

Laura Gray-Rosendale

excelsior editions

State University of New York Press
Albany, New York

Published by State University of New York Press, Albany

Excelsior Editions is an imprint of State University of New York Press

For information, contact State University of New York Press, Albany, NY
www.sunypress.edu

Production by Ryan Morris
Marketing by Fran Keneston

Library of Congress Cataloging-in-Publication Data

Gray-Rosendale, Laura.
College girl : a memoir / Laura Gray-Rosendale.
    p. cm.
 Includes bibliographical references.
 ISBN 978-1-4384-4709-4 (hardcover : alk. paper) 1. Gray-Rosendale, Laura.
2. College teachers—United States—Biography. I. Title.
LA2317.G635A3 2013
378.0092—dc23
 [B]
                    2012027402

10 9 8 7 6 5 4 3 2

ACKNOWLEDGMENTS

I cannot begin to express my gratitude toward those responsible for bringing this book to fruition. Thanks to the folks at SUNY Press—Beth Bouloukos, Fran Keneston, Larin McLaughlin, Ryan Morris, James Peltz, and Priscilla Ross. To Kass Fleisher, Michael Kimmel, Cathy Small, and Alexis Washam for early advice and support. To Linda Martín Alcoff, Jane Armstrong, Monica Brown, Sherry Greene Gelinas, Janna Jones, Rosemary Mild, Donald Mills, Tara O'Connor, and Karen Underhill for kindness along the way. To the District Attorney's Office of Onondaga County, New York, and the Syracuse Police Department. To the Verde Valley's Cancer Center, Dr. Deborah Lindquist and her staff, for seeing me through treatment. To all who have shared these experiences with me. Though your real names may not appear in these pages, you are this story's heroes and heroines. To my dear family—Mom, Dad, and Dave. And, finally, thanks to Steve, whose love makes this book (and this life) possible.

This is a true story. All this happened, more or less, as a famous writer once said.[1] This book represents years of research—consultation with journals I wrote, interviews with people involved, analyses of news reports, discovery of legal and medical documents, as well as the study of relevant academic scholarship. Conversations, time lines, and details have been altered where necessary. Some names have been changed.

PART
ONE

CHAPTER ONE

I probably dreamed that night.

It was probably the one where I'm in poetry class, listening to Dr. Yingling's soft voice read *The Wasteland*. Or that other one where I've been mysteriously transported into that cartoon show *Fantastic Four* with Lindsey and we're invisible or crazy strong or extra-stretchy and we're fighting off all manner of evil with our super-duper powers. There must have been the billowy touch of comforter over my face, that feeling of being burrowed so cozy deep it's hard to tell whether anyone's there at all except for the tiniest wisp of yellow hair visible on a pillow. There had to be big snore sounds, me waking myself up from half-remembered dreams.

These things probably happened.

But I won't remember them.

I'll remember this.

A fistful of my hair jerks me back.

There's a slabby male figure leaning over me, pants bunched around his hips.

I screech into the blackness, my fingers hunting for my glasses.
Pages are crackling on the floor.
A hand shuts off my scream.
I thrash, strain my neck to see a face.
It's gigantic, vacant, blank. Like a blackboard.
Outlined chin and jaw loom over me. I try to scribble in eyes, nose, lips.
But I can't call up chalk.
He moves his hand.
I scream.
Thick fingers jam up my throat. My tongue swells.
Leathery sweat fills my nostrils.

CHAPTER TWO

Unraveling mummies, togas with plastic ivy wreathes, and mouth-breathing zombies in melting faces shuffle the puke-stained wood floor. An artsy couple—she all in white, he in brown—flounces in.

She yells over the fuzzy music to no one in particular.

"We're not in costume! We're concepts! I'm a roll of toilet paper and he's a steaming pile of ex-cre-ment!"

It's Halloween at Red House, the architecture frat creatively named for its crimson exterior, and I'm leaning against a wall, inventorying the stiletto hole-punches I've made in the hem of my black velvet dress. My long black Morticia wig's plastered my blonde-streaked hair to my head. My black lipstick's turned a bizarre, vomited-up green color. Eyeliner is streaming onto my contacts, my pasted-on black eyelashes cemented together in gummy clumps. Thus my latest decision—to forego blinking.

This was a mistake. I knew I should have stayed home to work on that poetry paper.

I weave my way over to the black cauldron in the hallway—steaming with dry ice and jam-packed with plastic baby doll-heads and legs and arms—and ladle out a glass of grain alcohol and Hawaiian Punch. I sip. Doll toes rub my lips.

Then I see her—my way out of here stumbling toward me. My friend Missy—tonight all dressed up and resembling some manner of rodent more than usual (mouse? rat? vole? mole? rabbit? boomer?)—has the look of someone considering leaving.

"Poser-ville," I say, smacking my B&H Menthol Light pack so one junior-minty cig stems out.

"Gonna do a line?"

Missy's always about the coke. I shake my head.

"Let's get out of here."

I go toward the door, Missy skittle-scurrying after me. I begin to excavate the mound of coats on the stairs in search of my own. Then suddenly everything skews, goes sideways off kilter. It feels like a stone wall's crashing down on my shoulders. My back and knees crumple, and I'm biology-frog pinned to the floor. There's the stench of stale beer, vodka. There's a male voice that sounds like a combination of ugly baby and feral animal. His taller, dark-haired friend yanks him off me with a laugh.

"Sorry, he gets this way when he's plastered."

I pick myself off the floor, glance behind me.

"Tell your friend to keep his hands to himself." I hitch up my dress, attempt to exit without tripping. Missy and I edge into the night.

"You 'kay?"

"I'm so sick of these parties."

"Know what you mean."

Please. That girl doesn't have a clue.

And I'm still not done either. I promised my best friend Lindsey I'd go to one more party tonight. So I drop Missy at her dorm, hustle down Comstock alone, wend toward Lindsey's house on the border of Thornden Park.

Lindsey transferred to Syracuse University from Boston College about a year ago. We met when I auditioned for Thornton Wilder's *Long Christmas Dinner*, a play she was stage managing. I just liked her immediately. She has a gawky confidence, a smart, quirky sense of humor, can mold her silly-putty face into impossible expressions. Lindsey's also kind—piling up hours of time caring for a homeless man who lives in a fridge box, the Hermit of Chestnut Hill. She boogied from BC after smoking so much weed that everything spilled out of her head, including the fact that she was taking classes and had to put food in herself. But all that's so history. Now when you mention herbs around her you'd better be talking Celestial Seasonings.

Since she's Boston native and I'm New Hampshire, on weekends and holidays we careen highway 90 in her burgundy-colored Chevy Malibu boat. Lindsey drives like a pruned-up mafia guy, eyes barely peering over the steering wheel, gesticulates wildly. The first three letters of her state-issued license plate read "LEZ." This led some brainiac to key "ASSHOLE" on one side of her car, "LEZZY" on the other (all capitals). After that Lindsey was certainly within rights to get a paint job or request a different plate. Instead she raved she was honored to be taken for a lesbian, named it the Asshole Lezmobile, Lezzy for short.

Before I can knock, Lindsey busts open the door wearing giant, bulbous glasses, mismatched socks. I shed my Morticia wig and stilettos, pad with her up the wood stairs to her apartment. We perch at her table, slurp tea from earth-brown clay mugs.

"What are you? A hellacious witch?" she asks in a Chelmsford accent that'd make you swear the word *are* is spelled *ahh*.

"Morticia, you moron."

I don't tell her about my favorite Halloween costume ever, how I'd had my heart set on being a woodstove for years, how Mom made that papier-mâché costume with the paper-towel-roll stove pipe and crackling-cellophane fire, how I couldn't see in there, kept smashing into trees, fences, other kids. And I for sure don't tell her how wicked awesome I thought it was.

"Cousin It, more like it."

"Suck it, weenis."

Giggling, Lindsey sprints upstairs, zips into her costume, boomerangs back. Her stringy, half-Italian and half-Syrian, five-foot-two self is sporting black-and-white striped tights, a golden bowler-type hat bedazzled with multicolored glass gems, and a purple velvet minidress. Lind's black hair, usually pulled back with last week's broccoli elastic, now swings loose at her shoulders. She looks like the unlikely offspring of Ronald McDonald, the Burger King, and Grimace.

"And what are *you*? A messed-up Happy Meal?"

"Yeah!"

We drive to the party in the Lezzy. Lindsey wouldn't be going except she knows the guy who's throwing it. Maybe they went to high school together. He's swigging beer, trying to make some serious eye contact. Lindsey doesn't even notice.

A squat puff-marshmallow guy's fast-jabbering at me, something about being the most-serious-drug-dealer ever. His voice saws on and on, totally drowning out that old R.E.M, and I'm concentrating on the samples of Stipe's burbling brook of a voice sneaking through. This round dude is *blah, blah, blah*, a rifle being pointed in his face, the load of dough he rakes in each night, his fan club of strippers.

I make my best, tight, can-we-get-the-heck-out-of-here face at Lindsey. She smiles, nods in my direction. I spy her tell that guy we're leaving and he looks mounds of disappointed. I say good-bye to the squat dealer dude. He doesn't miss a beat, begins talking rifle, drugs, and strippers with someone else.

Lindsey yellow-brick-road skips over, puts her arm through mine.

"Now. The real fun."

She nabs my coat from the table, hurls it at me, wraps her faded army jacket around her. We pile into the Lezzy and Lind yanks her humungous glasses out of the glove box, shoves them on her face, zips her jacket right underneath her chin, readying herself for some sort of Secret Ops. But I have no idea what kind.

Next thing I know we're snaking down frat row in the Lezzy, headlights off.

"Them."

A prepped-out couple is walking on the sidewalk thirty feet ahead of us. Lindsey pulls up right next to them, slows down until we're barely inching along. She throws on the high-beams, downs her window. Lindsey turns her devilish head in their direction, snatches a cleaver-type chef's knife from her pocket with the other.

"*Bo-o-o-o ay-a-a-a wha-a-a-a!*" she cackles, swiping metal in the direction of their noses.

"What da . . . ?"

We don't hear his swear words cause we're gone, Lindsey putting the knife back in place, zipping up that window, killing lights, careening down Walnut. A band of about ten guys and girls are sloshed together on the corner.

"You like 'em?" she whispers.

"Lots."

The Lezzy eases to a clunkish near-stop. Lindsey lets down the window extra slow, and the group leans in closer, checks us out.

"*Bo-o-o-o ay-a-a-a wha-a-a-a!*" Lindsey screeches, that sharp gleam leaping out of her pocket.

Their expressions go from fear to puzzlement to laughter. "That's great. Totally . . ."

We don't hear how that sentence finishes either because we're on to our next victims. A half a dozen of these encounters later, we arrive at my apartment on Ostrom.

"Night."

She's the world's biggest dweeb and she's beyond friggin' fantastic.

"Careful with that knife."

"My work's done for the evening."

"Night, weirdo."

She shoots me a maniac grin, peels away. I walk in and my roommate, Sal, her wild Stevie Nicks–hair speckled with paint, is propped against the wall in her pj's, hoovering chocolate chip cookies. Last year when she and Miriam and I were roommates, they made up a significant part of our diet. Our new roommate Cathy's already in bed.

"Have fun?"

I nod as Sal hockey-pucks that box in my direction. I snarf three, shoot the rest back. Grainy news flickers on the screen.

"What do you guess Mir's doing right now?" I ask.

Miriam's my other best friend, a theater major who's in London for the entire semester, lucky dog. I thought to go too. But I didn't apply. I tell myself that this is because it would have screwed up my credits for graduating on time. And that's true. But the extra cost and my own inertia also factored in plenty.

Miriam's like a radiant-beating sun, a ball of pure energy with shiny black curls, splashing ocean eyes. She's never dated anyone seriously, won't smoke or drink. Plus Miriam's real kind and protective. One time some sailor on shore leave locked down on my arm when I tried to exit a bar. Miriam just glowered at him, *thwumped* him in the chest, pried his fingers away, called him an asswipe. That word sounded almost beautiful coming out of her mouth. Miriam's tried explaining how to read music to me, too, though I'm worse than terrible at it, can't seem to follow directions. And Mir's attempted to convince me not to study so hard. But I'm not so good at that either.

Miriam's a serious triple threat—a singer and dancer who can actually act, too. She, Sal, and I have a game plan. When we imagine ourselves in twenty years, it's like this. Sal's a world renowned painter. Miriam's a famous actress, dancer, and singer on Broadway. Who I am changes, but usually I'm some sort of writer-actress combo because of my dual majors in English and theater. The three of us are living together senior year when Miriam gets back. Until then, we put an ad in the paper for a new roommate and Cathy answered. We don't know much about her but she seems nice, pays the rent on time.

"Mir? Probably racing around London."

I nod, say night to Sal, trudge to my room, flip the light, slough off my costume to the floor, squirm into my long underwear, flop onto the futon. The floor around me is a yard sale of textbooks for my classes plus a script from Luigi Pirandello's *Six Characters in Search of an Author*.[1] In December I'll be performing the lead role of the stepdaughter for the Black Box Theatre, a student-run company. I could go over my lines again—but they're pretty well memorized, plus all night I've been thinking about poetry. So I skooch up my glasses and pry open my overhighlighted copy of *The Complete Poems of Hart Crane*.

Two hours later I wake with my face in its mildewy, used-book pages. My sleep-crusty eyes retrace the beginning of "Passage."

"Where the cedar leaf divides the sky / I heard the sea. / In sapphire arenas of the hills / I was promised an improved infancy." Lovely words—"the cedar leaf," "the sapphire hills."

I glance at the end—"What fountains did I hear? What icy speeches? / Memory, committed to the page, had broke."[2] Glum words—"icy speeches," "had broke."

And across those serious middle words about the "chimney-sooted heart of man" I've left some fabulous new lipstick drool punctuation.

CHAPTER THREE

For the next three weeks I'm consumed with Scene Study.

Scene Study is a huge deal. It's where you perform a play scene in front of the whole theater department, hundreds of people. Mr. R—he's the psychiatrist in *The Exorcist* who gets thrown up on by Linda Blair's spinning head, plus he's directed Al Pacino, Joanne Woodward, and Alan Alda (around here, he's the *shit*)—criticizes the heck out of you. It's supposed to be demeaning, painful, even downright horrifying. Sucking it up is what makes you a better actor.

Mr. R has never let an English major into his Actor's Workshop class before. Plus I'm an undergraduate and it's mainly graduate students in the class. But he likes me for reasons I don't understand. I have guts, he tells me, maybe even talent. My grandfather's age, he sports a weird, permanently evil eye—one that is three times as large and steady as his other puny one. When Mr. R took me on as an independent study last summer, he told me that I had a "good look" and appeared "Mediterranean." I bounced my head like I for sure understood, but I hadn't the faintest idea about what any of that stuff meant. He also told me I should lose the slouch. "Act like a woman," he boomed at me as if all those years of having his own theater teachers scream "Projection!" at him were finally paying off.

Then he asked me if I had ever seduced someone before. I said I wasn't sure.

The scene he chose for me for Scene Study is from that play *Extremities* by William Mastrosimone. The stage notes read that it was first produced in 1981 starring Ellen Barber, then in 1982 starring Susan Sarandon.[1] The time seems oddly timeless—"The present. September." The place is "Between Trenton and Princeton, New Jersey, where the cornfield meets the highway." The set is "the living room of an old farm house."[2] The stage is spare—just a dining room table and chairs, a sofa and table, several doors, a fireplace, a window filled with plants, stairs, a locked bike against the wall.

I'm doing this scene with a boy who has translucent hair, wire glasses, and Levis. He's way more comfortable building sets than walking on stage. I play the rape victim, Marjorie. He plays the rapist, Raul. Our read-through the other night was supremely mediocre. This guy just can't do rapist. There's also the problem of him being washed out and tow-headed—not exactly a "Raul" type. Plus my character's motivation makes no sense to me whatsoever. So I approached Mr. R about all this. He was trying to escape the theater building, heading toward Philomel's restaurant across the street.[3]

I told Mr. R I didn't have the foggiest idea what the heck to do with the scene. I explained that I have ten years of karate training, could kick the living crap out of someone if he tried to rape me. Why would I sit there and take it, just let it happen to me? All that time I never took my own contact-filled eyes off Mr. R's undulating evil one, staring sideways at me. I barely noticed that I was keeping him, let alone that I was holding him up in the middle of oncoming traffic turning onto Irving Street.

"It's harder than you think to fight off someone twice your size."

He moved toward the road's shoulder.

"Think about that."

I nodded, thanked him as he disappeared after his dinner. But that was a totally lame answer.

Now I walk from my bedroom to the kitchen, set the play on the counter. I fill our one saucepan with water, set it on the stove, click on the gas. Waiting for the water to boil, I read through the scene again.

Marjorie's in her bathrobe, looking at the breakfast dishes, putting on a kettle of water, making a phone call, spraying wilted plants with water. That's a lot to happen before the scene even begins. Yet the stage directions say—"Don't rush the action. It's a lazy day. There are no pressing concerns." Yeah, right. The stage directions close with "A wasp attacks her. She swipes at it. The plant drops. We hear pottery crack. She is stung by the wasp." Her first words in the scene are "Dammit to hell!" Then she grabs a can of insecticide, shakes it vigorously, studies that poor wasp meaningfully, sprays it. Even when it looks dead already, Marjorie keeps right on spraying. Then she contemplates the wasp's wings while burning them slowly with her cigarette.

I put the play pages between my teeth, bite down, open a box of spaghetti with my free hands. Mr. R keeps making a big deal about this wasp stuff, how it foreshadows her ability later in the script to turn the table on the rapist. Marjorie eventually sprays him in the face too, sears him with tea water, puts a noose around his neck, and stuffs him in the fireplace.

I sink a handful of noodles into the sizzling water, take the play out of my mouth, read each line several times. Marjorie's "Dammit to hell!" and Raul's "Joe? Hey, Joe? It's me. O. How ya doin? Joe in?" Their interaction goes on for almost three pages before the attempted rape occurs. She tries every tactic she can to get rid of him, finally lying and saying that her cop husband is asleep upstairs, will come beat him up. But the rapist is wise to her, doesn't believe her. "Maybe you're tellin me alittle lie eh, pretty momma? Maybe you think I scare easy. Go 'head. Go for the door. Let's see who's faster. So where's the other two chicks that live here?"

So Raul's been casing this joint for some time. I'm making a mental note that I have to tell my scene partner to remember this. Geeze, I have to think of everything. I set the play down, shut off the burner. I grab two scrap loop pot-holders, drain the noodles with the pan lid, slide the noodles onto a plate, set the pot in the sink, leave the plate on the counter.

I pick up the script again. The stage directions then read, "She runs. He latches onto her hair, brings her down, mounts her, and forces a pillow to her face. We hear muffled screams." Those verbs bother me—"latches," "mounts," "forces." He tells her, "Don't fight me. I don't want to hurt you. You're too sweet to hurt. Be nice. You smell pretty. Is that your smell or the perfume? Be nice. Wanna take a shower together first? I'll soap you up real good? Flip me a little smile, babe. I'm gonna fuck you frontways, backways, and ways you never heard of."

This is beyond yuck. I set the play down again, look at my naked spaghetti, grab a jar of sauce, dump half onto the tepid mass, set it back on the counter. I'm not squeamish as girls go, but the words are so darn graphic.

I wish Mr. R was not making me do this.

Method acting requires that I have a motivation for every line. To do this, I'm supposed to recall experiences that will help me understand this woman's situation. I take one of our three forks from the silverware drawer, noodle-wind through the sauce. I take a bite. It's cold, slimy. I take another.

I need to reflect on all of the grim stuff I've been through. You would think at twenty there would not be much to pull from. But I have a few things to try. There's being sent away at fourteen to Northfield Mount Hermon (NMH) boarding school, paid for with Grandpa and parent money scrabbled together.

Mom had her reasons. Our sleepy, no-stoplight town—Mason, New Hampshire—exemplified New England charm. The dirt road we lived on was more pothole than anything else. There were annual summer strawberry festivals with makeshift parades, cider-press Falls, winter snow angels and hot Ovaltine, wet-earth lilac springs. Houses were heated with the wood we chopped ourselves, and all the dogs roamed happy and leash-less. But it was understood that I'd have to leave there if I was going to get a good education or make anything of myself. And I know Mom had other reasons for sending me away, too, like the swelling stomach of that sixteen-year-old Mormon girl at the end of the road.

I nudge the remains of the spaghetti and sauce into our open garbage can with my fork, set my dirties in the sink, put the jar in the fridge, turn off the kitchen light. Play in hand, I walk to my room, close the door. I kick off my sneakers, plunk Indian-style on my futon, which is flat on the floor, pushed against the far wall. I remove my contacts, put on my glasses, stare down at the pages.

Leaving my brother Dave, four and a half years younger, was like forgetting an arm. And it meant other seriously crappy things, too—like saying good-bye to our mother-and-daughter yellow Labs, Honey Bear and Lady Tawnee Pooh Bear of Mandalay, the latter whom I had named, both of whom I loved fiercely. Gone were those hours spent identifying every little wildflower sprouting up in the woods. Gone were those nights in my sleeping bag, all of my wide dreams and prayers playing out across the endless glitter-tossed skies. Losing that stuff hurt. When I went to NMH, I was thrown onto a superhighway, sharing classrooms with the sons and daughters of supermodels, foreign diplomats, famous actors and actresses, political figures, wealthy businesspeople. I knew I was supposed to want to become them. And over those high school years, I learned to develop that want. But I also knew I would never be them, that maybe even the wanting itself was somewhat suspect.

All that was kind of hard. Still, it wasn't rape-scene hard.

I search my room for inspiration. A dozen or so melancholy books with incomprehensibly wordy titles and colons are strewn about my room. To the head of my bed, there are stacks of flashcards wadded together next to a Latin textbook and dictionary. My luggable computer sits suspended against the far wall on a door held up by milk crates. Perched atop the computer looking down on me is my first doll, Ursha, whose yellow hair I scissored while playing beauty salon. Next to her is a soil-colored teddy bear with Master Mind black peg eyes. He was a gift from Mom just before I left for boarding school. Something about my impending departure made her remember she had forgotten to get one for me as a child. By the time the bear arrived I was beyond too cool for stuffed animals, and the bear had lived, unnamed, in a box in my closet. But now that I'm in college, no-name teddy bear has a prominent place in my room. Apparently being cool isn't as important anymore.

Come to think of it, trying to be cool in boarding school had been a confusing disaster. For a few weeks there I tried (and failed) to be bulimic like the other girls. As I recall, I had real emotions like wanting to be considered cute and fear about not fitting in.

There was pain there. But not enough for a rape scene, I'm quite sure.

I ought to be able to draw on my parents' divorce. You'd think it would be harsh to see your parents who have been married for over twenty-five years split up. Though it blew up my brother's world, mine stayed more or less intact. I was already half-away from home, independent. Lots of times—and I am certainly cow crap for thinking this—I'm edging more toward being relieved about it than anything else.

I'm getting nowhere with this. I should do some of my other homework. I rifle through my book bag, take out my latest book for poetry class. We've moved from Hart Crane to Marianne Moore now. I open to "A Grave" and read these lines: "Man, looking into the sea—/ taking the view from those who have as much right to it as you have it to yourself—/ it is human nature to stand in the middle of a thing/ but you cannot stand in the middle of this: the sea has nothing to give but a well excavated grave."[4] Intriguingly bleak, yes, but I just can't concentrate on it. I catch myself wondering if I can use someone else's poem as motivation for this *Extremities* scene. Then I shove Moore back in my bag, return to scouring my mind for painful memories of struggle that I can use. It's making me a little anxious to realize how few experiences I have to choose from.

Am I lonely? I've been boyfriend-less since I can't remember when. Ever since my art major boyfriend Geoff and I broke up a year ago, I haven't been able to imagine dating anyone else. He'll always be my first love. We met freshman year. He moved in across the hall with his battered clothes, unwieldy canvases and paints, hideous pet tarantula. Still, there was just something right about him, something I couldn't ignore. From our first meeting, we were pretty much inseparable.

I slide out of my clothes, grab my white long underwear-sweats from underneath my pillow, put them on.

Things between Geoff and I went off track somewhere, got too serious. Breaking up was wrenching for us both. It's a year later, and I still love Geoff, feel a little sad not to be with him. We say we're friends. But we don't hang out much anymore.

I open my door. Sal's and Cathy's rooms are dark. They must still be out. I walk down the hall to the bathroom, turn the light on, squeeze toothpaste onto my brush, move it around my mouth. I spit, rinse, look in the mirror, see my tired eyes looking back at me from behind my glasses. I shut off the light, walk back down the hall to my room, close the door, sit down on my bed.

It's also a little weird to be the only one home, not to be into what everyone else is doing on a Saturday night. Sometimes it makes me feel lonely. But I'm not one of these "gotta have a man" girls. I like studying. That's who I am.

What am I going to do about Scene Study? I guess my parents' divorce will have to do.

In later years, whenever I remember this night, I'll be overwhelmed with a desire to stop time, to pause and hover over this scene, over this college girl in the last hours of her ordered and clement life. Her troubles may confuse her, but they do not bewilder her. Until her heavy-lidded eyes close in sleep this night, her life will still be arranged chronologically. Whatever her pains, they are still subject to the ordering logic of remembrance and identity. For this last night, she is a college girl and that explains her.

Sometime in the next few hours, her memory-making abilities will change. Her point of view, her sense of time, will come to resemble that of a veteran of war, much like the hapless Billy Pilgrim from Vonnegut's *Slaughterhouse-Five*: "Somebody was playing with the clocks, and not only with the electric clocks, but the wind-up kind, too. The second hand on my watch would twitch once, and a year would pass, and then it would twitch again. There was nothing I could do about it."[5]

That's what her night would be like, later. I'd love to remember her in her last hours of pacific sleep. I can't, though—not really.

But here's what probably happened.

I must have tossed Mastrosimone's *Extremities* scene next to me on the floor. I likely put my glasses back on the windowsill just above my head. I must have cracked the window, killed the light, pulled my frilly lavender comforter down tight. A raw November air must have spilled over me.

I probably switched positions, twisting sheet and blanket round me, my breath coming on even, deep. Slurry voices likely streamed into and out of bars and pizza joints. Bodies slumped their way home. The sounds probably died out.

The computer screen with its pulsing cursor likely smoldered an iridescent, wavy green. I left it on most of the time: somewhere I'd read that all halfway decent writers did this. The whole room was probably bathed in mustardy light when I flipped onto my stomach. My white, cotton gym socks lying on the floor by the foot of the bed, scrubbed off during sleep, might have even had a dim, green glow.

I probably dreamed that night.

But I won't really remember any of that.

Instead, I'll remember this.

CHAPTER FOUR

A fistful of my hair jerks me back.

There's a slabby male figure leaning over me, pants bunched around his hips.

I screech into the blackness, my fingers hunting for my glasses.

Pages are crackling on the floor.

A hand shuts off my scream.

I thrash, strain my neck to see a face.

It's gigantic, vacant, blank. Like a blackboard.

Outlined chin and jaw loom over me. I try to scribble in eyes, nose, lips.

But I can't call up chalk.

He moves his hand.

I scream.

Thick fingers jam up my throat. My tongue swells.

Leathery sweat fills my nostrils.

My mind searches out a sketchy trail, finds it and follows. Wait a minute! That albino-y guy from Scene Study. He has a wide face! He wears a leather jacket! This is some sick prank. Ticklish hummingbird laughter sparks through my head. That's enough. I call *Uncle. Uncle!*

But, no. I'm wrong. It's not him. This man is larger, stronger. My mind Hot Wheels loops. My body stalls out, freezes. My hope goes missing. His fingers move inside my mouth. Wait. So careful. Now. Now! I bite down on finger flesh.

"Fucking bitch."

His blood's on my tongue. Knuckles sledgehammer my nose, lips. Metal taste rams my nose. This is my own blood now.

"Shut up. Got it?"

Shoved against his shoulder, I cannot move.

"Es."

Fingers leave my mouth. I scream.

Guys partying downstairs, please hear me. I kick at the floor, throw punches in back of me. My fist grazes a head. It's covered with something soft. Like milkweed silk. Or stockings.

Fist thwaps. Cracking in my nose. My mouth chunks up with blood.

He heaps onto my back. Thunder shoots through my spine. He shoves my head into my pillow. A scramble of cotton plugs my mouth. I can't. Move. Hushed. Holler. All wheeze, hack. No air. No air. In here.

He jerks my head back against his shoulder. Gulp-gasp for. Air. Something sharp, cold. Slicing my neck.

"Feel this knife? Do what I say or I'll kill you."

No way out. My body, electric. Confused weather patterns. Rasped breaths. Shuddering heartbeats. Everything tapering down.

I reach ahead. Yank that clock out by its cord. Time stops. Evidence hands stuck there. On the three and the five. I'm going to die here. They'll need to know when. This bed. Closet door. Cut glass door knob. Sheets. These are the last objects I'll see.

"God, pleeez."

"Don't do what I say, you're dead. Understand?"

"Es."

Warped paperbacks trapped up in the milk crates. Can see part of my closet floor. That pair of brown flats Dad bought for my birthday. Strange color. Never been able to find the right outfit for them.

Hands shove me hard onto my stomach. Push my face into my pillow. Wrench my arms behind me. Sits on them heavy. Like a cord of firewood. My scream's soft sob now. My hands worse than any kind of useless. Metal jabs my throat.

"Take them off."

My neck gone stiff. My muffled answer all vowel.

"O."

That knife slices.

My head travels. Centimeters side to side against the pillow.

"Fucking cunt."

Stubby fingers rip off my long underwear bottoms. Yank them down around. To my knees then tear. My panties down. To meet them. Fingertips run up my crack. Sharp pressed to my neck.

"If you make a sound, dead. Understand?"

"Es."

Alarm screaming inside me. No one's coming. No one going to save me. Lifts the sharp. Away from my throat. Gasp. Can't see. Eye swollen shut. Something drops on bed. Maybe the knife.

I'm going to find it. But he is. So much faster. Pins my wrists. Down against my back. Elastic snaps. Pulls down. No. no no. but these no's are. just inside my. head now. his limpness shoves hard. against where babies come from. thrust. slam. push. nausea courses. through my body. good eye filled. with tears. stares at that closet door. cut-glass knob like a diamond. reflecting shine from a streetlight. i can't see.

he stops. pulls away. lift my head and. air. breathe air.

what. what's happening?

"Damn it."

catch at air. he's above. still jamming. hands to back.

i'm tracing. the shadow that runs. along my closet door. i'm looking. above me. a tiny part of the upper corner is. lit up by. that streetlight. that corner. the brightest thing I can see. so far away. but i'm going there.

sharp metal. cuts my throat. my eyes rush. from light corner back to bottom of closet door. i can't. i won't.

I have to leave. I can't be here anymore. I fracture. Pieces of me split off from the college girl, become airborne. I am winged, escaping up to that corner—little wisps, feathery scraps and shreds long jumping through the streetlight's halo.

I'm not with her now. I'm above her in the streetlight. I tuck knees under chin, rock back, forth. The cut-glass doorknob shines below in the streetlight's glow. And up here breath's full and free, goes on forever and ever. Up here anything might be possible—even perfect worlds, places full of kindness, peace, and hope.

Below me the college girl cries in the dark. That shiny metal jabs her neck raw. The college girl's face is eye-level with those Latin flashcard piles in that no-end darkness. Squinting from above, I try to make it out with her. Like knowing the answer could save us both. Is that a word on top or a meaning?

"On your knees."

He releases her arms. They've gone sore from being twisted behind her, pinned by his full weight. I watch the college girl snail onto hands, knees.

"Sit back."

She sits back, trembling, her heel bones shoved against her bare bottom. She looks down at her thighs, two curious charcoal blobs.

"Put your hands in front."

The college girl moves her head, searches above her. From the college girl's kenneled angle there's only that light itself. She tells herself it's getting brighter and brighter. But I'm up here and I know it's not.

I watch the college girl place her teeny deserted fists side by side. She starts speaking. Her upper lip's swollen and split, leaking onto her bloody chin. The college girl's wishing so badly she could get some words out, though she can't figure out which ones or what good they'd do. She just knows she has to.

"Why're you doing dis?"

His body is rigid.

"Don't fucking ask me that."

Her fists fade in front of her.

"I gif it to you. Computer. Money. Anyfing. Take anyfing you want."

He laughs. Her talk keeps on.

"You don't need to. You could jus thalk to me. I might . . ." The college girl has to say these words, though they're rancid garbage on her tongue. I know as I watch her from the safety of the street-light that she has no choice.

"I might like oo."

She's thinking if she reasons with him, he'll understand his mistake, that he'll take his knife, his pants. He'll be like I'm so sorry, my mistake, miss. She's thinking then she can erase him from this room and he'll never, ever be able to pencil his way back.

"You'd never like me, girl like you."

Something shatters in the college girl. She wonders. What kind of girl am I? How does he know me? Who is he? The college girl's mind uneven-record spins around and around. Nothing catches. She flashes on her ex-boyfriend, Geoff. She mouths what she desperately hopes are smart new words. They're magnified in the college girl's mind from that play page she read hours ago.

"My boyfend. He'll be home sfoon. You can leave. I haven't seen your face. I won't tell. I sthwear. Promise."

His laugh is like tires scraping gravel. It's as if he knows Raul's part spot-on cold, as if he skinned that character and zipped himself inside.

"You don't have a boyfriend. Haven't had one in months."

He knows me, the college girl realizes. But how? Her mind tumbles through all the voices she's heard. I'm absolutely sure, she tells herself. I don't know this voice.

"Stop talking."

From the streetlight I listen to her stifled chokes. I see her shining eyes tearing in the dark. Metal slices her neck. Blood slicks down the right side of her throat.

"Peeez, pleeez. Don't kill me."

He's fumbling in his pocket. Looking down from the street-light, I see what the college girl cannot. He has something in his hands. He lowers it in front of her face.

"Don't strangle me, pleeez. I fromise. I'll be quiet."

He sniggers. Maybe he's laughing because of the college girl's fear. Maybe he's laughing because of her childish failure to anticipate what's coming next. I watch as his hands lash her wrists together tight. The rope is cold, plastic. It cuts grooves into her skin.

Telephone cord, she thinks. Did he pull the telephone from the living room wall? Is this my own phone cord being used against me? Then a more urgent thought hits. If it is, if I ever get out of here alive, I won't be able to call the police.

There's nothing else left for the college girl. She says a tiny prayer. Someone, anyone. *I need you.* Please hear me! She screams as loud as she can. But it comes out debarked dog, just wheeze and cough.

He pulls the college girl's head back by the bangs, jams his fingers down her throat. A side of fist pummels her lips. The college girl realizes. No one's going to hear me.

I watch from above as the college girl makes a decision. If I have to, she tells herself. I'll do it. I'll give in to save my life.

"Peeez. Peeez. I won't fight. You any ore."

The college girl gags. His weight shifts against her as he searches the foot of the bed. From the streetlight I see that familiar wad in his hand. He removes his fingers, shoves it deep into her mouth. Her shriek, muzzled groan. Through her bloodied nose, she takes in the thick, dry smell of her own foot.

The college girl's breathing's harder now. She tries to jostle her sock from her mouth. Tears are caterpillaring down the college girl's cheeks. She sucks at the air from her mouth corners. She extends her neck toward the streetlight. Delicate spidery rainbows shimmer before her, jump rope along her lashes. And she's sure. There's never been anything more magnificent, more full of glorious-dazzling, fairy light magic—never been a more heavenly beautiful. Am I dead? the college girl wonders. She's turning ghost. Her eyes cloud over, dim out. She's near to gone.

For her, there will always be a blank here. But from above in the streetlight, I see it all. He violently shakes her lifeless limbs. And time passes. Seconds maybe. Or minutes. Then the college

girl's chest trembles. She splutters back. Into the world. And everything's. Everything's panic.

Quick wheezes escape her socks. Big fuzzy forms at first and
then sharper. Her nose—blood, snot, and shattered bone. Her
small, bare bottom is still pointed up in the air at him.

Some of me will stay here in the streetlight for days, for months.

Some of me will stay here in the streetlight for years.

But most of me—God, no—I'm pulled away from the streetlight back into her body again. He pushes his hard against.

me ripping. my lips apart with his. hand and pounding. into
me. crying. against my socks. please no. he thrusts. and thrusts.
over and over. seems like forever. then he goes soft again and. he
cannot keep. himself inside me. and he shoves his fingers. around
my hole and. i'm screaming against. my socks.

wetness seeps round me. through. outside me. and i'm peeing
all. over him. and he. misunderstands and. thinks this is. glad wetness. no. no. no. my pee is. turning him on.

"Like this, slut, don't you?"

stomach lurches. at his words. but. no time to tell. him. about
his mistake. this is my chance. now. i'm going to. do it. suck air.
from edges of mouth.

if i make it. out. alive. have to be. able to identify. who he is.
kick him. hard in right. shoulder.

whip. head around.

baseball cap. light hair sticking out. against the black. outline
of leather. jacket beneath. light shirt. kind with collar. cotton dress.
long. or short sleeves. can't tell. white male. twenties. or thirties.
one ninety. maybe over two hundred pounds. five-ten, six feet. his
face. nothing. still blank. as. chalkboard.

"Don't look at me."

jammed against. pillow. can't. breathe. no air. but i. saw.

he rams. himself against. wrong hole. hard pushing my butt.
flesh tears apart. him.

getting harder. stomach tosses. heaves. floor. drops from
under. me.

i am. sea cucumber. i eject my insides out. over and over.
strings of pasta. chunks. of tomato.

violent bursts. of vomit. flow. back into. my stomach. throw it all. up again. him thrusting. moaning. time elastic. warps. stretches. loses sense. insides rip. crack.

i am. over.

his body. still. tears himself. out. pulls up. underwear.

new sounds. boots. scuff wood. sharp crack. door bursts open.

bright beams. move. through. black.

i see. dark forest. copse of trunks.

no, no. not trees. legs. so many legs.

more men. here to hurt me.

i cannot remember. how to count.

gasp and. screech. against socks. mouth sides grab. air.

i scream. make no sound.

CHAPTER FIVE

he runs. out of my room.

gone. he is. gone.

scattering thuds. cross floor. look up. dry twist pain. the tree legs are. clear cut. gone now.

Except one.

no. no. please please no. don't. shriek soundless. that flashlight. moves. closer. i play caught-lizard-dead.

"It's okay. It'll be okay. I'm a policeman. We're here now."

it's the police. not here. to hurt me too. he moves closer. and even though. i know he's a man. i give him. a different name. i name him Tall Tree.

Tall Tree takes my sock. out of my throat. fingers graze lips. i wince. Tall Tree stops. starts again. slowly pries my mouth. apart. my jaws decide to. bite down on those fingers. but i hold them back. sock gone and i scream and i scream until my scream starts to match this chasmy ache, until my throat loses sound, until it can't scream anymore. Tall Tree doesn't try to cut off my sounds. then i fall into deep quiet.

"You're going to be okay."

Tall Tree's words float. there. but college girl and I won't. trust them. neither one of us can believe them.

Tall Tree takes a step toward me. he bends down. i'm scared but i won't, i won't stop him. his palm brushes back my bloody hair. my neck rages with pain. Tall Tree covers my shoulders. with my comforter.

"Keep you warm. Come to the dining room. You'll feel better in the light."

Tall Tree walks. behind me. he holds that softness. closed round my neck. my bare bottom, my unsteady fists still bound. i stumble out the room. old chandelier's so glittery. that i can't open my slit-punched eyes at first. when i can everything's unrecognizable, bloody blur. i trip. Tall Tree catches me.

"where. is he?"

my voice, no kind of venomous. just whispery hiss.

"who is he? how did you sfind me?"

did my scene-reading conjure a demon? i taste sour vomit on my chin. bludgeoned cheeks sting. silent sirens shoot streamers of red and blue against living room walls. sounds of bodies struggling. flesh is striking flesh.

My gauzy eyes slowly start to focus.

But some parts of me are still in the streetlight. I'm not all here.

I see Tall Tree's navy uniform. He places a chair in the center of the room, leads my limbs over to it. I follow. He puts slight weight on my shoulders. My body sits.

Tall Tree leans down next to me. His eyes glaze over. Maybe he's weary. Or fighting back tears. Or he doesn't see me but instead his daughter or his wife or his coworker or every other raped corpse he dreamt he could breathe back to life.

"He's not going to get away with this."

Tall Tree's choked-up voice makes him sound like he means it, and this time I think the college girl and I might actually believe him. He eyes me.

"He's not really your boyfriend, is he?"

I suck at the air. My tongue barely forms the word.

"O."

"He says he's your boyfriend, that you were just having a fight. When we tried to cuff him, he punched us, ran out of here fast as he could."

I try to scavenge syllables, some Scrabble letters to explain what he did to me. Over there. In that room. But not all of me is here. Some of me is still in the streetlight.

"I dunno him."

Tall Tree looks at me sideways. He starts to say more words but he doesn't finish. A female police officer crosses. In my head I name her too. She's Little Tree. She's about my little height but with a muscular build, short brown hair. Little Tree's hazel eyes blaze like a universe of stars.

"We got him!"

She glances down at her right elbow. It doesn't quite line up with the rest of her arm, like it's bad-bruised or broken.

"Fucking bastard."

Little Tree stops, sees my swollen lids following her.

"Jesus, Jesus Christ. 'Scuse me, miss."

Hundreds of volcanoes are erupting under my skin. My mouth twists, lips tear—my new smile. My voice rattles.

"Yeh, fucking bafstard. Fucking bafstard!"

Little Tree rubs at her eyes. Dark hairs flicker in the chandelier light. She laughs. Then Little Tree's laughter joins my screech and both of us are laughing together. My hands slap each other clumsy and I'm crying. Tears slide out from behind my puffy lids. Little Tree looks at me like she's trying to solve a tricky math problem. But I can't help her. Not all of me is here. Some of me is still in the streetlight.

CHAPTER SIX

Little Tree tears her eyes away, looks at Tall Tree. He motions her to the other side of the room. I try to make my ears like Superman's but I can't quite make out what the Trees are saying. It goes something like this.

"Did he have ID?"

"Yeah. He IDs as . . ."

Tall Tree sights me over his shoulder. From there things go murmur. Little Tree nods in my direction. Soon things turn sense again.

"That's the same?"

"Could be."

Tall Tree glares hard at the wall in front of him, shakes his head.

"Take him to the station."

Little Tree's heading down the front stairs and Tall Tree's starting toward me. But me-screaming noises are flaring up again now and I want to douse them but I can't, so they just flame on and on. How long exactly before they go ember, I don't know. Then Tall Tree speaks again.

"An ambulance is downstairs to take you to the hospital. Gather your things when you're ready. Maybe your roommates can give you some clothes, so you don't have to go in there."

For the first time my thoughts turn to Sally and Cathy. I've been selfish, thinking only of myself. Did he get to them first?

"Where's Sthal? Is fshe okay?"

"Who? Your other roommate?"

I nod yes.

"Don't know. Cathy's downstairs. She's real scared but okay. She heard you scream, ran downstairs to the neighbors. They called the station from there. She's real worried about you."

It hits me. Cathy, someone who answered our ad, may have just saved my life.

"Tell her fank you."

"You okay to sit here? Don't move. I'll be back here with her in just a few minutes."

I nod. Tall Tree disappears down the stairs. I look over at Sally's room, see that thin wall we share on the right side. There's no way she didn't hear me. Sal's hurt in there. Or dead. Light's leaking out the door bottom. I push off my chair, move toward that door. I pound with my fists but that sad pounding's more like tapping because my arms have gone Jell-O useless. No response. I turn the 'knob. Press.

"Sthal? STHAL!"

CHAPTER SEVEN

The door cracks a few inches. Then sticks.

Behind it I can see the back of a dresser.

I peep my head through the opening, watch my head blood smear on the door jam. A desk's behind the dresser. Behind it, there's a bookcase. Behind that bookcase, there's Sal. Alive. Her lips tremble. Her eyes see me. She begins to haul her furniture out of the way.

And right then I know. Sal was raped first. After he was through with her, Sal probably piled all she had against that door to keep him from coming back.

Sal continues her movements. But she's not here. I watch her indigo eyes braid through me, the room, me again. And I want so badly to bring her back. Her voice is calm as iced-over pond.

"Oh. Hi."

I squeeze through the door opening. Every light in her room has been thrown on. A shambled stain sludges across Sal's wall mirror. I stop. Back up. Look.

There in the mirror. My blonde-streaked hair drenched

through with blood. I always thought blood was the color of Valentine's Day chocolate boxes. It's not. Blood's black when it's puddled all together here like this. Eyes, gray and purple, bruised, nearly swollen shut. Lips shiny, with blood. Blood lines necklace my throat.

"My Od!"

Some parts of me are still in the streetlight. I'm not all here.

But the college girl's all beat up. I don't recognize her anymore. I touch her carnaged cheeks with my fingertips. Sally's face appears in the mirror behind me, stares straight ahead. I notice my wrists are still tied, spin around, put them in front of Sal. Sal unties the knots, loosens the cord. There are new scarlet channels there. I rub my wrists with fingers, I move farther into Sal's room.

"Police here?"

"Dey got him. Sthal, are you okay?"

I try to hug her, bundle her in my arms, but she's stiff.

"I'm fine."

But she isn't. Maybe some of her is still somewhere else too. Sal's absence from her sunken body's scrambling up my insides. What did he put her through? And my mind just can't think so I can't find the right words. But I want to say so many things. Like I love you, Sal. Like the nightmare's done. Like I don't know how. But we've done it. We both survived.

Then I notice. Sal's working awful hard not to meet my gaze in the mirror. And for the first time I look at her bruiseless eyes. At her tearless pajamas. At the foot of her bed reflected in the mirror, sheets and comforter still mostly tucked. And I start to have new, different thoughts.

Maybe he never came in here, never laid a finger on her. Maybe she's crumpled-up and scared but otherwise okay.

"Was he here? Did he hurt you, Sthal?"

She ogles the floor. After a while she speaks, but the voice that comes out isn't her own anymore. It's someone else's.

"No. I'm okay."

Still Sal won't look me in the eye. And questions crash in on me. I don't ask them. But when did she stack all this furniture against the door? Was it when she heard the officers struggling with him in the hall? Or when she heard him breaking in? Or when she heard my cries for help, heard him threaten my life, heard him raping me? When was it?

The walls are sweating. I can't stay here with her.

CHAPTER EIGHT

Cathy's standing in the dining room. She throws her arms around me, presses her teary cheek onto my shoulder.

"Are you okay?"

"Caffee."

I can't think of what I'm supposed to say.

Some parts of me are still in the streetlight. I'm not all here.

I wish I knew her better, wish we were closer friends. But I don't and we're not. She's just a sweet girl who answered our ad.

"I had to call the cops and I couldn't do it from here in case he heard, so I went downstairs and the cops came real quick, got here in minutes."

She leaves, returns seconds later cradling a folded white sweatshirt, matching pants.

"They'll be big for you but I want you to wear them."

"Caffee, fank you for saving me. I'll get 'em back to you, promise."

"You keep 'em."

"Fanks."

Sal's gaslight eyes follow us from the doorway. Cathy wants to know.

"Who can I call to meet you at the emergency room? Someone in your family?"

I don't think. I just say.

"Indsey. Call Lindsey."

CHAPTER NINE

Cathy rings Lindsey. I hear her voice murmuring in the kitchen. I feel pain pierce my temples. I reach up, stare at the blood left behind on my fingers. Light froths and bubbles in front of my eyes. The air turns to yellow and black spots, and the room seems to steam.

I feel cloth dabbing my face, shrink back from the pain. I don't know the body attached to the hand. I squint over at my room, now awash in bright light. Looking at it scares me, but I make myself. Through swollen eyes I see my futon askew in the middle of the room, flashcards, Mastrosimone's *Extremities* script, clothes on the floor. There's a pink animal with a trailing-long tail, but it's not moving and the tail's too long to be a real tail. It's my clock pulled from the wall and even though I can't see its hands I feel safer knowing that they're stuck, that time's forever stopped in there. I squint over at the wall clock behind Tall Tree but it hasn't stopped. Its hands seem to be flying backward.

I hear Tall Tree saying he wants to respond to my questions from before. His face comes into focus.

"Might have been stalking you. Could've been for a few weeks."

There's an iron taste on my lips. I smell vomit and urine, alcohol and leather. The dabbing on my face has moved to my eyes now. I yelp. Tall Tree speaks to whoever's been wiping the blood from my eyes.

"That's enough for now."

I can feel that body move away. Tall Tree's talking.

"Not positive on this but we're pretty sure he knew the layout of this place, was targeting you specifically."

The room spins and the chandelier casts a dappling light, like sun through leaves. My eyes beat and my head twitches. I try to move to the edge of my seat, to ease the pain from the cuts on my thighs, the deeper, throbbing pains shooting through my inside parts, now split and torn. There's leaking there and I know it's blood, too. The throbbing won't stop.

I try to push myself up and Tall Tree steps toward me, towers over me, eases me back into the seat. The room ripples, turns from bright light to dark and back again. His words swing in. His words swing out. Of my grasp. I ask the question I've had with me since it all began.

"Why?"

He looks troubled, shakes his head, doesn't say anything.

Nothing I can see—not the room, not the people, not me— nothing makes sense anymore. I can't stay here, be here anymore. I'm frantic. I must find a way back to the streetlight. So I focus real hard and I tell parts of me to take flight. But they don't.

I watch Little Tree come into view, motion to Tall Tree. They move away from me, out of my view, and lower their voices. But I make out these words.

"Looks like he broke the glass on the back door, put his hand through, unlocked that first door, used a hoe from the basement to prop it open. Must have done that so he could get out quick. Went up those back stairs, busted up that chain lock."

"What about that bolt?"

"Wasn't locked."

"The roommate said they never use the back door so the bolt's always thrown."

There's a silence. Then Little Tree starts again.

"I don't know. Maybe one of them went out that door, forgot to relock it. Or, since he knew the apartment, could be he's broken in before while they were home, unbolted it from the inside then."

All those words turn to crisping static-sound again—no meaning—so I try to find the Trees with my eyes. I twist my neck, feel a charge run through it, wince. I'm throbbing again.

I squint, watch her mouth making sounds. But they don't make sense. So I tell myself to concentrate extra hard and I do, and soon her noises turn to words.

Tall Tree's standing back next to me again. He's talking.

"He stepped in paint. One of you a painter?"

"Sthal."

He nods decisively, moves away from me again. I see them there. Orange boot tracks on the floor. I will my breath steady but it won't listen, whooshes out in fluttering bursts instead. And that other body's near me again. Cloth's cleaning the blood and snot from my mouth. I'm whimpering. Tall Tree speaks to Little Tree.

"First he went to Cathy's, realized it wasn't the room he was looking for, walked into hers."

He was looking for mine, for me. This was no accident, no random act of violence. I was it, the one he was after. Me. But why? Why?

Cloth's catching on the cuts around my neck. I pull away. The hand tries again, gentler this time. And I sit as still as I can and I listen. I don't know how he tells it all to her. But Tall Tree manages to convey that they think he planned it all, had several screwdrivers, yards of cord, that he probably never meant to burglarize our apartment, that he came with one purpose, to rape me.

I can't stay here, be here anymore with the throbbing. I must find a way back to the streetlight. So I focus real, real hard. And this time I can feel parts of me growing lighter, getting ready to lift off. But then everything flitters and vibrates, buzzes, cuts off and away.

I'm awake. I must have blacked out. I try to remember what happened but it's as if my thoughts have just blinked off, leaving only hollow darkness behind.

I lost time. I don't know how much. I have no idea what brought me back. Maybe I got stuck, hit some hard stop that locked me back into the world, dropped me back into place, back into the stream of seconds and minutes and hours again.

I haven't been off hovering, watching everything through the soothing silence of distance. I haven't taken flight, soared up to that streetlight. I just blanked out. The streetlight doesn't want me. And I can't go anywhere else. I can't escape anymore. A door that was open has shut for good.

Tall Tree's face is close to mine now. He's talking.

"You there? You okay?"

His breath brushes my cheek. I make hand motions, gurgles. Evidence, I know it's going to be important now. I manage to say these words, though I don't know how.

"The knife. Maybe in his pockfet. Maybe by my bed. Wherever it is, pleeez find it."

Then I'm reeling again, losing time.

CHAPTER TEN

I snap back.

I'm carried down by Trees. Or ambulance drivers. Or I stumble. Then I'm in an ambulance on a stretcher covered with blankets. Or sheets.

I'm throbbing and I'm utterly alone. Or I've got someone with me. I can make out two man shapes in the front seats. Their voices spool in and out of the darkness. Plastic, antiseptic-type scents jostle the air. I'm hollering against glass, metal cabinets heaving with supplies. Lights shred the dark. My lips glop blood onto my gums.

"I've got this. I want to sit up."

Sirens shriek over my sounds. We pass beneath streetlamps. Streams of white light freeze, then liquefy. I lash and scream. I wrench my neck to see windshield behind me. Muddy city unfolds between the men like a crinkled map. I arch my neck to look out the window in front of me.

I wake, throbbing. I've lost time again. Streets are dying out behind us. The ambulance lurches to a stop. A male body opens a door. Cold hits me. Arms haul me up. Glass doors slide open. I close my puffed eyes against the brightness. I'm hoisted, dropped into a wheelchair. I've got to get out. I'm pressing myself up.

"I can sthand."

Hands push my shoulders back down. I try again. They press harder this time. And I'm rolling. My bloody hair's bitter cold against my neck. Then I'm in a new room. My lips are throbbing. Near me there's a body without face or voice. But it has hands. Those hands clutch mine tight. Now a female Voice comes from those hands. It's saying it's here to help. There will be a rape kit. I remember reading about that in a book once. Maybe in a feminist philosophy class. Probably something by Susan Brownmiller. I'm blaring no. Or I'm weeping. Or I've gone stone silent. A person in a white coat arrives. Male voice comes from that coat, says it's a doctor, says I'm hurt bad. Coat's got a young man's face. I'm embarrassed for that. There's dark hair, glasses. There's beard. Or moustache. I'm telling Coat I don't want this.

"No. Don't look at me."

Coat says he must.

"Get me a woman. A female futhking doctor."

Coat says none are available this time of night. Coat says he's got to do it.

"I won't flet you."

Coat yanks the sweats off and I'm clawing, gnawing and Coat's yelling at me, trying to pry my twisted legs apart but Coat's going to lose because they're welded together. And even if I told my body to trust Coat, to let him take the sweats, my legs wouldn't listen because they answer to their own separate brain. It controls them now. I kick Coat in its face part. Or chest. Or arm. And someone's shrieking like a cornered rabbit. I wish I could comfort her. But I can't.

I wake to my own wailing. More time's been lost. Voice is saying words about everything being alright. Cold metal enters me. Pain shoots from my vagina up my spine. A comb moves slowly through my pubic hair. I thrash.

Voice says it's important for the law. I know Voice is right, that I have to do this. But I don't like Coat or Voice, hands that touch me, eyes that see me, see me here like this. Bulbs flash on and off. Coat's taking pictures. Or a Tree. Male hands position my body. They prop it up, they pull it down, they flip it over. A box records gashed face, busted nose, slashed neck, scraped arms, channeled wrists, bruised thighs.

Lindsey's there. She's in this room. Or down the hallway. She's holding my hand tight. She's hugging me safe. Lindsey's saying lots. Or nothing. She's weeping. Or her eyes are sandy desert. Or Lindsey's nowhere near and I can't get to her. I scream for her. Or I ask nice-girl politely. No one hears me. No one responds.

Awake again, more time's been lost. Time rides a bicycle without training wheels, falls and rescrapes its scabby knees, gets back up. Now I'm sitting, back mashed up against wall on a wooden bench, scent of bleach, cotton, and blood in my nose. I've been told to stay there by a Coat. Or Nurse. Or Tree. I have to wait for results.

Nurse walks over. She's wearing a shirt with excessively cuddly panda bears. Or sugared-up children playing jump rope. Or noisy, garish squawking parrots. They are magical—the bears, the children, the parrots. I'm waiting for them to leap off Nurse, squiggle their way out those hospital doors. I'm hoping they'll take me, too.

"We tested all of the samples."

Nurse's eyes move from my bloodied eyes to my smashed nose to my busted lips to my sliced-up throat. Her forehead turns to wide wale corduroy. This combined with the bears, children, or parrots makes me laugh. I'm throbbing and Nurse is watching me.

"We don't have pregnancy results yet."

This possibility never occurred to me, his grisly fetus growing inside me but now that it does, laughter reverbs through my skull, squirts out in bursts. My sounds won't stop.

"No STDs."

"What?"

"Sexually transmitted diseases."

[44]

The laughter's more frantic now, but I'm crushing it down real hard inside. I never thought to think about these things—none of them. I've been thinking about how to stay alive, not even thinking about it, just trying to.

My lungs are constricting and Nurse is pressing her clipboard tight to her chest, heavy-squashing the bears, the children, the parrots, too. Her suffocating them bothers me, but I tell myself to calm down, not to say anything about it.

"Evidence of vaginal and anal penetration. We're still waiting to hear back on fibers, hairs, fluids."

I nod. Or I moan. Or I offer no response.

CHAPTER ELEVEN

I come back. I'm with myself again. More time lost. It's a few hours later, Sunday, late morning. Lindsey's with me in a police station. When or how we got here, I don't have worked out. Lindsey drove me in the Lezzy. Or I arrived by Tree car. I do know I brought no-name teddy bear. I tell Lindsey that he's an eye-witness, here to answer the hard questions.

A policeman looks at me. He's got a midnight-blue uniform. He's been speaking. But my mind's molten and it won't focus. It should really bother me that I don't know what he's saying because I won't know how to respond, but then my mouth starts moving and it's saying *knife, phone cord, raped in the front hole and in the back one too.*

"Your pictures are here from the hospital."

I wipe at my eye with my coat sleeve, stare down at the blood smear. I hear my voice.

"How'd dey turn out?"

I think to say other things, too. Like can I have copies to use as headshots? It sure costs a wad to order those glossy professional ones. But I don't. Everything feels wrong and humor isn't working.

"Miss, write out what you remember. You know, everything that happened."

He motions to paper and a pen on the table between us. The air smells like old brick, sweat. My gums ache. I watch as my hand moves against the pages, the lanky blue lines. I don't know what it's saying, what it's doing, but I notice my script growing like vines across the margins. My fingers, my wrists are throbbing.

Then my hand stops moving. It's done, everything spent. No no no. It can't be because if it is, everything will be gouged and scooped out, cutting cold. I'm for sure not crying. I watch the pen being pried from my fingers, the pages disappearing.

I come back again. I've lost time. Now we're floundering around corners in the Lezzy, parking outside Friendly's on Marshall Street. Lindsey's in the driver's seat next to me.

"You need to eat."

I might be nodding.

"I'll get you a milkshake."

Lock the doors.

It could be I say that last part. Or it could be those words just rumble around in my head.

Click. No no no. I can't do this. Can't be all alone with the parts, with the throbbing. I see them in the rearview mirror, the pummeled face, puffed-up eyes, soaked-up-blood hair. They were there. They saw.

Students file past in dress-coats, boots, wool slacks. Book bags slung over their shoulders, they slog their way down the slurried sidewalks. Some see me seeing them, look at the sky. Turn back. Stop. Stare. At me. I'm shrieking.

"Go ahead. Look at me!"

They look down. They look away. They move on. I scrub my sleeve on my face. They have classes to get to. I do too. Let's see. They are—Peoples and Cultures of the World (Dr. Rodriguez), American Poetry: 1914–1945 (Dr. Yingling), Advanced Actor's Workshop: Scene Study (Mr. R), Latin (Dr. Mills), and Interpretation of Drama (what's-his-face).

Lindsey crosses the street, unlocks the car. Her eyes are staring at my face. She places a shake between my hands, wraps my fingers round it.

"Drink."

I wag my head. The car clock reads 11:08 a.m. It's been eight hours and three minutes since I pulled the plug on the clock.

"Do it."

Straw between bloated lips, I drag in hard. Strawberry wipes down my throat. It tastes like stardust.

I come back again. I've lost time. Now we're in Lindsey's apartment. A few of my clothes are here. Lindsey got them. Or the police. I eyeball the chipped linoleum on the table from her parents' pre-remodel kitchen. It's fifties diner style and I sure do love it.

Lindsey has two roommates. One is a man. One is a woman. And they are boyfriend and girlfriend. They are older. They are graduate students in political science. Or sociology. Or anthropology. They are not here. They have a black, wall-crapping cat named Bono, and I'm throbbing.

"You need to take a shower."

"I can't."

Or maybe my mouth never flubs out that answer. Maybe my mind just thinks and thinks it. All I know is that I won't let it happen. I'm not going to be left all alone here, stuck with the parts.

"You can do this. I'm right here."

She leads me to the bathroom and she lifts off my glasses and she places them on the edge of the sink. Or the back of the toilet. Or the window sill. She peels off the sweatpants, T-shirt, and sweatshirt molasses slow. I want to help. But the parts won't budge.

The tub's got *Where the Wild Things Are* claw feet and the floor's a hodgepodge of tiles, a black-and-white version of a picnic tablecloth. She ferries my back and legs over the tub's edge. She tries to hold me up, to stop my bones' rattling. She turns on the water. It gushes down from way up there.

"Is it warm enough?"

My head nods. She grabs soap from that built-in dish. Gray remains cling to the corners. She says nothing. Or help me. Or try to relax. Or it's all going to be all right. Or there are no sounds except water falling.

Her fingers are fearless. They wash arms legs breasts vagina face back butt pearly-pink painted toes. The parts pulse with pain and I want to bound out, shake all over the claw feet and the table-cloth floor, try to leave all the parts behind. But I know I can't. So instead I totally tell them off. Don't you dare kick or hit her. Or else. And they must be scared of my threat because they do it. They settle still as they can.

She rinses the parts. Beads bounce off plucked chicken skin. The parts pitch, shudder against the scalding mist. She rubs shampoo through dried blood, untangles my hair with her fingers, piles it big and high on my head. The shampoo smells like bunches of wildflowers. That hairdo must look hilarious and I hear my throat giggling. I think I hear her laughter too. For a brief moment, I'm okay again. But then a pain shoots through deep inside me and it all rushes back, the memory of what has happened, and my limbs unfasten. I'm a jumbled-up wreck on the tub floor. My brackish tear water mixes with the rest. Lindsey lifts me in her arms like a little child, holds my bouffanty head under the rushing stream. I look down, and see those suds foam pink with blood. I watch them flee down the holes in the drain.

I hear water stop. Lindsey aims my shoulders away from the tub, puts her arm around my back. I lean on her, step over the edge, watch the parts rain onto the picnic-tablecloth floor. Lindsey swaths them up in a giant white towel. Then she leads the parts into the living room, eases them onto a dirt-colored brown couch, hands me my glasses.

"Just sit right here. I'll get some clothes."

She disappears up the stairs.

I'm alone. And suddenly everything feels awful again, just like in the car when I was last left all alone and stranded with the parts, but I tell myself that I have to, I must, I have no choice but to keep it all together. I'm not going to let it happen. I won't lose it. Not this time. Every single thing on my face hurts. I gently put on my glasses. I lean over carefully, slide Lindsey's old pocket watch off the side table, flip open its gold lid. The roman numeral hands read one and fifty-five: 1:55 pm. Ten hours and fifty minutes have passed since I pulled the clock plug in my bedroom.

Can that be right? I check to make sure it's working, that its arms are going forward. I listen to the seconds tick away beneath the glass.

Time's passed. I know it has. But I can't corral my memory shards, bring them back to one another. I can't make anything make sense. Nothing has a place or an order anymore. My see-sawing memories tilt in and out of view. I think I'm going crazy. I have to find something to hold onto, something solid. These last ten minutes. I'll hold onto these. I know what happened in these minutes and I won't forget them.

I'm storing everything away. Lindsey's fingers as she washes the parts. The parts pitching. The mist. The shampoo bouffy-do. The pink suds and the towel. The pocket watch. I repeat each of the details so they leave an imprint in my mind. Then I stare down at the white towel, at my shaking fingers, at the couch that is mostly brown but also has specks of blue and purple, at the old wood floor, the shiny pools of water and blood the parts left behind. I take in the taste of sugary strawberry and metallic blood still on my tongue, the smells of soap, shampoo, crusted blood. I feel the bruises on my lower arms, the pain shooting up my back. I will remember every last part of these ten minutes. I'll remember exactly how Lindsey bathed me, how much she loved me. I'll remember how she cared for me like I was her own.

Lindsey rushes into the room, tosses what looks like a folded mix of her clothes and mine on the couch next to me. I try to figure it out. Is that my underwear? Is that her T-shirt or mine? What about those sweatpants? Lindsey tells me to pull the parts through all those openings but I can't help her because I can't move. So I watch as Lindsey moves the parts for me. She pulls the feet, the calves, and the thighs through all that cloth. As I see the correct cloth appear on the correct parts, it seems to make a sense that brings with it a kind of contentment. That's underwear. Those are sweatpants. She pushes the head through another cloth opening, then each one of the hands, then the arms. That's a T-shirt. That's a sweatshirt. I stare at the thin black tubes left next to me. They seem strange. But then I remember, slide on one sock, then the other.

CHAPTER TWELVE

Lindsey's telling me. Call your parents.

I don't say anything back. Like how much Mom and Dad hate each other. Like if I call, I'll be forcing them to interact, making everything worse. I manage to shake a no.

"They'll want to help."

She's right, though I'm also pretty sure they won't be able to. She's handed me her black phone with the extra-lengthy cord. I see my index finger trace a phone number. It's ringing.

"Mom, hi."

"Hi, honey."

A silence strings across those miles between us and I'm scrutinizing that cord. I'm afraid of phone cords now. Lindsey's standing in the doorframe and she's mouthing the words "tell her" and my mouth is moving.

"I'm raped."

"What?"

"Raped."

Moments tick by slowly. I wait for Mom there, lost in that quiet. I see streetlight and I see diamond-cut glass doorknob and

I smell leather and I taste hunks of blood. And I'm throbbing. But then the quietness begins filling and mighty fast. Mom gasps and she weeps and she screams and she sobs. Shrieks rip through me. I'm throbbing and some part of me is damming up. Or maybe it's drowning. She's asking how and who and am I okay and do I know just how much she loves me. And I say I don't know and I don't know and I don't know. And I say I know, Mom, don't worry, for sure I know. Mom says some other stuff I don't much follow. After that it goes something like this:

"My poor little girl."

"Isth, it'll be okay, Mom."

"Why you? It's a mother's worst nightmare."

I look at the frayed knubs at the carpet's edge. Her voice is smaller now, thinner and farther away.

"Worst nightmare."

I can feel my vagina stinging where it's torn up and that stinging is really bothering me. But for some reason I'm thinking mostly about just how badly I've messed up, how I've done that thing a good daughter should never, ever do. I've made my Mom's worst nightmare come true. All I want is to make things better for Mom. But I can't figure out how to undo what all happened to the parts. And I don't know how to express this pain, guilt, and heavy-miserable sadness, this big anger for what he did to me, or this smaller anger for the fact that we aren't just focused on that right now but instead on Mom's nightmare. I don't know how.

"I'm, I've gottha go, Mom. Love you."

"I love you, too. We'll . . . we're going to talk again soon?"

"'Kay, Mom. Bye."

Her cries muffle, cut off as phone plunks on receiver. Lindsey's asking.

"What'd she say?"

I'm not real sure so I don't say. I just look at Lindsey.

"When's she coming to take you home?"

I think on this for a second. I know what I've said hurt Mom, that she never had time to range over subjects like gathering up the parts, taking them home. But that's my fault, I think. I didn't plan this out like I should have. And now all I have are these questions like, What if I'd planned the call better? What if I'd given her more time to react? What if I'd had more comforting things to say? My mouth's no longer filled up with my own sock, stretched open, but my lips are useless. My nose and my chin are throbbing.

"I don't fthink she is."

Lindsey's face looks like she's just seen a kitten dismembered with a chainsaw.

"What do you mean?"

I don't know how to explain. So I just look at her. I watch her head shaking like she can't stop it, like something's just not adding up, not making sense.

"Try your father."

I dial information and I scrawl down his company's main number and I get an operator and I ask please connect me to Dad and I'm being connected and it's ringing.

"Dad?"

"L."

Lindsey's staring at me, but this time I spit out my line fast so she won't have to remind me. I say it on cue, just like I'm supposed to, and I'm a little proud of that.

"I was raped, Dad."

There are no Daddy sounds.

"Dad, I'm sorry."

Nothing. I try to stuff my whimper.

"Please sthay something, Dad."

His voice starts, snaps and falters. I can feel him beginning to shut down. I know I'm losing him too, just like I lost Mom a few minutes ago, and it scares me bad. But then I hear him and he's coming back, regaining himself and I'm so glad for that, because maybe now he'll be with me and maybe now I won't feel so all alone. Maybe we'll work together, make it better, make me better. Maybe we'll beat it. Maybe we can beat this thing.

And now Dad's talking a whole lot and superfast and my mind's carouseling around so I can't get what he's talking about, but it's got something to do with what must come next and who should be contacted and who's in charge and who holds the strings and who must have input. What are their names and what are their phone numbers and who is going to contact them?

Images from my bedroom hurtle in on me. The walls undulate, quiver.

"Will you contact them? Or will it be *your mother*?"

"I don't know."

"What about transferring to another university, L, someplace where no one knows? You could start fresh, over."

My eyes track the rusty canals on my wrists. No, Dad's not with me. He's nowhere near me. He's ten steps ahead of me, thinking about management, about how he can exert power on the situation. He's thinking about how now I could go to another school, maybe even a better school, and I'm throbbing.

I'm a tiny bit ticked at Dad for all those steps in his thoughts he's taken ahead of me, away from me. And I'm a little mad that just like Mom he hasn't just offered to pick me up, bring me home. But mostly I'm wracked with guilt. Now I know that I didn't do what I should have done. I should have kept it quiet. What happened to me must be hidden. I shouldn't have involved Mom and Dad at all. I've made everything way worse because now Dad will have to talk to Mom, and he's anxious and angry about that. I can't settle what to do and I don't know what to say, and I can't make it better for Dad either. So I stop.

"I've gottha go now."

"Love you, L."

"Love you too, Dad."

I set down the phone. Lindsey's been watching me, her eyes round and big. She's not asking what Dad said.

"Do you want to call your brother?"

I waggle my head. No way I'd drag my little brother Dave into the nightmare too. The divorce is already hurting him plenty, and he's under pressure not to get homesick at boarding school, to bring home straight A's, to do great for the varsity tennis team.

Lindsey glowers into the distance. I study her face, but I don't know what she's thinking. Her chin moves up. Her chin moves down.

CHAPTER THIRTEEN

Only big blank exists between when I called my parents and right now. No longer tethered in time, I've lost it again, slipped and fallen through new hours. My glasses are on. A pain slices up the small of my back. I stare at the clock on Lindsey's bedroom wall. It reads 11:53 p.m. It's been almost ten hours since the last time I recall seeing something that told time.

It's late Sunday night and I'm lying in Lindsey's futon bed, covered in two thick blankets and an old quilt. Lindsey's asleep next to me. All of the lights are on and still it doesn't seem nearly bright enough in here. I rub my wrists. The channels are there, now brown and scabbing. I remember the cord and I shiver. I order myself to stay awake so that if I hear any suspicious sounds I can call the police with the phone right on the floor next to me. He said he would come back, that he would kill me, so I have to stay awake, and the knife I nabbed from Lindsey's kitchen is under my pillow. I'll use it if I have to.

Time ticks over. It's Monday morning, 12:01 a.m. It's clear that my logic, my reasons for needing to stay awake, are totally flawed. He's not going to show up. He's in jail, still locked away. He can't really come back here and hurt me.

Unless he's posted bail. Unless he's back on the street. And once this possibility occurs to me, logic flitters away entirely, just like time. None of the parts can have faith in logic. They have to be awake so I have to be awake. And this lost time problem's getting worse. My mind's splintered and I'm falling, can't stop. If only I could grab onto something to stop myself, to help me catch up to myself in time.

I need a way to keep better track of it, I think to myself, to put pushpins in my memories. Maybe I can do this if I set them down permanently in ink. If I write in my journal, maybe I'll be able to capture some of these lost seconds, minutes, hours. That's what I have to do, but I can't write in my journal right now because it's downstairs with my Latin book, poetry book, the Pirandello script, and other stuff that came from my house. I can't figure out how it all got here. And I can't go downstairs alone in the dark by myself because there's a chance he could be there. I could wake Lindsey and ask her to come with me, but when I look at her face, there are new, dark blotches under her eyes. So I determine to stay extra quiet and I stare at the circle of light on the ceiling.

And I try to imagine what I would write if my journal were here. My mind bumbles through the missing hours. I went to the bathroom. I made Lindsey come with me and wait outside the door. I can recall the pain of peeing, the raw, glass splinter-knifing awfulness of it. There was blood in the toilet water. It turned my bright-yellow pee orange. And there were chunks of my insides, too. I watched them float there for a minute then flushed them away. Heaving nausea grabbed hold of me.

It's late Monday night, 11:33 p.m. Almost twelve new hours have tumbled past. I'm in Lindsey's room, sitting at her desk. Lindsey's asleep in her bed and all of the lights are on. I've wedged a pillow underneath me so the pain isn't as bad. My journal, extracted from that pile downstairs during daylight hours, is now in front of me. I have to try to record what's happened, recall things.

I flip through the earlier pages crammed with my daily entries, my notes from acting classes, my plans for self-actualization (try really hard to meditate, to appreciate nature more fully, to be a better, more caring friend), random ideas for plays and short stories, lists of things I should accomplish.

Time buckles. I glance back at Lindsey's wall clock. 11:43 p.m. Ten minutes just gone. I can't come up with anything to write. I'm hoping some memory will come back to me, something I can fill in. But I have nothing. What on earth have I been doing? Clocks have been moving on. I was here for it all. I must have been. Or did I go somewhere else, somewhere I can't recall? Have I been here for any of it? I don't know.

I've got to try to account for this time. So I do some lost-time math. I go with what I haven't been doing. I haven't been sleeping. My eyes are still puffy from where he hit them. They're also red, itchy. I have that brittle body, gliding through spider webs feeling of not sleeping for days. I have no memories of dreaming.

I cannot recall eating or drinking much. Maybe there were bites of crackers, sips of ginger ale. And imagining those things being there reminds me of something I do remember. Of being eight years old, of soaring, splotchy-eyed fevers, of Mom's soft voice and hands, of my mind turning gushy in the vaporizer mist.

That was a comforting memory. I'm feeling better now. I imagine writing it all down in my journal. But the pen in my hand doesn't move. I feel my lips crack into a small smile as I watch the page swimming in front of me. I'm going to write something. Time finally captured. Time stopped.

But then I feel it, the roadside-wasteland, all of this emptiness. He broke into my room on Sunday in the early morning. Now all of Sunday is over, most of Monday too. Nearly two days have come and gone. No one's come to hug me. No one's come to get me and take me home. I imagine writing these things down too. But I don't.

I can dimly recall trying to read. I know I thought I had a test to study for, that I had to read a textbook, like a college girl. At first I wasn't sure what class the test was supposed to be in. But after a while I must have determined that it was anthropology because I began reading that textbook. I remember letting my eyes roll over those weighty names of places and people, looking at the pages with pictures. But I had to stop reading before too long, because my eyes still hurt from where he hit them. I remember not remembering anything I'd read.

I have no other details I can fill in. I have nothing.

It's Tuesday morning now, 2:35 a.m. I'm back to Lindsey's desk and my journal. I wedge the pillow under myself again, tell myself maybe there are fewer pains down there now. Maybe things are getting better.

I try to do some more lost-time math. Almost three new hours have passed. I don't know what happened during them. I have that jarring in and out of wakefulness while still being awake feeling.

It's nearly Thanksgiving. Mom hasn't offered to take me home yet. Dad neither. I'm still here. No one has come to get me. A question keeps pressing in on me. I try hard to push it away, to forget about it. But I can't. Why hasn't anyone come? Why isn't my family here with me? My chest's caved in and I'm shaken all the time now. A lump of lonesomeness lives in my throat. Mom and Dad's not being here is bothering me. But I won't talk about this to Lindsey. I know with every hour that passes she thinks it more and more. There's something not right. The girl's parents should be here. I for sure won't raise this subject with Lindsey because I'm kind of embarrassed for my parents, for how their actions reflect on them, for how they reflect on me—say something bad about what kind of parents they are, what kind of daughter I am.

We both know exactly what Lindsey's parents would have done. They'd have been here as soon as they heard. No matter how strong Lindsey seemed on the phone, what she might have said or done, how busy they might have been, how full of their own plumbless sadness about what happened to her, they would have dropped it all. They would have jumped in the car, driven the five to six hours without stopping. They never would have let their daughter sit here, wondering and waiting.

It's not because Mom and Dad don't love me. They do. But I'm a new problem they can't figure out how to handle. It's important, I think to myself, to be conscious about this, to remember. Right now my parents are going through something truly awful themselves. They are probably nearly as freaked out as I am. They may not have a clue what to do either. Even though they'll want to, it's very likely that they won't be capable of helping me. They won't be able to make things better.

But knowing this fills me with fear. After all, if they won't be capable, who on earth will be?

It's still Tuesday morning, now 9:02 a.m. I rub my nose lightly. I remember the crunch, the blood, the metallic taste. I'm sitting on Lindsey's bed, my knees pulled up to my chest, my head against a mound of pillows propped against the wall. I should really go over my lines for *Six Characters in Search of an Author*. The performance is just a few weeks away. I thumb through the script but I can't make sense of the words. I decide against it. Instead I do some more lost-time math. Almost seven new hours have passed.

I remember a few things. Lindsey called my Mom. I heard Lind tell her that I'll be at her parents' house in Chelmsford, and that she needs to get over there and pick me up. I could hear in Lindsey's voice just how pissed she is. Lindsey told me to pack my things so I grabbed books, the Pirandello script, clothes. Lindsey squeezed them into one of her old suitcases. We're leaving.

It's Tuesday night, 6:45 p.m. I'm in New Hampshire in my old room in the basement. A small, ghostly pain moves through my body, disappears. All of the lights are on. The door is locked. The windows are locked.

I try to calculate how I got to 6:45 p.m. Things grayed out again. Well over nine new hours have passed, and I don't have the first idea what happened during them. That phone call Lindsey made to Mom, us packing some of my belongings, these are the last things I remember. There are no other memories. How this can be I can't understand. Surely something's defective, very wrong with me. For a moment I try to envision myself as a college girl home for the holiday, but all I can see is this bewildered figure in a basement wondering how she even got there. Where is that girl I was? I'm not a college girl. I don't know what I am.

I'm doing some more lost-time math. I know I have to find a way back, and that nothing good will happen until I can start keeping track, start remembering things. Lindsey must have driven us from Syracuse to Massachusetts, though I have no recollection of that drive. We must have arrived at Lindsey's folks' house, though I don't recall being there. I should start writing these things down. I can't keep anything straight in my head.

Mom must have been there when we arrived, though I have no memory of seeing her. I try to imagine what might have happened with me and Mom. Maybe our eyes locked and she held me steadfast and tight against her. Maybe we cried. All of these things are likely. But I don't know if they happened. I know Mom drove me to New Hampshire, though I don't remember her doing it. I know I must have eaten and drank, though I don't recall these things happening either.

I do know this. I'm alone now. I'm without Lindsey. And even though I'm not in Syracuse anymore and he's nowhere near here, I'm still not sleeping.

CHAPTER FOURTEEN

The hours come and go. I know I really should study my lines for the Pirandello play. I have to be ready for that performance coming up. But I can't because the words are squishy. I still haven't managed to write anything in my journal since it all happened. This time I'm going to, though. I'm really going to do it. I grab a pen. I open my journal. I write:

Tuesday night, 11:22 p.m.

I look at the words there on the page. They're not much, but they're something. I pause, try to think. What's happening? What's relevant? What's worth recording? All I can think to say is that this is Thanksgiving Break and I'm sitting up in my old bed in the basement. But writing that seems stupid, so I decide I won't write that down.

And my mind seems incapable of calculating lost-time math anymore. So instead I slip out of bed to look outside, push my nose too close to the window, flinch back, eyes watering from the pain. It's still sore. I search the night. I can't see anything bad or wrong out there, just stars, moon, a dusting of snow. But, I know now. Somewhere, somewhere close enough to get to me, there's something terrible in that night.

As I pull back from the window, my reflection draws away from me. I look. The light hair, the glasses, the eyes still puffed behind them, the nose bent sideways. I wonder whether I can or will ever be a college girl again. I don't know this new person. I'm not sure I want to know her. Thinking about her reminds me of other things I don't want to think about.

I recheck the locks on the door, on the windows. I crawl back into bed, sit upright, cover pulled tight to my chin. I look at the fluorescent light and I listen to the dog run door banging in the wind. I inch my right hand out from under the blankets. I grab my journal. I have to keep things straight. I have to have a record. I look down at the journal where it says *Tuesday, 11:22 p.m.* Before the Tuesday, I scrawl *It was.* Now the line reads: *It was Tuesday, 11:22 p.m.* By the end of the night, the journal entry looks like this:

It was Tuesday, 11:22 p.m.
It was Wednesday, 1:23 a.m.
It was 2:02 a.m.
It was 3:00 a.m. It was 4:09 a.m.
By now he would have come. By now he wouldn't be here anymore.

When the sun comes up on Wednesday morning, I reread my entry. This isn't good. This isn't good at all, I think. It's all in the past tense, as if I was never there for it. All I have is marking time and words about him. I have to do something to remember better. If I don't find a way to preserve my memories, I won't have any. I'm going to lose them all. So I make a decision. I will carry my journal around with me. I'll try to fill in what has happened right after it occurs, so that the next day I won't have only blanks to look at. Still, mostly I don't know what to write except the time.

It was Wednesday, 11:01 a.m.
It was 2:30 p.m. Fed Tawnee. Pet Tawnee. She's older than I remember.

It was 10:06 p.m.
It was Thursday, 3:12 a.m. Not sleeping. I'm scared of this
basement. Going to Mom's room.

I get scared, crawl in bed with Mom. Every light's on. There is,
I think, a warm happiness as her hand runs across the top of my
head, brushes over my hair. I float into consciousness. I float out
again.

Later Thursday, I write more:

Thursday, 8:15 a.m. Back in my room. Changed out of pj's.
4:22 p.m. Ate. Almost threw up. Thanksgiving, no Dad.

There might have been a largish bird, the taste of sausage-and-
mushroom stuffing and pucker-sour cranberry sauce, the smells
of Mom's chocolate pie, all cumulous-like and irresistible. But I
don't know. I was just trying to keep the food down. Later, when
I try to recall what the foods were, I'm frightened to realize I can't
remember.

Mainly I remember this.

Dad's not here. Most signs he ever lived here have vanished—
his yellow beekeeping suit, sawdust-caked radial arm saw, fetid
Gold Toe socks. I catch myself thinking about family bicycling
trips across the Cape, four-way living room hugs, visits to Kittery
Maine Lobster Pound, crazed two-on-two dining room soccer
tournaments, sparkling-sequin Boston Ballet Nutcracker Christ-
mases, Dave and I racing around Faneuil Hall, searching for Mom
and Dad's gifts, spending all we had on bubbling-fizzy Pop Rocks,
glow-in-the-dark yo-yos, bags of Superballs. Outside the orchard's
shriveled apricots, peaches, apples lay unburied. They have frozen
forgotten to the ground.

After dinner, after washing dishes, drying them, putting them
away, I return to my journal. I think I should write something
more here. But I'm not sure how to write what I have to write. And
even if I find a way to write it, I'm not sure what I should do about
it. I make myself scribble these new words.

6:03 p.m. Dave is staring at my mouth.

Dave's home from school for Thanksgiving, too, and he's looking at my face and lips a lot. I don't know what Mom and Dad have told him and I don't want him to be scared or sad or love me any less, so I don't talk with him about what happened.

More hours move by, night hours and early morning ones, too. I find I can't say much more about them. They come. They go. I record them in my journal.

9:44 p.m. 11:23 p.m.
1:15 a.m.

I look at *1:15 a.m.* on the page. It doesn't explain much, so I decide maybe I should write what I'm doing, too.

I'm looking at the clock plug.

I study the new line:

1:15 a.m. I'm looking at the clock plug.

This is not a pink clock. This is a black clock, my parents' old one. This clock's plug is in the wall. It's been in the wall a long, long time. It's only ever been unplugged for a few minutes to make space for the chair Mom and Dad bought me for Christmas in eighth grade, to plug in a bedside reading lamp next to it, the one I got on sale from the college bookstore freshman year.

By the end of the night, the entry reads:

9:44 p.m. 11:23 p.m.
1:15 a.m. I'm looking at the clock plug.
2:30 a.m. 3:11 a.m. 4:16 a.m.
He could have been here. But he's not. And I am.

Later that day I reread those last words. *He could have been here. But he's not. And I am.*

They make sense to me. They say something that makes sense. I pause. I think. There are new words I need to write in my journal now.

11:38 a.m. Visit Dad.

I don't know how I get to Dad's place. He lives in a condo now, footsteps away from the company where he works. Dad's trying real hard to act happy. But I know he's not.

Dad has two roommates. One is a twenty-six-year old, ex-aerobics instructor. She wears leopard-skin spandex leggings, high-heeled sandals, cherry-red nail polish. She acts hot for Dad. This is icky. Sometimes Dad acts like that back (even ickier). The other roommate is a kind, bald, divorced guy with two little kids who visit on weekends. Dad's fridge is bare except for one family-sized syrupy fruit cocktail jar from Sam's Club. His freezer's crammed with microwavable burritos.

Dad says he's working on himself. He tells me he's joined one self-help group for people who drink too much, another for people who eat too much, another just for men. I ask Dad why he goes to the first two since he doesn't drink much and he's not even near to fat. For the company, he says. Then I ask Dad about the last one. Dad says that he and his inner man have been too long separated, that from now on his life is about him. It's his time now. Mom plus his own mother damaged him. All his masculine energies have leeched out. He needs time and space to heal. I ask Dad what they do together, those middle-aged men all plopped together in a meeting room. At first Dad refuses to answer because I'm a girl, but after a while he tells me a little. They're trying to get in better touch with their mannishness, he explains. Sometimes they cry and they shout. Other times they march into the woods, beat on drums with sticks.

I don't understand. But I nod anyway. Dad and I don't talk about what happened to me. I can't remember how I get back to Mom's house from Dad's. But by the end of that night, I add:

4:11 p.m. Back home.
10:24 p.m. Study Pirandello.
11:59 p.m.
Saturday, 4:16 a.m. Still here.

I pick up Pirandello again, scan my lines, try to concentrate on each word. I say each one back to myself. They don't make sense to me but centering on getting each of the words right makes me feel better somehow, like I have something important to do, something that matters. And it helps me make it through those early morning hours between when he would have been there and when he would have left. And I make it. I do it all by myself. I do it without climbing into Mom's bed. But I'm unrelentingly afraid and wide awake for each second he would have been here. Every last one has ticked its way through me.

Later that day I write 1:27 p.m. I look at the time sitting there on the page. It doesn't convey what I need it to, what's happening here, what's going on with Mom. So I decide to add some words:

1:27 p.m. Mom's so sad.

I watch Mom. I feel so bad for her. She's an injured angelfish trapped in an undersized tank now. Mom moves from one ice-cold room to the next while old Tawnee follows her. Her palette with raisined-up watercolors and her dirty old brushes scatter the dining room table. Forgotten pulled weeds and frosted leaves obscure her gardens outside.

Mom cries lots now. She's got to manage her life, all those people at work, without losing it. And Mom going to therapy sessions after work now. She's confronting her issues just like Dad. Mom signed up for a women's rafting retreat trip out West. Men are jerks, Laura, she says. I need to be in the healing company of other women. Mom's turned my childhood bedroom into a Woolfish "Writing Room." It's packed with a new lacy daybed, an army of cushions, a rich wood desk, a computer. All signs of my little girlhood now live in boxes in the attic. Only those black-and-white faced harlequins with their satin outfits and jingling hats remain. And they'd be plenty hard to move because they're just plain spooky-looking.

Mom closes the door, sits writing children's stories, drawing lively ladybugs and flowers to go alongside them. Mom says she might send them to a publisher. It's not a sure thing she'd let them publish her work, though. She'd only consent if she can be the illustrator, too. Lots of writers are forced to work with crappy illustrators. Complete creative control, that's what I would demand, she tells me. Then her eyes fill with tears.

I pull my sweater sleeves long to hide the cord scars and I listen to Mom, watch her closely. They'd both said the word "divorce" plenty, she says. Still, she can't quite believe Dad did it, just up and left. She stoops her head, wiggles it back and forth.

I continue my entry. I do what I can do. I mark more time.

3:03 p.m.
5:25 p.m.

Then I pause. Maybe I ought to record something positive. So I revise a little. Now it reads *5:25 p.m. Ate. 5:45 p.m. Kept it down.*

No nausea, no vomiting. I tell myself that this is good, something to be glad about. But I don't feel glad. I need to write more, to explain more. Maybe doing these things will help. I add new words to my entry:

6:12 p.m. It's like Chutes and Ladders.

I catch myself thinking about Dad and Mom a lot. The analogy seems childish, but it's the best I can do. They're like the busted-up boy surrounded by jar pieces and broken cookies at the bottom of the longest slide in Chutes and Ladders. I wish I could make them all better, bring back their bone-warming laughter, their easy, maple syrup smiles. But I can't. So I try to listen a lot, not talk too much about what happened to me. Most of the time that's pretty easy because they don't ask. When I wish they did a little, I push that thought down, lock it away. As if they aren't already busy dealing with their own problems right now. And even if they weren't, they wouldn't know what to say. No one does.

I pick up the Pirandello script again. There is no understudy who can play my role, so I have to do it. It's important that I do it. As I look at my lines, I realize I remember them. The play memorization has somehow stuck with me. I have memories about a character's words. It's not the same as having my own memories. But, still, I'm grateful for them. By the end of the night, I scratch a few more things on the page:

8:01 p.m. 12 midnight. It's Sunday. Miriam. I miss Miriam.

Just a few weeks more and my other best friend, Miriam, will finally be back from England. Maybe Miriam will know what to do. And next to those words, I write in *Sunday, 4:11 a.m. I'm still here.*

I'm still here. The words seem obvious, banal. But I can't come up with anything else. Plus, they're true, mostly.

Hours later I add more words to my journal.

7:23 a.m. Frost's "Birches."

I'm outside alone, and it doesn't feel scary. The woods are all snowed in, hushed. Clotted snow slops from the fir trees. My down coat catches on old prickers as I tramp on long-frozen lady's slipper carcasses. Clearing the trees, I mark up the fresh snow. Tawnee trails behind me, leaving grizzled paw prints too. I stare at the galena sky, at the swung over snow-white birches on the field's edge, the shattered icicles on the ground. These birches remind me of that early Robert Frost poem that we read in middle school by the same name in which he describes the birches clicking on each other in the breeze, turning colors in the sunlight.

Its first few lines are "When I see birches bend to left and right / Across the lines of straighter darker trees, / I like to think some boy's been swinging them." The narrator knows what's true—an ice storm is responsible for birch branches being brought low, sagging to the ground. But he likes to imagine that a little boy's been swinging on them. In Frost's story, the boy was supposed to be doing his chores, getting the cows back in, but decided to play a game instead. And since he's the kind of boy who lives too far from town to learn baseball, this swinging-on-birches game is the one he plays.

I've always loved this poem. There's a great line about the boy's technique, how he learns "about not launching out too soon," how to balance on the branches, to swing lightly. I could also identify with that small-town boy's plight, too, all bored and baseball-less. Every time I've reread that poem—and in New England schools it gets assigned over and over—it's felt like sunbeams sweeping through me. Tiny mist-clouds sit like a fluffy icing over the snow. A dark flock cuts across the grayness.

Somewhere hidden under all that white there's that swimming hole I'm sitting beside in a wrinkled picture, an eleven-year-old me in a green bikini splattered with pink flowers. There's that sheep laurel I'm standing next to in that black-and-white photo, a fourteen-year-old me with immense platinum hair, jean jacket, and headphones. There's that oak sapling I'm looking at in that candid photo, an artsy eighteen-year-old me, eyes rimmed in kohl eyeliner, in a white blouse, a flouncy blue miniskirt, off-white flats.

I take out a cigarette, clamp it with my lips. They hurt less now. I put a clicking flame to it. I suck in. Whipping-cold smoke fills my mouth, my lungs. I seem to be smoking more. I plod back to the house. When I get there I pour some coffee, drink it. Mom and I pack up the car. We get in and Mom begins to drive and I can feel her looking at my cheeks, my nose. And I can hear them, too, the new clenches in her throat, the runs and catches in her breath. These things worry me, not so much for me but for Mom. She's watching me, needing me to be okay, wanting to say something reassuring. But she doesn't talk about these things, and I don't either. Instead I pick up my journal again and write:

9:05 a.m. Mom's driving me back to Syracuse.

Thanksgiving Break's over and I need to get back. I have papers to write, exams to take, a Scene Study to do, a play to perform. Mom and Dad keep asking if I need more time. They want to know whether I'm ready to go back to Syracuse. Dad says don't do it, don't go back, Laur. Move closer. Take some time off. Find another school to go to so you don't have to think about it, won't have to talk about it. Mom says do what makes you feel good, honey. Mom says shut up, Bob. Don't tell her what to do.

Whatever that thing was, the sky-wide something I hoped could be made better by coming back here, it hasn't been. Was it home? Was it family? Maybe. I don't know. But it wouldn't matter anyway. These things aren't anymore. They don't exist.

I can't go back to my apartment. And it wouldn't be right for us both to stay at Lindsey's. So when we get to Syracuse that night Mom and I stay in a hotel, the Genesee Inn. We share a queen-size bed and Mom lets me keep all the lights on. By the end of the day, my journal includes a few new things:

5:55 p.m. Ate room service. Kept it down.
7:14 p.m. Woke up. I must have been asleep.
8:20 p.m. Had a glass of water.
11:07 p.m. Studied Pirandello script.
1:03 a.m. Read Frost's "Birches."

I sit in bed, my back supported by two pillows propped against the headboard. Mom sleeps lightly next to me. It feels strange to be back in Syracuse, just blocks away from my old apartment. I try to picture it in there, my computer, my desk, the milk crates with all the books crammed inside, my bed, my awful bed. Thinking about it makes my stomach toss a bunch, drop away.

I know something that will cheer me up. I take out my broke-back copy of Frost's *Mountain Interval*, originally published in 1920, turn to "Birches." And I read it. I don't read it like I tried to read the textbook for that test or like I read the Pirandello play, to memorize lines. I really read it. This is the very first time since everything happened that I really read anything. I take the poem in carefully, read it from beginning to end.

I stop. It all hits me at once like a fire hose to the face. I'm such an idiot. How could I have been so foolish as to believe that I ever understood this poem? I guess up until now there's never been any reason to question my reading of Frost's words. Iced-up birches like this, no matter how they got that way, were magical things. But the poem's not about playful birch-swinging or a small-town boy. It's about something else. Frost says what he means plainly enough early on in the poem. I just couldn't see it. He describes his hope, his wish, his preference: "I like to think some boy's been swinging them." But right after writing this Frost admits that there's a truer, darker story that must be told: "But swinging doesn't bend them down to stay. / Ice-storms do that."

Ice storms do that. Ice storms maim birches, and the trees don't necessarily recover: "bowed / So low for long, they never right themselves: / You may see their trunks arching in the woods / Years afterwards, trailing their leaves on the ground." Happy swinging this is not. In spinning his fairy-tale version, Frost's narrator is actually acknowledging the true pain of the ice storm's reality. Though he wishes the bent birches could be the result of play, he knows better. Instead, he's acknowledging that trying to deny what really happened won't work. It won't make the truth go away.

I pause, reread the poem slowly. And this time through I notice something else. For Frost's narrator the maiming of these birches is no isolated problem. It exemplifies a more general fact—that life itself is a series of painful surprises: "And life is too much like a pathless wood / Where your face burns and tickles with cobwebs / Broken across it, and one eye is weeping / From a twig's having lashed across it open."

I think about Frost's words. It's not just that a twig hits you in the eye. It's that this twig hits your wide-open eye while it's taking in the world. And after that hit, you won't ever again be quite the same. It will change things. Like how you see, what you see. It changes whether you see at all. I close my eyes. Wet and hot builds there. I write a final entry for the day, lines from Frost's poem that now chill me:

> . . . *they never right themselves.*
> *You may see their trunks arching in the woods*
> *Years afterwards, trailing their leaves on the ground* . . .

CHAPTER FIFTEEN

Whole days disappear while Mom and I stay at The Genesee Inn—the rest of Monday, Tuesday, Wednesday, and Thursday, too. I talk to a woman in the District Attorney's Office. She tells me he's out. Just days ago he paid the $25,000 bail. He's in this city somewhere, could be anywhere. The woman says that he had no trouble posting it, that this doesn't surprise her in the least. I ask her why. She asks me whether I recognize the rapist's last name. I say that I don't, that he's a stranger. She explains that he's from one of the oldest, wealthiest families in Syracuse. I tell her thank you, hang up the phone. But I don't want to know these things. I don't want to know anything about him, about his family.

Being so close to where it happened scares me. My thoughts keep busting apart. Or hammering on the same things over and over. My mind keeps at its calculations. I think about how long it would take someone to get from my old apartment to the Genesee Inn on foot. Ten to fifteen minutes maybe. By car, three. He might be here already, somewhere in the hotel. I wouldn't know it. He could be the light-haired bellhop downstairs, the light-haired man who delivered our room service. And just thinking about him, not knowing exactly what he looks like, makes me think about my bedroom, about all my stuff still sitting there, unmoved. I'm nauseous and my heart is pounding. So is my head.

I stare at my lines for the Pirandello play. Going through with performing in this play seems very significant, like if I can manage to do this maybe I'm going to be okay. In the hotel Mom and I order room service. We go for short walks down the hotel hallways together and I can't breathe, make Mom rush back to the room with me, lock the door.

But one morning I get daring, agree to Mom's suggestion that we eat one breakfast downstairs in the restaurant. Its glass windows look out on the street, at the gray sidewalk slush. I gnaw at an English muffin, my eyes flitting around the room, looking to see who's in it with me. I'm safe. Just waiters and waitresses, lobby attendants, old men with newspapers, a few parents and their nearly college-age kids. But then I'm losing my breath, all of my parts throttling in on me at once, and I'm telling Mom give me the room key, rushing back, locking the door, drawing the curtains. And I'm sitting on the bed, staring at that door, waiting for a knock, asking who it is. Mom's saying it's her and I'm letting her in, quickly locking again.

Sometime during all of those room service meals, those forays into the hallway and downstairs with Mom, those long night hours lying anxious and awake in the hotel lamplight, I make a decision. I just can't do this. I want so badly to be brave, to not have this change who I was, who I want to be. But I can't be here. I can't remain in Syracuse.

I will still perform in that play. Everyone's worked so hard on it. I won't let them down, can't let myself down. I have to keep my promises, need to be responsible. But once the play is over, I'm taking the rest of the semester off. I hate to do this because it's an admission of defeat. I tell myself that I ought to be able to get over my fears, should be way stronger than this. But I can't and I'm not. I try to convince myself that this is okay. It has to be. It's what I can manage. It's just a few short weeks I'll miss, and then I'll come back to Syracuse stronger, more capable of handling everything, in the spring semester.

I make a point of squaring everything with my professors. They know what happened to me and they are kind, don't make me feel worse—any lesser than or more sullied—than I already do, and I'm thankful for this. They say we'll make it work. They say they'll help me. They'll send my final exams to New Hampshire, and I can complete them at home. As long as I send everything back by the end of the semester, I won't get incompletes. This is good news, very good. I tell myself that I'm lucky, that I'll be able to work harder than my classmates, write better papers because I won't have all those other distractions—like parties, like friends, like grocery shopping, like going to class.

But I know. I am no lucky one. If only those were my distractions. I'm not capable of going to a party. I can't walk on a street alone. I can't go see friends or make my way to a grocery store. I can't go to classes. I can't do any of these things. I can't. Knowing he's out there, that he could be anywhere, this is my distraction.

My next entry reads like this.

Friday morning. Talk to Mr. R.

I know exactly what I have to do to complete all of my classes except one, Scene Study. And I don't know what to do about it, so I call Mr. R, and I reach his secretary and I tell her my name. She says hang on a second, puts me through to him. Mr. R asks how I am and I say I'm okay, my cheeks, my nose, my lips, my other injuries are getting better, and I want to schedule my performance of Mastrosimone's *Extremities* scene. Mr. R says he's very glad to hear I'm doing alright because he's been worried. I say yeah, thanks, and I'll drive back from New Hampshire before the semester ends to do the scene. I don't say I won't be able to drive myself, that I'll have to have someone who loves me stay in the hotel with me all night long with every light on, that this someone will have to walk me to and from the class. Instead, when Mr. R takes a breath I add that if that option won't work, I'll do it the first day of next semester. I feel like I can really understand the scene now, I say, am capable of doing a good Marjorie. I don't say that it scares me to think about why I understand Marjorie now, that I'm a little jealous and angry at her because she escapes her rapist and I didn't.

Mr. R clears his throat. Mr. R says that he doesn't think it's a good idea. He'll grade me on my other work in the course, but not the Scene Study performance. I need to take more time, get help, he says. But I can do it, I say. I really, really can. Not now, not for a long while, he tells me. Mr. R explains that I won't be able to get enough critical distance to do it justice.

I don't tell Mr. R that I need to do this *Extremities* scene very badly, need to know myself capable of performing it. I don't say that part of me still believes that I can make things right again if only he'll let me do this. I don't say that what I really want to do is rewrite my life so that it's more like the play. I don't say that I don't just want to play Marjorie, I want to *be* Marjorie. Marjorie is strong and Marjorie is tough and Marjorie doesn't get raped and Marjorie survives and Marjorie gets revenge. Instead I mumble my agreement, thank him for his time, hang up the phone.

Later I rewrite the entry to read *Friday morning. Mr. R says no.* Then I add the words

Friday early afternoon. Get my stuff.

My Aunt Anne, Mom's sister, arrives from Pennsylvania. The air's like a corpse and I'm standing on the sidewalk outside the house where I used to live, where it happened. I know everything's thrown out of place and wrong up there, just like he left it, so I don't look at it.

One of my hands is holding a cigarette and the other's submerged in the pocket of the secondhand mancoat I bought a few days back. It's four sizes too big (it's absolutely perfect), and I'm carrying Lindsey's old jackknife in my pocket for protection, in case he shows up here. All my knife openings and closings have slashed up its silky pocket lining. I wriggle my fingers through the tears.

I hear Mom and Aunt Anne. They're going up the stairs, down the stairs, with my stuff. It's like they're cleaning out the closets of a dead girl, making room for a live one to move in. And they're stacking everything from my bedroom in the car trunk, saying words. The futon where he raped me. The computer with its cursor. The milk crates clogged with books, one with the

Extremities scene on top, the scene I won't be performing. Seeing it there, I feel a tightness press at my chest. No-name teddy bear. My doll, Ursha. The mirror. The pink clock stuck on three and five. My clothes. Those flats Dad bought me, still missing their outfit.

Mom's ash-blonde bob shudders as she stumbles on little snakeskin-heeled feet. Aunt Anne, with her jet-black layered cut, sets Mom upright. Mom and I get in the car and Aunt Anne thunks the trunk shut. Frozen rain comes down. I sit in the backseat next to all that's mine. Mom's and Aunt Anne's Philly accents shear over one another. Their words fizz then pop. Fizz. Pop. But I won't speak. I can't make my way into their dialogue or their silences anymore. Aunt Anne blabbers deep Molson Golden Girl and American Express sounds just like in her radio and television spots. The "girl with the golden laugh," they write about her in *People*, *USA Today*, and *New York Magazine*. Her throaty-deep giggle is seductive. But Aunt Anne's not laughing now. Gray tree limbs snarl against the sky.

Mom and Aunt Anne move me to Lindsey's apartment. I'm thankful to them for doing this, Mom taking off work to bring me back here for the play performance, Anne coming all this way to move my stuff. But, honestly, I don't give a rat's butt about my junk. Them going in there, getting it, hauling it away so I don't have to—these are kind things. But mostly I'm thankful for what their doing these things means. It means that they love me, want to protect me, want it to be harder for him to keep his promise to come back and kill me.

Friday late afternoon. Get ready for play.

I determine to go through my lines for *Six Characters in Search of an Author* again. This play focuses on a rehearsal for a play during which six people show up, tell the actors that they are unfinished characters who have come to life and must find an author to finish their story. The actors and director agree to act their story out, but the characters challenge the actors' choices and eventually demand to play themselves. I think about how this play questions the structure of theater itself—how stages are set up, actors interact, authorship functions. My lines go in and out of focus.

This idea of an unfinished character doesn't seem at all strange. I feel unfinished, too, just a bunch of experiences I can't make sense of, have no control over. Like the characters, I feel as if I don't know where things are going, like I'm not the one writing my own life.

Friday night. First performance.

My cheeks, lips, and nose are still a little swollen. But I tell myself that they're not, that I'm all better now, as I stand off stage, waiting for the play to begin. And suddenly I'm just not at all sure I can do this. He could be in the audience. But Lindsey hugs me, tells me that he's not, that she's watched every single person walk in and there's no one who fits his description. So I try to steady myself while she holds my hand. And when I hear my cue, I walk onto the stage. Everything's brightness out there, as if nothing beyond the stage can get in, as if nothing in the whole wide world can ever again hurt me. There's a numb throbbing down there, but I let it go. I'm not the raped one right now. I'm someone different, something else. My voice is saying some words. I'm relieved that they aren't mine. I let them go, too.

I won't remember what happens up there, just have the sense that it felt right and good to follow through on my commitments, that for a few moments I almost felt like a normal college girl. When I get off the stage, Mom's there and she's crying, saying she's real proud of me, and I tell myself that maybe I will be, maybe I'm going to be alright.

But I can't ever manage to shake them, all of my mixed-up-uneasy feelings that there's something deeply wrong with me, something that doing the play has highlighted even more. How can I manage to remember someone else's lines yet not remember what's happening to me? How can it be so easy for me to be someone else, so hard for me to be myself?

Mom drives us back to the Inn. Before I get out of the car, I search the darkness for any signs of him. Mom watches me. She looks frightened for me, and her mouth opens. But no words come.

CHAPTER SIXTEEN

I return to New Hampshire. More days pass, but I do not write about them in my journal. When I try to fill in the missing pieces, I can't. I don't know what's happened. So I resolve once more to write more about things as they happen. I don't write as much as I told myself I would. But I begin to write in earnest. And I start to think of my journal not just as a place to capture memories, but as a place to be heard, to preserve what's true. When I make my first full entry, it's like surfacing to breathe after holding my breath underwater for so long I'd begun to panic. The entry goes like this:

Sunday, December 11

> *I woke screaming from a nightmare. The last thing I remember were words written on a wall in human blood, warning me—"three days left to live." The locks were bolted, I was sure of that. I also knew it didn't matter.*

Not a fun night, but I'm beginning to be able to write about it in a voice that resembles mine. Other entries follow.

Monday, December 12

I dreamed I was Marjorie. I put on a kettle, sprayed wilted plants with water. I wasn't rushing the action. When the rapist showed up, I kicked him in the crotch with my high-heeled boots, punched him in the face. Sal, Cathy, Miriam (back from London), and I tied him up, stuffed him into the fireplace.

Then there was a wide smattering of applause. I couldn't tell where it was coming from. And then I realized I was on a stage. Beyond it was all drippy fog. But through that swirling fog I was sure could see the Trees—Little Tree and Tall Tree—their bones all back-in-place and healed. Lindsey and Dave were standing next to them, smiling. And Mom and Dad were there next to them too, holding hands. And Susan Sarandon, who played Marjorie in the play version, was behind them. I'd swear Farrah Fawcett was standing there with her, too.

Tuesday, December 13

Lena McBride, the DA who's handling my case, called. She said that the perpetrator entered a sixty-day alcohol and drug abuse treatment center. He can't leave there, so he's not on the streets. My neck eased, jaw loosened. She said that this is strategic, so his attorney can build a case that he raped me during an alcohol-induced blackout, that his client's judgment was impaired, that he can't remember, get him out of serving time. Even if a jury won't buy those arguments, she told me, at least it'll look like he's getting help for his problems. She said that I need to be prepared for these things. My neck turned thick, jaw locked-down. I didn't feel prepared.

Thursday, December 15

Two hours of sleep and in my waking dream I was on a highway hitchhiking. I've never hitchhiked before in real life. But I was hitchhiking. Someone was with me, someone I'd never seen before. I couldn't tell if it was a man or a woman, but I felt a comfort with this person. It was like the combination of myself and this person made us whole. A man in a tan Buick picked us up. The driver wasn't him. I know what he looks like enough to say it wasn't him. But this man had bad, crazed eyes. And after I saw those eyes, my comrade became defenseless, tied and gagged in the backseat, but still there.

The driver was fighting me, not with his hands but with his mind. I knew if he gained control of my thoughts, he'd gain control over my body. So I thought as hard as I could. And it was really working. But then the driver spoke and he had my attacker's voice and I lost all power and the world was spinning and I was tired, frightened, half alive. I screamed but no voice came out. He was saying that he was going to rape me in the library, that amongst all that knowledge, he'd commit this act of ignorance. I woke up afraid of books.

Friday, December 16

I got a letter from Miriam today forwarded from my old apartment. She says that "The flat's adorable. I can see Big Ben, the whole city lit up at night," that she "saw the most amazing Shakespeare last week." She said "Miss you! XOXO, Mir." I think about time, how many minutes and hours and days have passed since it happened, how much I cannot recall. Just a few more days and Miriam will be home and she'll talk about how much fun she had in spite of missing us all so horrible-bad and she'll recall London's battalions of nasty puddings but then she'll see that something's not right with me and she'll ask what's up and I'll tell her what happened, that my parents are already broken, that it's taking a big toll on Lindsey. And Miriam will hold me, cry with me, listen. Miriam will know what to do.

I stay up late each night and into the mornings. I write in my journal, I write my papers, I write my exams. I revise my papers, double check my exams. They need to be perfect. At night, when I do sleep, it's mostly in ten-minute stretches, and I'm in Mom's bed and we keep all the lights on. Lots of times I wake up trying to yell, my voice choking in my throat.

CHAPTER SEVENTEEN

It's days away from the sparkling holiday. There could have been fire sounds, a hot storm of sputtering and popping, the tastes of Mom's cookies with the Triple Sec prune filling (an old Russian family recipe), the smells of fir tree all freshly cut. These things probably happened.

But I won't remember them. I'll remember this.

I'm at Mom's, sitting on the wooden step dividing the old house part from the addition Dad built, rearranging lukewarm apple-cinnamon oatmeal in a white bowl. The television is on. But I can't see it. The woodstove, overflowing trash bin, and galvanized ash can are in the way. A man's talking on the TV. A plane exploded over Lockerbie, Scotland.

I stand up, walk over, look. There's landscape, stripped and charred. Distressed cameramen and reporters scuttle around like confused ants. The man says that 259 people exploded too. The man says that people on the ground were killed. The plane originated in London. It was packed with American college students.

Four from Colgate, four from Brown, two from Seton Hall, two from SUNY Oswego, one from Hampshire College. Thirty-five from Syracuse University.

If you need to find out whether someone you know was on the plane, the man says, call Pan Am. So I repeat the number until I get to the phone and Mom asks what I'm doing, but I don't know what to say or how to explain, so I point at the television and I try to dial.

A recorded male voice answers and it reads names, precise and solemn, name after name after name. At first there are names I don't know. But then they come. That tiny opera singer with the sweet smile and long, wavy dark hair from my dorm freshmen year. That incredible playwright guy and his ballerina girlfriend from dance class. That tall, pale-skinned actress with the auburn hair from that play last semester. Gone.

And then I hear it. Miriam. My former roommate, my other best friend. Who's from before, who's going to live with me and Sal again, who'll know what to do. No, no. Miriam's still in the air, moving over water and land, peeling back time, and she'll be home soon.

But I heard. My deflated kickball head rolls in my hands. And I know I should do something but I don't know what, and my mouth seems like it'll move and it'll for sure tell Mom what's going on but it doesn't, just stays locked shut. My legs lead me past the sprawling, overgrown fern in the window, out the front door—no jacket, no mittens, no hat—and Tawnee squirts out behind me. We shred through the orchard, rip past snow-caked stone walls into the woods.

I fall into wet snow. Squirrels dart downward. Tawnee barks at them.

Miriam won't sing a song. Miriam won't do a pirouette. Miriam won't perform in a play. Miriam won't ever anything. Ever again. I'm there in that chilly blanket of flurries for a while. Maybe for minutes, maybe for closer to half an hour. Then I wipe my face on my mancoat sleeve, push up from the cold. I walk back.

Later I write it in my journal. The black ink keeps running where my tears fall. It dries that way.

Wednesday, December 21. Miriam died.

CHAPTER EIGHTEEN

Tuesday, December 25. Christmas Day.

In my dream the world was burning. I was in New Hampshire watching it from the living room window and my legs wouldn't move. Trees lit like torches were falling on people and their flesh was melting. I watched their silent screams.

Friday, January 6. Medical reports.

My medical reports came in the mail. No semen was detected. There was my blood and blood that was not mine. They found hairs that don't belong to me. They found out I'm not pregnant. I ought to be grateful for this, I know. Instead, I threw up.

Wednesday, January 11. Back in Syracuse. Met with the DA Lena.

The DA Lena is talking to me. She's tall, has auburn hair and muscular calves, a face splashed with freckles. She's telling me to wear something conservative, feminine when I appear in front of the Grand Jury. I'm trying hard to describe the one good dress hanging in my closet without using the words "garbage bag." It's like my mancoat, I tell her, long, black, big. She nods, says it should be okay.

The DA Lena is trying to make me understand that we need to go over my testimony, asking if I'm ready, and I'm telling her that I'm ready. But I'm not.

Our conversation goes something like this.

"I'm going to ask you a series of questions, Laura. Are you okay with that?"

I nod.

"What do you do?"

"I'm a student."

"Where and what are you studying?"

"Syracuse University. I'm a double major in English and theater."

"Where were you on the morning of November twentieth at approximately three a.m.?"

"Asleep in my bed."

"How were you awoken?"

"Something I heard woke me up, and there was a man standing over my bed."

"What did the man do when he saw that you'd seen him?"

"He pushed my face onto my bed, held a knife to my throat, said he'd kill me."

"Let's stop a second. You need to say that he 'held a sharp object to my throat that he said was a knife.' There were two screwdrivers and a putty knife found at the scene, no knife."

"No knife?"

"Laura, it's more than likely that what he told you was a knife was actually a sharp screwdriver."

"But he said it was a knife."

"All I'm saying is that since there's no knife in evidence, better to be more ambiguous."

"Okay."

"What did the man do when he saw that you'd seen him?"

"He pushed me down on my bed, held a sharp object he said was a knife to my throat, said he was going to kill me."

"Then I'll say 'Then what happened.' And you answer that question."

"He told me to take my pants off."

"What happened next?"

"When I wouldn't, he hit me a lot, told me he'd kill me. When I still wouldn't, he did it himself, shoved himself in me, and I screamed, told him no over and over again."

"Stop. That's good. But, and I know this is hard, you have to use the actual words. You need to say that 'he put his penis in my vagina and in my anus.'"

"I'd rather not."

"It will help our case if you can be specific. Can you do that?"

I nod.

"Let's try again. Then what happened?"

"He told me to take my pants off. When I wouldn't, he hit me over and over again, told me he would kill me. When I still wouldn't take my pants off, he ripped them off, shoved his penis in my vagina and in my anus. I kept screaming, telling him no."

"You were resisting?"

"Do you have to ask me that?"

"They just need it confirmed—that this wasn't consensual."

"A stranger broke into my home, bound me up with cord, gagged me. In what universe could this appear consensual?"

"It's obvious to you, to me. But we can't count on it being obvious to a jury. I know this is hard, Laura, but try to just answer the question. You were resisting?"

"Yes."

"You screamed?"

"Yes, until he gagged me, then I couldn't anymore."

"Just say 'yes.'"

"Yes."

"Did you kick him?"

"Yes."

"Did you punch him?"

"Yes."

"Did you keep saying no?"

"Yes."

"That's good, very good. You'll do just fine."

"But what if I start crying, have trouble answering the questions? If I do something wrong, he could go free, right?"

"That's true, but we're going to do everything we can so that doesn't happen."

"If he doesn't go to jail, what's to stop him from hunting me down and killing me?"

"Let's focus on what we have to do now. You alright?"

The DA Lena squeezes my shoulder, and I nod. Not one thing about me is alright.

CHAPTER NINETEEN

Dark hours now I sleep in Lindsey's futon with her. All lights must be on. And there are bruises on Lindsey's legs and arms where I've kneed her, slapped her. I'm appalled about this, can't understand why on earth I'm hurting her. So I say I'm so sorry, Lind. I totally don't mean to. I'll just move back to my own room, no biggie, really. But Lindsey says cut it out, that I belong here, with her, now.

Lindsey knows how I won't ever go into an unlit room by myself, how I try hard to hold my pee until it starts to get light outside, how I don't sleep on my stomach anymore because next time I have to see him coming at me. And she knows the knife I grabbed from her kitchen is still tucked under my pillow. But we don't talk about these things.

When her boyfriend Jim visits, I move to a mattress end to end with hers, we all sleep with our heads together, and each of them clasps one of my hands. I try to never let my eyes close because if I do, blood-spattered images smash in on me, play over and over like a filmy-black looped cassette.

CHAPTER TWENTY

Friday, January 13. Grand Jury.

I sit on a wooden bench outside the court room and Mom's here with me. She's saying she loves me and it's going to be okay. Even though Mom's being here means more than I can begin to know how to express, Mom has no idea who I am anymore. I don't either. And I don't believe her. Nothing will ever be okay again.

The DA Lena is speaking to me. She says remember to answer the questions with a yes or a no. She says don't forget that the knife is not a knife, it's a screwdriver or a putty knife. Forget it. Just call it a "sharp object." She says remember to say "vagina" and "anus." She says remember to say "kicked," "screamed," and "hit."

Mom's cringing, cambering in more with each new word DA Lena says, and I want so badly to make it better for Mom, to take away her hearing, to protect her. But I know now that I can't. So instead I tell myself to recall the things the DA Lena said. I'm on-purpose not wearing my contacts or my glasses so I won't have to see the jurors' faces.

Someone grabs my hand, leads me to a room, to a wooden

chair in a wooden box. I try hard to make believe that it's made out of old Lincoln Logs and I tell myself that this actually makes me feel a little better even though I know it really won't. The box looks out on the lawyers and the jury and I for sure am going to be sick and all my air's running out, can't get enough. I can just make out a black blob-like thing next to me.

Everything gets quiet and the DA Lena approaches me, and she asks me if I'm okay, if I'm ready, and I hear myself answer yes, and one by one she asks me the questions we practiced and I try to answer them just like she told me and the questions are mostly in the same order as when she asked them before.

With each new answer, I'm rattling more with the shame. And even though I promised myself I wouldn't cry, the gunky mascara and eyeliner are landing on the front of my garbage bag dress. I want so badly to be brave, to answer all the questions like I'm smart and capable. But I can't.

By the end of those questions, I'm sobbing, cannot speak anymore. The DA Lena says thank you, nothing further. I blot my chin with the tie wrapping up my garbage bag dress. The black blob says you can step down now, miss. An arm leads me from the wooden box, down the middle aisle and the DA Lena motions me to follow her out of the courtroom and I do. Mom's there waiting for us and she makes for my sake like she's stopped crying. But we both know she hasn't.

The DA Lena starts talking.

"You did good, Laura."

I know that's a total lie, but I'm thankful for it. We leave Mom and the DA Lena leads me to an elevator, excuses herself for a moment, and when she moves away I don't know what to do. I'm unraveling, pulling apart and I can't see anything. So I stand still. But then I feel eyes on me and I hear new voices. I can't tell where they're coming from.

"That's her, that's *the girl.*"

The voices mold in that air. If only me not being able to see the world would mean that the world couldn't see me, too. If only I could go missing then no one would know—where I was, that I was. If only no one ever knew that I was. Then no one could think of me as raped-girl.

But I can't make myself disappear. I'm stuck here and I can't change this. I'm the poor thing, the girl who can imagine, the one trying to stop her tights-covered knees from knocking together, her eyes from flooding. I am the girl. And everyone knows. The girl is less than nothing.

CHAPTER TWENTY-ONE

Friday, January 13. He's indicted. Tuesday, January 17. He pleads not guilty.

Not guilty—like it never happened, like none of it ever was. But, then how? How can I be here, like this?

CHAPTER TWENTY-TWO

More time passes. My insides are shuffled and I can't ever sleep. Lindsey pallbearers me to and from each class. Or we go over in the Lezzy. Or I try to walk myself. Cars pass by and I look at each driver's face. I hear footsteps behind me, turn around, make sure it's not him. When I think about what happened, about the "not guilty," the right side of my brain spasms, feels like it's close to a rupture.

Thursday, January 26. The gentleman.

The phone's ringing. Lindsey picks it up, says some lady wants to talk to me. I grab onto it.

A voice says hello. It's a woman voice. The voice says that it's the dean of some college at the university. I imagine her goggle glasses, mouse-brown mom-perm, ill-fitting suit.

"How are we doing?"

"Okay."

"We've been concerned about you."

She asks me what I know about the rapist. I say I don't know much but that he's a stranger, that he's not a college student, that he's from Syracuse. But the truth is I know more—his leather jacket, his laugh like tires on gravel, his face like a chalkboard.

Then her voice starts to sound like someone talking to an extra dunce-y toddler. She says she knows his grandfather well, that everyone does at the university, that he's a wonderful man.

The woman has many questions to ask me, she says. Did I know that his grandfather is the president of the city's single-largest employer? Did I know his grandfather is on the university's Board of Trustees? Did I know that this man is responsible for the largest sports complex on the university campus? I've been there, I think, for football games, for concerts.

I can't understand why she's saying what she's saying. Or why I'm listening. I don't want to know about him. I don't want to know about his family, their connections. I don't want to know how much money they've shoved at the university.

Then she goes oleaginous, like what she's about to share is an extra-special secret. But I'm no fool. I know it won't be.

"He brought his grandson to fund-raising event recently. Such a nice, polite, well-mannered boy. Well-dressed. A gentleman."

My breath's bellowing in my ears and my blood's clamoring inside my wormy capillaries through to my clogging-up arteries, and I wish I could think of some way to shut her up, to stop all of her terrible talking. But I can't.

"Why are you telling me this?"

"You have a right to know. And, honestly, it's hard to believe he'd do something like this."

My mouth's maelstrom-muttering.

"He was caught raping me."

Her throat sounds stuck. Her orchestrated exercise not having gone as planned, she takes a short recess, starts again. Then she asks whether I know that he has a girlfriend, a friend who is a girl. Did I know that this girl called her office when he was arrested, said it's a mistake, that he's not capable of doing this?

My body is prickling with full-on hate. Because what he did to me is all there is. It's all I am anymore.

"Why are you calling me?"

"We want to make sure that you're okay. We care."

I know they don't really care how I am, that they're after something, want to figure something out. It could be whether I can be swayed not to testify against him if I learn who he is. It could be whether I'm going to make trouble for the university. I'm turning to powder.

"I'm not okay."

"We're sorry to hear that."

"Thanks."

I hang up that phone, stare at my fingers. Lucky me. My rapist is rich. He comes from money, old-boy connections. My rapist is important because he comes from a family that controls lots of things that happen at my university. My rapist is nice. He's smartly dressed, polite, well-mannered. My rapist is a gentleman. My rapist pled not guilty. He couldn't have raped me.

The syllogism:

Major Premise: He is smartly dressed, polite, a gentleman.

Minor Premise: Smartly dressed, polite, gentlemen do only good things.

Conclusion: He must do only good things.

Except he isn't and he doesn't. I know I should be storing all of this information in my head somewhere, that everything should be a whole lot clearer to me now—who his family is, what the university wants me to think, what I'm up against. I don't understand what to do with any of this, can't bring anything into clear focus.

When I find words again, I tell Lindsey what I know now about who he is, who his family is, what the university's official line is on him. Lind listens, opens her arms fields-wide, holds me as I quake against her. I feel her spine bones through her T-shirt. She's not eating enough and that's because of me, my fault.

Then Lindsey turns to war mode. Together, she says, we'll put all of our smarts together, and we'll figure out what to do with all we know. This is good, really. We're informed. We know how to arm ourselves, which weapons to use. I say okay, you're right. I say I'm not going to spiral, promise. But we both know. That she's most likely not right, that I'm already corkscrew-curling up, circling.

CHAPTER TWENTY-THREE

Lindsey's taking me to the therapist. I have to go because Mom and Dad say I need to talk to someone, and clearly they'd rather it wasn't them. I write about it in my journal.

Tuesday, January 31

Today I went to the Medical Center to talk to the therapist about the rapist. It's not lost on me that "therapist" and "the rapist" are spelled the same. A baby's runny discharge smell was in the air. It was repulsive but comforting, made me feel less alone, like birth was there, not death. I thought about being alive, about someday having a child, showing it a world that's beautiful and kind. I watched as an irritated mother slapped her son on the head and I met his eyes.

Tuesday, February 7

I went back to the therapist. Her office has two windows shrouded in slatted blinds, three diplomas on the wall, four saggy bookshelves. The brown-panel walls are covered with rows of books with words like "ganglia" and "nervous system" in the titles. Seeing all that brain-related stuff makes me wonder if I'm crazy, if mine's not working right.

She smiled when she saw me, a pretty smile. Not pretty actually, just unassuming, but not exactly passive. She was definitely smiling. I deliberated. Should I take off my coat? And then somehow I did in the course of the hellos, but then I felt vulnerable because Lindsey's old jackknife wasn't ready in my pocket.

She didn't turn on the lights. I don't know why. It could be she's trying to save electricity or has an eye condition that makes her sensitive to light. But it makes me uneasy. She crossed and recrossed her flesh-colored stockings a lot, asked if I was sleeping alright. I told her I sleep when I'm exhausted but I wasn't sure if that was alright. She yawned, glanced at the wall clock above my head. I wanted to ask her about her nights, too, her sleeping, but I didn't.

I'm not sure I need her. But she's costing my parents a bunch so I forced myself to talk about the incident and doing that made me cry. Then she asked whether I see men as objects, if maybe that makes them project that onto me so that I, in essence, create my own objectification. I really had to go to the bathroom but I held it and I tried to think about her question, which I didn't and still don't understand.

Tuesday, February 14. Valentine's Day.

I feel worn. She asked me to tell her everything about that night, so I tried to be as specific as I could, answered all her questions. But I didn't tell her that I have new little creases around my eyes, that my friends say that they're a cloudy gray now (some say "sharp"), that there are new lines near my mouth from him gagging me. And I didn't tell her that therapy doesn't seem to be changing anything.

Tuesday, February 21

    *Today I told her I was angry. She yawned, asked me,
"Why are you angry?" I thought to say "Because you
yawn." Instead I said I'm angry because I can't seem to
find my way back to before. I said I'm angry about what
he did to me, his family's money, Miriam dying in the
sky. I said I'm angry because my parents aren't sure what
to do with me now. I said I'm angry about that dean
woman calling me, how people seem to want to tell me
all about my rapist's great qualities, how I think maybe
the university administration is against me, wants me to
keep quiet. I said I'm angry that no one can find the knife
he held to my throat, that this bothers me a lot because
it's crucial evidence. Plus, if he never really had one, then
he couldn't have ever really slit my throat after all, just
jabbed into it lots. And if that's true, maybe I could've
and should've fought harder. I said I'm angry because
it happened in my own locked house, in my own bed. I
said I'm angry because it was some rich stranger. I said
I'm angry because back in my tiny town where I grew up,
I'm one thing now, will only ever be this one thing—that
college girl from up on Old Ashby Road that she went off
to Syracuse, got herself raped.*

    *I said I have to go to the bathroom. So she led me
down the corridor to the one with the sign No Patients
Allowed. She likes me. She likes me a lot. I said thanks
and she left me there. I switched on that overhead light,
checked each stall to make sure no one was hiding. I
locked the bathroom door, went into the stall and locked it,
thudded the toilet seat down, hid my knees under my chin,
rocked back and forth. I picked fluff from my sweater.*

    *I left the stall, stared at the mirror. The college girl's
gone, I thought. But I still look like her. I lathered my
hands with pink soap, rinsed them, dried them with a
paper towel. I missed the can, left it on the floor. I lathered,
rinsed, dried with a new towel. I gathered the lost towel,*

threw both towels in the can. I repeated these things until fifteen minutes had been spent on my watch, wandered back along the hallway. I said I guess we're done. If that's what you want, she said. I told her it was.

Then I wrap my misshapen black scarf around my head so just my eyes are peeking, peer out the door. Sixty days are gone and he's out of rehab now so before I step out the door, I look left, right. I check again. I step onto the street, make sure that no one big, male, with light hair is there.

I walk fast. I quick-check behind me. I walk faster and and soon that walk turns full-out jog and I keep on with that jogging until I get to Lindsey who's waiting for me two blocks over at the slushy crossing of University and Madison.

"How was it?"

"Fan-friggin-tastic."

She laughs, softly laces her arm over my shoulder. I inhale. Breathe in deep. We march up the hill past Walnut, leave the rows of rental houses, cross Ostrom, press the edge of Thornden Park. Lindsey heaves her backpack to her left shoulder, takes out her keys, lets us in. We dump our debris in the hallway. She hits the kitchen light, places a mound of vegetables on a cutting board, lifts down a pot. Lindsey says it's sauce time and she asks about therapy, chops onions, minces garlic. She tehee-snickers at my descriptions of the therapist, assembles little islands of fresh tomatoes. She talks about some bozo who said something idiotic in class. She sautés the onions in olive oil, adds them to the simmering pot. She sprinkles in oregano, black pepper, bread crumbs, parmesan, salt. She pauses over the pot, closes her eyes, lets her nose drink in the rich steam. Lindsey cradles a spoon, brings it over.

"Taste."

I taste, her eyes like frizzling sparklers.

"What does it need?"

My gums warm with tang, sweet. This is liquid sunlight, and that jarred stuff's just chunky smog.

"Nothing."

CHAPTER TWENTY-FOUR

Monday, February 27. Convenience Store.

I can't seem to ditch her, the college girl gawking at me in the mirror, as if nothing in the world could possibly be crushed, broken. She's a fraud with that baby face, long blonde hair. Much as I abhor her, though, the college girl's familiar. She's someone I used to know.

If you look at her closely, you can see I'm here too—the new real me. Her eyes are hollowed-out. Her nose has a lumpy bump. There's the mancoat barnacled to her now. Most days she doesn't wear contacts or glasses so she won't have to see her friends' discomfort or strangers' pity. Her hand never escapes the mancoat's right pocket, her fingers opening and closing that jackknife, her thumb tracing its blade edge.

I've ducked inside a convenience market with an orange-and-yellow sign. I'm standing in line, about to buy my typical lunch, tuna-with-lettuce-on-rye-dill-pickle-on-the-side. I check behind myself in line, sight a golden, tousled-type with moppy curls. He seems to be smiling in my direction. He wants to talk to her, the college girl, the one who goes with the face and the hair. But she's not here anymore.

The knife wants to be used. He's out of rehab. This could be him. There's a voice speaking, bitter and black. It's mine. It's making a statement, not asking a question.

"What."

But, no. This one's too lean, too muscular, too tall. It's not him. It can't be him. Still. His face blank as chalkboard. The boggy eyes, Moppy's spotted them. His smile fades.

And for just a split-second, I'm the college girl again, wanting to be cared about, to be liked. But then it disappears and the flatness returns. Moppy seizes his waiting sandwich, his change, stomps out the door. My lungs are on fire and I seem to have forgotten to breathe, and how long that's been going on I just can't say. It's not fair to put these things on the Moppy, I know this. But I do it all the same. Thinks he can look at me, like that's all I am, like that's what I'm here for.

I pitch a five at the deli counter. A hand passes back change along with the tuna asphyxiated in plastic wrap. I shove the coins past the mancoat's lining ribbons. Customer eyes move over me. I wonder if they see it, the padlocked and crippled here. I wonder if they sense it, that I'm the rumor, the one talked about on the local news I can't bring myself to sit through. Lindsey watches it, though, says it mentions the things about him that I already know, that he's from a wealthy Syracuse family that's thrown lots of money at the university, that he's in his twenties, not a college student.

Why? How? Did he see me somewhere? Was it at a coffee shop, in a play, walking to class? And, if he did, when was he watching me? Was it while I was eating at Philomel's, when I was crossing the street, leaving my house? Could he be the man who biology–frog pinned me at that Halloween party? I don't know. I have no answers.

But he's out of rehab. So I keep reminding myself to breathe and I fast walk. Or I slow run. Because I can't be seen. Because I must get home safely, stay alive. I make my way through the drizzling wind.

CHAPTER TWENTY-FIVE

Wednesday, March 1. A Room of My Own.

I tell Lindsey I'm ready to sleep by myself now. It's not true. But I can't live with the fact that my legs are still kicking her, my arms hitting her. So I screw up my courage, ask Dad to please drive out here to wrench the door off my new room in the attic, install a metal security door, put three sturdy locks on it.

One at the top.

One in the middle.

One on the bottom.

Dad comes for part of a day. He buys a special new gray door made out of metal. He buys wood, nails. He cuts a piece of plywood to fit the opening left by the spiral staircase that leads from the living room to my room. He nails it into place. Now no one can get in without me hearing him, without me knowing.

And I really want to tell Dad. That this door's everything I've ever dreamed of in an entrance. That it'll be just like living in a meat freezer, but I'll be warm and locked in from the inside. That I love them, that piece of wood, those nails. That he can't leave me.

That I'm so scared, Daddy. Please stay.

But I bulldozer over these thoughts, flatten them down. No way could I say those words. Dad hugs me. He leaves.

At night I try turning the lights out, but once they click off, I freeze. My heart lashes and blood bangs through my ears, so I keep the lights on and I don't sleep. But if I do by mistake, Lindsey's kitchen knife's still safe under my pillow and I tell myself that when he breaks down the door, I'll be ready.

My three a day smoking habit turns to a pack and a half. And I lift weights until my arms shake, row on my rowing machine as fast as I can to nowhere on an invisible lake. My muscles are getting stronger. I'm still afraid to be alone in the shower with the parts so I wear more perfume to cover over my new smelliness. I forget to brush my hair and teeth. And I write and write. I write about what happened. Terrible though it is, I have to do it. Because just like at the police station when I gave my statement, if my hand stops scribbling, everything turns heavy again.

And I dream. Lots of times in my dreams I'm hurting things. Some of them are mine. I'm slicing each of the parts super-slow with a knife. But some of the things I hurt aren't mine. I'm killing things—a few animals and babies, but mostly I kill strange men. In these dreams, I'm not outside myself, witnessing myself commit the crimes. I'm plunging the knife into flesh, feeling blood slosh through my fingers. I wake up afraid of myself.

I have other dreams, too. I'm in London and I'm pleading with Miriam not to take that flight and she's promising she won't and she never sets foot on that plane. We take the next flight out together and when we get home everyone who loves us is waiting at the airport. And in the blinking Sandman-seconds that pass between my asleep and my awake, I believe. That Miriam's still alive. That I've never been raped-girl.

When I'm not writing or dreaming, I'm reading or doing homework. I spend five times as long as my classmates on my assignments, over-check everything a zillion times. The papers I turn in are twice as long as the required length, and they make my professors look at me strangely, like they know something's really off here.

CHAPTER TWENTY-SIX

Friday, March 10. Ayden's House.

The DA Lena tells me that I will have to pick him out of a line-up. He'll be looking at me looking at him through a one-way glass. She says he won't be able to see me, but I don't believe her. I ask the DA Lena why this is necessary. We've got our work cut out for us, she says, because he has the best lawyer in town and that guy's likely gathering evidence about me, who I am, who my friends are, what I do with my time. The DA Lena says that if I can identify him quickly, this will add to my credibility as a witness, help our case against him. I tell the DA Lena that I might be able to identify him. I remember some things. Like the milkweed silk or stockings that turned out to be his baseball cap, the light hair sticking out in the darkness, the giant weight of his body, the smell of leather.

But I'm not taking any chances. I know that these things might not be enough. So Lindsey and I are making our way through the gray to a house sunk in snow somewhere near the corner of Euclid and Comstock. We look to see whether anyone is around. There's no one. We knock.

It's Ayden's house. He's one of my ex-boyfriend Geoff's art studio friends. Since Geoff's still in classes with Sal, he knows what happened. But, like Cathy and Sal, I haven't seen him. I'm guessing the idea of it makes him freaked out. I couldn't imagine contacting Geoff. It would just hurt too bad. Ayden thought he might be able to help, though. So he got in touch with me.

Ayden throws open the door, searches past us to see if we're being watched, shoos us inside. We sit on his shivery porch piled high with folded newspapers in bags, pyramids of beer bottles. He grabs a muddy-brown yearbook off a card table, places it in my hands, his sighs water-logged heavy. He rambles off to the kitchen, and I hand the book off to Lindsey, wrap my mancoat tighter around me.

Lindsey inspects each page and I watch flakes fall outside. Ayden comes back, thumps cups of hot cocoa down on the table, lifts the book from Lindsey's fingers, begins to rifle through it. Pointing at a picture, Ayden slashes the silence.

"That's seven years ago maybe, but gives you an idea."

Ayden places the yearbook in my hands and Lindsey's watching my face and I need to do this, I know, have to do this, but I just can't, can't look at his picture because I'm scared that it's not just a picture but that it's the real him and that he for sure knows and he's going to kill me. Lindsey rotates the book toward her, looks at it a long moment, glances back at me.

"This totally sucks but you've got to. Study this face."

She turns the book back toward me and my eyes flash, fling from Lindsey's face to Ayden's, back again.

"Can't."

"You can. Now, look. Look at his eyes."

Lindsey steadies my arm. I breathe in. How I manage this, I can't be sure. But I do it. I look. Just at the eyes. There's void enough in those eyes that there would be plenty of room for gusting anger and colossal idiocy to build a duplex inside him over the years in between. I tell myself to focus on the hair next. Next to the eyes is slightly wavy pale hair.

I tell myself to focus on the mouth. The mouth is open, teeth are bared. I hear his laugh in the darkness and I remember him behind me lashing my wrists, gagging me with my own socks, thrusting, moaning. The book's sliding from my hand.

"I can't."

Ayden pulls the book away, scrutinizes his fingernails, then looks at me.

"Did this help?"

The answer to Ayden's question is I don't know. I'm not sure I've learned much by eyeballing this picture. It has made me aware of another frightening possibility, though. If they rustle up a bunch of frat guys, stick them next to him in a line-up, I won't know what to say, where to point. He looks like every other tall, big, light-haired, beer-guzzling college student. Except now he'd look older. I try to imagine that face aged. But when I do it's just like every other twenty-something guy with a frat past.

There's no way I'd say any of those things, though. I don't want Ayden to think I'm not grateful for showing me this. I nod.

"Yeah, thanks."

Ayden's staring at me like he wants to say something else, like it's something important, like he doesn't know how to start.

"Have you been watching the news, reading the papers?"

Lindsey shoots him her best don't-you-dare-go-there look. I don't know why. I say what's true.

"No."

Ayden keeps avoiding Lindsey's eyes.

"You should, you know, if you can."

I nod. We hug, say good-bye. Lindsey leans into the door. It gives way. The sky has lost all its sun. The snow falls faster. We clomp our way home.

CHAPTER TWENTY-SEVEN

Saturday, March 11

It's Spring Break. Lindsey and I drive back to her family's house in Chelmsford, Massachusetts. Mom's coming to pick me up again. Around me is Lindsey's family kitchen. Everything's a snug, chocolate brown. Oil paintings of pebble piles line two walls. Lindsey's mother is feeding me last night's lasagna. She's saying something about literature. She's saying something about how astonishingly long it's taking for her to finish her graduate degree at Harvard. If only she didn't also teach full-time high school English. She says it's just as well, though. There's no way she could ever leave those kids. She loves them too much. Her smiling eyes are that snug brown too.

"Who's your favorite author?"

I shrug.

"Come on. Who do you like?"

"Hemingway's alright, I guess."

"He is."

She grins, rests her hands on my shoulders.

"How are you, dear? Really?"

It happened in late November and now it's the middle of March. I'm doing a little better now. But when I think about the eyes, hair, and smile from Ayden's yearbook, suddenly all of the things that come to mind aren't that great, like I'm an old town dump that's been looted, like I'm like a wide-eyed-pickled Mütter Museum fetus jammed in a jar. By the time I've thought up these answers, though, I'm more cloud on the verge of downpour, and holding back tears reminds me of weeping while he raped me, and that remembering makes me worried I'll lose it for sure. She hugs me.

A girl's voice singing the Stones' "(I Can't Get No) Satisfaction" pours out the shower, down the hall. It's loud, clashing. I try to imagine it more off-key. I can't. Lindsey's Mom's eye-rolling.

"Welcome to our funny farm."

Lindsey's Dad jangles in the front door, hugs me, winks a smile.

"Great to see you, honey. Ahh, gosh, not this nonsense again."

He's opening the fridge, appraising the edibles. A Lindsey-dervish, in a floor-length black skirt, roadrunners into the living room. She does a piano bench slide, raises her hands spectacularly over the keys, glances back at us, bows her head as if in special-silent prayer. Her little black painted toes barely graze the pedals.

Then she's pounding on that thing like a maniac, fingers tracing out her latest composition, but somewhere along the way it's morphed into a busting-out rendition of Billy Joel's "Piano Man." It's a hideous mess of drawling tones. I try imagining a more ridiculous version. I can't.

". . . La dah dah diddy dah. La dah dah diddy dah, dah, dah . . ."

Her head bobbles side to side, her hand punching up the air every few words. I try to imagine how she could be any more of a full-out goofball. I can't. And the Stones voice just keeps growing louder, ever more horribly off-key.

". . . I can't get no—no, no, no. Hey, hey, hey, that's what I say . . ."

Then there's yelling in a Jaggery, British accent.

"Shut up, you wicked flippin' ham."

"You shut it, Batshit Jagger."

Batshit Jagger, creampuff turban and flowery fuchsia slippers, dashes out of the bathroom, wrestles squealing Lindsey to the floor. Then a miniskirted, heeled sister dashes in, steps daintily out of her shoes, smiles back at us, plops atop them like she's leaping into a mound of crunchy-dry leaves. A squirmy mass of knees and elbows rumbles around the living room floor.

And for a few minutes, I forget.

Because we just. We can't.

We can't stop laughing.

CHAPTER TWENTY-EIGHT

Saturday, March 11–Sunday, March 19. Spring Break.
Return to New Hampshire.

I don't write anything else in my journal over Spring Break. But I walk through the woods a lot with Mom, past roaring cascades, bloodroot shoots filled with crimson pulp, their tiny white bellflowers not far behind. I sleep in my old room downstairs with all of the lights on. I read through the nights, fall asleep in half-hour patches, hugging a book to my chest. When I recall the eyes, the hair, and the smile from Ayden's yearbook I start to tremble and my parts feel battered. But I breathe and I try to focus on happier things, like all those Canada mayflowers with their shooting-star stamens that will soon pop up in the deep woods, like all the new books I'll read over the break. I think about Ayden's suggestion about reading the papers, too. And when I return to Syracuse, I write an entry.

Monday, March 20

I dreamed that he was everywhere. That one night

he might have been one man, with one voice, one skin, one identity. But in my dream, he could change those things. He was in a car driving by me, honking his horn. He was seated at a table next to me and my friends in a restaurant. He was black, short, and fat, wearing a red ski hat, leather gloves, driving a silver car. He was white, skinny, and tall, dark eyes like knives. No matter what shape he took though, I wasn't fooled. I knew. I knew it was him.

CHAPTER TWENTY-NINE

No one knows I'm here right now, not even Lindsey. I told her that I'd get a ride home after classes from a classmate because she'd be worried if she knew the truth. That I'm sandwiched between the stacks in Bird Library. That the ground around me is carpeted with all of the local newspapers published during the last few months. That I'm foraging through the pages.

I pass stories about low-income housing, the latest in women's sportswear. I pass stories about arson, how to force tulip bulbs. Then I see it. "A man was accused of brutally raping and beating a Syracuse woman." That's me. The one "brutally raped," the one "beaten." I am "a Syracuse woman." That's strange. I'm not from Syracuse. I'm from New Hampshire. And I'm a Syracuse University student. Why not "university student"?

I read on. One story says that this man was charged with first-degree rape and four counts of second-degree assault. It describes a struggle during which two police officers and a police captain were injured. It says something about the police showing up at 3:56 a.m., that they kicked open my door, that the man was found standing over me, a screwdriver in his right hand. This screwdriver was the knife that was really just a screwdriver. Another story says that when the police first tried to cuff him, he was "resisting wildly." As if he thought he'd never get caught, I think, like he believed he could get away with it. And he was willing to break more than my nose to do this. He broke a few police bones, too.

The stories are awful but I can't stop reading. It's like I'm staring at the aftermath of a head-on collision. But this collision is my life. The articles say some things I already know, like the fact that he's from a very wealthy and powerful family. They say that his grandfather is the CEO of one of the largest employers in Syracuse, that he's a major player in local politics. They say some things I don't know, too, like that his grandfather is actually President of Syracuse University's Board of Trustees. This doesn't sound like good news. That dean woman on the phone was right even though she said things I didn't want to hear. He's from an old Syracuse family that's very respected and well-connected. They have gobs of money. Reading these letters, seeing them on these pages, makes everything realer somehow.

I read on. Another article says that the rapist's father is himself an attorney in Syracuse. It also asserts that the father was recently arrested for something involving possession of a controlled substance and a prostitute. And I wonder to myself. Who are these people? What am I supposed to make of all this? Are they old money socialites whose thin façade has been ripped away, wealthy people falling from grace? Or was the older generation respectable, the later copies becoming more faded, less and less capable of retaining elements of the original? Another article asserts that the woman, me, "said her hands had been bound with telephone cord her attacker pulled from his pants pocket." My ears are heating up. The word choice makes me angry. I "said." It's as if I made an entirely unsubstantiated claim, as if maybe he never had the cord with him, as if maybe he never was found at the scene of the crime next to me with my bound hands, as if maybe I thoughtfully bound my hands myself in anticipation of his arrival.

I read on. One article says that the woman, me, was treated at Crouse Irving Memorial Hospital for "scratches to the neck and leg and released." My face is woodstove-hot. Word choice again. A bloodied, busted nose, blackened eyes, a sliced neck, a head covered with blood, pulverized lips, and bruises all over my body have been rewritten, my rape reduced to little more than light cat claw marks. Another article states that the woman, me, told police that the man hit her several times in the face and held a sharp object against her neck as he raped her, that "the man stated several times that 'he was going to kill me, he was going to slit my throat, strangle me and break my back.'"

It was more than "several times." And I didn't just *tell* the police, that it happened. It all happened. *It happened.* There's walloping pain building in back of my right eye and something's about to blast off inside me. I can't figure out what it is at first. Then it hits me. My nonstop fear and numbness, something's mowing through them. There's big, big emotion building in me. It's clear and bright. I'm raging like never before in my life.

I read on. In addition to rape and assault he's charged with first-degree attempted sodomy and first-degree burglary, felonies, and fourth-degree criminal possession of a weapon, possession of burglar's tools and resisting arrest. "Police recovered two screwdrivers and a putty knife." All of this has happened and he's pled not guilty, but he's guilty and we have all the evidence we need to prove it and why are we waiting? What on earth are we waiting for?

I want him to pay, pay for what he did to me. I want to read the article that doesn't exist yet, but will someday very soon. I imagine picking up that paper, reading that lead story. The writer will describe how the case went to trial, how many people testified against him, how much evidence there was to convict him. The author will write that he's been found guilty of raping me, and that he's going to jail for a long, long time.

That eye pain's more piercing and needlelike now and I'm white-finger gripping the page. I set the paper down and I pick it up again, try to read it all once more. So I can remember, recall precise details, exact phrasing, so I don't forget anything that might be important. But I don't get too far through it this second time, because the burn in me is spreading fast. I'm losing all breath. The letters are turning smudge. There are still so many things I do not understand. And I don't know what to do with all of this new information. It's overwhelming. But I remind myself that it's good. Now I know how the media are representing what happened to me, that I'm a Syracuse woman, not a university student, that "I said" he bound my hands, that the many injuries I sustained have been rewritten as "scratches." Now I know the exact charges he's facing and has plead not guilty to. I'm glad I know. I needed to know. I needed to understand what I'm facing, to understand what I've become.

I take those newspapers, recklessly out of order and crinkled, shove them back into the stacks, throw my mancoat tight around my shoulders, twist it round my middle, wrestle my hair back into a My-Little-Pony tail, rush down the stairs, past the library security scan.

I'm stopped at the library's glass doors. The dark, it's already fallen out there. I haven't been caught out alone at night since it happened, calling Lindsey for rides whenever the sun's within several hours of setting. But I'm here and it's dark and I chose this. So I muster my courage, push through the door. I slip off my mittens, light a cigarette, peer up at the moon. It throws silvered-up light on the old fraternity at the corner, the science building. And I'm afraid.

On a pole next to me a blue glow sizzles. Beneath that pole is a phone box. The university recently put in its first blue light system. When a person is in danger, she's supposed to run to the first blue light she can find, pick up the phone, be saved.

I could have used a blue light, a phone box. But I didn't have those in my bedroom. The only alarm I could sound was my own suffocating voice. When the police arrived, they bust in soon enough to save my life, but too late to stop him.

Tonight I will do it, I tell myself. I'm going to get home on my own. I think about John Cheever's character in his story "The Swimmer," how he strings together swimming pools through neighborhood yards to make his way back to his house.[1] Though it's not the most direct route, I can puzzle together a series of blue lights to get home. I cross University, run fast onto College Place, through the cloudless pitch-dark to the next blue light near a bus stop. When I reach it, I collapse against the pole, try to push off my panic, stare ahead to the next one. I can just make it out in front of the frat house at the corner of Euclid. I try to shake the quivering fear, steam over all the snow and ice until I can touch the next phone box. Once there, I search the street, catch up to my breath.

I can't see any more blue lights from here. But I know there's one a ways down Ostrom outside that dorm. So I race across Comstock, turn onto Ostrom, pass Thornden Park. My lungs sting with each cold breath.

When I finally reach that blue light, my whole body shuddering and heaving, I realize. The blue lights only make me feel safe for the few brief moments when I am right beneath them. There aren't many of them and they're not creating nearly enough safety to make this worth it. I determine to pass the rest of them by. I'll make my way home alone without them. I run straight down Ostrom, not another blue light in sight. And for a few minutes I make believe. That I am something worth six million dollars and nuclear-powered bionic. That I can out-swim the biggest of waves, out-climb the tallest of mountains, out-run the strongest of winds. That I am so much swifter than this night's bursting blackness could ever hope to be. But even as I am pretending these things, I cannot ignore the truth. That I'm really super-scared and that I'm shaking hard and that I'm so little and, yes, that I'm a girl. That I can't change any of these things. Still, facing this night alone, not depending on other people or the false security of the blue lights, I feel a bit better, a tiny bit closer to brave, to safe.

When I get home I write my favorite entry since it happened. It is short, but not like before. I know and will never forget what it means:

Wednesday, March 22. Blue Light Special.

CHAPTER THIRTY

Friday, March 24. Town Hall Meeting.

In the past couple months the number of reported rapes on north-eastern university campuses has spiked dramatically. Television news programs like *Dateline* and *60 Minutes* are hungrily scouring campuses, trolling for raped female college students willing go in front of cameras, spill their stories to national audiences.

Since Syracuse University has had multiple attacks in a few short months, producers have been showing up, sniffing around. Some of them have learned about me, pestered my friends about whether I would be willing to speak with them. But my friends say no. They know there's no way I'd be willing to go that public about what happened to me. I do think it should be talked about, but I have this fear if I ever speak publicly about what he did, he'll hunt me down and murder me. Nothing's happening with the case. And he's still somewhere out there, free.

This national spotlight on Syracuse University has made students here more and more vocal about rape as an issue. Due to this pressure, the university administration is holding an afternoon

Town Hall Meeting in the basement of the Schine Student Center. Part of me really wants to be there. Part of me wants to be as far away from there as possible.

My new friend Celia, a sharp-witted political science major with shiny black hair, from a well-to-do Italian family in Upstate New York, suggests that we go. Celia and I were Miriam's two best friends—and Miriam had always told us that we were idiots for not getting to know each other better. Wanting to honor Miriam's memory, Celia's taken it on herself to seek me out. She knows what happened to me, and it doesn't weird her out. She's treated me to coffee and lunch several times over the last few weeks, we've spoken about Miriam, she's asked me about what happened. She's cared, too, really listened. Miriam was right. We do hit it off. And I'm hoping having Celia around will take some of the pressure of caring for my gloom-fest of a self off Lindsey.

Miriam would want me to be at this meeting. But I'm genuinely scared. Celia says it's totally understandable, but there's no reason to be. She'll be right there, and no one will know who I am. You can just sit and listen, she says. And, if you don't want to stay, we can get up and leave anytime.

For reasons not altogether clear to me, I agree to go. I nab my mancoat and we slide our way through the slush to the meeting. The room is a soot-somber purpling black, lights just illuminating a stage and its claret backdrop. There are two seats open toward the very back of the room. As we sit down, more students surge in. Some move in chairs from other rooms. Some sit down on the ground between the tables, form zigzag lines against the walls. Some squeeze in with their backpacks, jamming themselves into the far corners behind us.

The room's packed. A man I've never seen before wallows toward the stage. From his navy suit, red tie, and starched white dress shirt I can tell he's some sort of drone bee, a hive-protecting-administrative-type from Counseling or Student Activities. He's probably fabulous friends with that dean woman who called me, the one bent on convincing me of my rapist's niceness. Drone Bee's smile is pasted-on-rigid. Perched behind him are five white-haired men wearing the same uniform, like yellow-eyed snowy owls ready to swoop down on a marsh, fast-gobble up a mess of skittering mice whole. The Snowies look at one another, stare out on the audience, shift positions in their chairs.

The Drone welcomes everyone, says we're here to talk about the recent sexual assaults at the university and issues of safety. He takes off his glasses, wipes his forehead with a iron-pressed hanky, gestures behind him, explains that the Snowies are members of Syracuse University's Board of Trustees. Then Drone Bee places the kerchief in his pants' pocket, puts on his glasses, riffles a sheaf of papers, moves one to the front of his pile. He reads a set of statistics about the growing incidences of sexual assault in the fraternities, in date rape situations, on campus as women are walking to and from their cars and homes at night. Voices whip around the room.

The Drone slides off his glasses again, sets them on the podium. He scrunches his eyes at the light. He reshuffles his pages, inches his glasses back on. He mentions the details of a few high-profile sexual assault cases that have occurred in the last year. He reads about one date rape. One fraternity rape. One stranger rape. Before my brain knows what my body's doing, I'm on my feet.

"That's me."

Every sound stops. Heads action figure-twist in my direction.

"I was raped by a stranger, the grandson of someone on the Board of Trustees."

I realize I'm hoping one of those Snowies is the grandfather, that he's hearing my strength, that he's feeling guilty and wrong for being related to, for helping to create, his grandson. My voice grows heavy, thunderous.

"I'm not a statistic."

By now my brain has caught up to my mouth. It's wondering what the heck I'm doing, and it's telling my mouth to shut up already. There's nothing at all smart or safe about this. He's going to track me down, kill me. But my mouth isn't paying attention to my brain. It won't hold my tongue—no way, no how. It's like the darkness of this room is a different darkness, like maybe it will wrap me up and protect me, make me anonymous. Like I could be any woman with long, light hair in this darkness.

"I'm a person. I have a face, a name."

Drone Bee whirls around toward the Snowies, pivots back toward the audience. He shelters his now annoyed eyes so he can see better. He can't figure out where my voice is coming from. He gapes back at the Snowies who've begun their low krekking, swiveling their heads, fluffing up clumsily. The Drone looks back at us. His old face is a painful-raw red. There's a kind of loathing in the next words he uses.

"Your experiences, Miss . . . they matter to us."

A female voice from the middle of the room shouts out.

"Hell if they do."

Claps and whistles bounce around like sparks. Voices fill the room.

And now I know with a deep-water clarity. I'm not all alone. What my mouth's been saying, what my brain and Drone Bee have been trying to shut down, was never just about me. It's about us. Us, who have survived sexual violence, told it's better to keep quiet, just move on, not make a fuss. Us, who love them, know what they've been through, that their voices must be heard. I didn't realize it, but I brought myself here for this reason. The voice is a woman's behind me.

"Stop feeding us this line."

Then there's a man talking up in front.

"What're you doing about it?"

I'm still standing. The Snowies clap their beaks now, hoot at one another. The Drone makes one last, futile effort. His voice yells over the crowd.

"Let's settle down now. You have to try to understand . . ."

Another man shouts.

"They're just here to cover their asses."

Something powerful is happening. Smart, articulate, committed people are jumping up all around me, and they're speaking to Drone Bee and the Snowies about things that never get said, about their girlfriends' rapes, boyfriends' rapes. They're saying it's not just a woman's issue. It's everyone's issue. They're saying that if men are part of the problem, don't leave them out of the conversation.

They must be part of the solution. They're saying that it's the result of wider cultural problems, systemic social inequities and oppressions. They're saying that women, children, people of color, people from economically disadvantaged communities, bisexual and transgender people, gay men and women all suffer sexual assault in disproportionate numbers.

The Drone scuffles his feet and his voice splutters "well" and "um." He says something about the blue lights and the University's "investment" in "campus safety," but no one is buying it. They're saying it's not nearly enough. They're telling the administration to take action, to do something lasting, real, meaningful.

I sit. The room's *Alice in Wonderland* shrinking. And I know that as much as I needed to say these things, I must leave now, right now. I can't stay. Celia chases after me as I blunder toward the door at the edge of the room. Drone Bee's eyes trace my silhouette. He might be gratified by my exit. But when I glimpse back his face doesn't register it. He's trying to make sense of what I'm leaving behind. I'm launching myself against the two weighty wooden doors, stepping outside. I'm fireball-burning. Celia grasps my arm.

"You okay?"

My breath's turned draggy.

"What did I just do?"

"You told them the heck off."

I joggle my head.

"I just told hundreds of people who I am. What's wrong with me?"

"It was too dark to see your face. You're safe."

I gawk at her. I am so many things. And all of them at the same time. Huge and alive. Tiny and frightened. Warm and elated. Polar cold and paralyzed. I won't go back in there for anything. But I can't go home either. Celia grabs my arm, pulls me toward campus. I feel really grateful to Celia for doing this, because otherwise I know I might just stay ugly-lawn-ornament stuck on that piece of sidewalk forever. We walk together and before I know it, have a chance to notice or reconsider, we're on those more isolated paths, ones I've been scared to walk, afraid of seeing him. As we stump along through the squeaky-cold snow, I feel it, my stride stretching, my shoulders settling back, my back lengthening. I'm more upright.

And I catch myself hoping. When the cold weather passes and the crystal ices melt, maybe it happens. Maybe some birches begin to straighten their branches a little.

CHAPTER THIRTY-ONE

On Wednesday, March 29, I hear. I was chosen as the 1989–1990 recipient of the Newell Rossman Fellowship for Excellence in the Humanities. I handed in my materials last October, and most days since then I haven't thought about it, tried not to hope too much for it. But it's a real résumé-builder, plus it'll help pay for my tuition and I can be more self-sufficient, won't have to depend on Mom and Dad for money as much anymore. Things are starting to look up.

That night I even allow myself a half-hour celebratory study break from my nineteen credits—Natural Sciences, Honors Seminar (to prepare for thesis writing), Fiction Writing and Interpretation, Shakespeare, Nineteenth- and Twentieth-Century British Women Novelists, and six credits of Intermediate Latin. I still have a long night ahead. I want this 4.0. I need it, and I'm going to get it.

Even though I'm tired, I'm so excited for each of my tests. I'll write and write and write and soon I'll be hovering above a subject, grasping it, and tearing it apart. Then I'll put it back together as something new. I love the writing. How it frees my mind. How it makes me busy. How it keeps me from thinking, from remembering, about other things. I see that pink clock buzzing at me, ticking through all of my precious study time. Stupid clock, I don't care what it thinks. I toss my sweater over it. And I fall asleep thinking. I got the Newell Rossman. Yes!

I don't write much in my journal during the next week. But I read Virginia Woolf's *To the Lighthouse*. And I read Shakespeare's *The Tempest*. I decide to write my senior thesis on Charles Baudelaire. I take all of his strange writings out of the library, start making my way through *Les Fleurs du Mal*. I try to get the perfect subjunctive straight in Latin, too—active, *portaverim* (I may have carried), passive, *portatis sim* (I may have been carried).

My professors congratulate me on the fellowship, seem genuinely excited for me. The Honors Director calls me into his office, gives me a huge hug, tells me there's no one more deserving. And I even agree to go out with Lindsey to Cosmos Pizza and Grill on Marshall Street to celebrate. The place bustles with tired-faced college students, waiters in grease-covered aprons. We guzzle our sodas, slippery pizza slices. And I feel like I've achieved something, like right now people aren't looking at me as the raped-one, that instead they see the college girl. I'm not the same college girl I used to be. I'll never be the same, exactly. But for the first time in months, I feel good about myself. I feel like I'm going somewhere.

CHAPTER THIRTY-TWO

My new confidence lasts exactly eleven days. They are good days of exhausting study. I'm back to my old routine of reading until I fall asleep, this night Shakespeare's *Midsummer Night's Dream*, my very favorite of his plays. I slip in and out of shimmery dreams—skies thickly blazing with starlight, sticky firefly-summer nights, fairies casting hocus-pocus spells that rearrange the world. Bono the wall-crapping cat purrs against me. I run my hand along his back, his slinky tail. We both fall asleep in the blinding light, Shakespeare's collected plays open, its pages like a blanket against my stomach.

I startle awake. The phone's ringing, going to wake everyone up, so I push the book off, root around for my glasses, inch them onto my nose, rummage the floor for the receiver, pick it up.

"Hello?"

There's light breathing.

"Who's there?"

Then voice.

"Do you know what time it is?"

My heart stops, eyes scud around the room. The pink clock's cramped-up hand's on three, the long one just past thirty. It's time. My own hand's iced to the phone. He's back.

The smell. The leather. The taste. The metallic blood in my mouth. And I can't. Move. I strain my ears. Wait. For more information. For confirmation that I'm not hallucinating, that he's not apparition. That it's really him. That this isn't just another nightmare. But there's nothing else. Just dial tone. He's gone, but I still feel his heaviness. His breath. They bruise the air around me. He knows where I am. He's found me.

After this phone call, all of the good things that have been happening cease to matter—running through the night, the Town Hall, the fellowship, the 4.0. I don't think to write in my journal. I have trouble recalling things—like my phone number, like what day it is.

I can't sleep at all now. Lindsey has to remind me that I have classes—what they are, where they are, when. I forget food. When Lindsey insists I do eat, it doesn't stay down.

Days pass. I run across the card Tall Tree gave me. The name on it reads *Captain Richard Pull*. I remember that he said I should let him know if I ever needed anything. I might need something, so I phone him. I really, really don't mean to cry, but I do.

I tell him about the phone call, that it sounded like his voice, that he asked me the time, that it was just around the time he was raping me, that he knows where I live, that he said that night if anyone ever found out, he would hunt me down and kill me. I wouldn't bother you, I say, but I'm so afraid. He says he won't let that happen. We could ask for a phone tap, but it'll be lots of red tape, take too long. So, here's what we'll do. We'll get an order of protection against him, he tells me.

I say I don't understand what that is. He says if the rapist comes within five miles of me or the university, if he breaks the order, he'll be arrested. If he contacts me, harasses me by phone, anything like that, he'll be sent back to jail. I say that I want it and he says he'll have the papers sent to me right away and I say thanks. I forget to remind Tall Tree about his promise to me from that night, that he would find the knife. But I wonder how he'll be able to find it if it never existed.

When the papers appear the next day, I sign them and I send them back to Tall Tree. The police issue the order of protection. And even though I'm supposed to feel safer, I don't, because it doesn't change the facts. He knows where I am. He knows how to get me. If he wants to kill me, it won't do anything to stop him. I don't sleep and I don't eat. When I do make it to my classes, my professors are saying important words for my final exams. But I don't know what they are because my ears don't hear things anymore. And he's there—sitting two rows behind me, at the desk right next to me, in the quad. He's standing in every doorway, walking down every stair, watching from every corner.

He's there, even though he's not.

CHAPTER THIRTY-THREE

Wednesday, April 12

I had no breath. I knew I had to cross University Avenue to get to Latin class. But I couldn't do it. Everything was unhinging. I was losing my knees, could see myself tumbling toward the pavement. I didn't fall, though. Cars passed and it scared me to look at the drivers' faces. But I did it. Not him. Not him. Not him. Still, I couldn't catch a full breath. I made myself cross the street, climbed the stairs to the Hall of Languages, past Miriam's name carved on the Remembrance Monument for the Pan-Am victims. I heard footsteps behind me, stopped, turned. It was a girl with dark hair. Not him. Definitely not him. But for how long?

Friday, April 14

I write it here so that there will never be any doubt: If I die, he killed me.

Tuesday, April 18. This New DA.

A man phones, says he's from the DA's office. He tells me that a new attorney has been assigned to my case. I ask about the old one, the DA Lena with the calves, the freckles, the auburn hair. He tells me she's getting married, that her work is load shifting. She'll no longer be involved in the legal proceedings.

Hearing this makes me nervous. The DA Lena knew my case and she cared about me, making sure the case went forward. Now this new lawyer will have to be brought up to speed and I could easily just become forgotten felt-y dryer lint. Now there's an even greater chance that he won't ever have to pay for what he did.

The man tells me to come down to the District Attorney's office as soon as possible to meet my new attorney. The order of protection has changed nothing. I'm just as scared as ever to be out in the city alone. But the next day I force myself to do this. I find a bus schedule, make my way downtown. The snow's gone now, bunchy grape hyacinths stabbing through soppy earth.

In the waiting room I flip through issues of *Good Housekeeping*, discover new techniques for dressing up a glazed ham, for creating party favors, for baking birthday cakes with crushed Oreo cookies on top (to resemble soil), gummy worm heads poking out. And, for a few moments, I really try to imagine. I try to wish myself into that chirpy-happy life.

Then a woman with rich black hair tied back in a bun calls out my name. I stand up, try to manage something like a smile, start to pull my hand out of my mancoat pocket. But she says she's not my new attorney, she's a secretary, and to follow her. Her heels strike the floor decisively. We pass rows of cubicles. She stops, leaves me. A woman with midlength brown hair stands up, holds out a wide hand, says it's nice to meet me. Her shake is firm, her voice deep. She introduces herself as Megan Rue. I don't say it's nice to meet her because it's not. This DA Megan is a complete stranger, and even though I'm sure she's capable, I can't imagine starting this all over again with someone new. I wish so, so badly that I could have my old lawyer back.

This DA Megan tells me she's been studying my case, that she was hoping we could talk about it, that I should take a seat. I sit. She says that the Grand Jury went fine and next we'll move to trial, but first there will be that line-up. I'm thinking about how facing him through a one-way glass, let alone in court, scares me and that I still don't really get this need for a line-up. But I can't gather up the energy to question it anymore. My roommates will be summoned to testify, she says. And they'll bring in other people who know me well—my friends and family, my teachers, my psychiatrist. His lawyer will bring in witnesses too—his own psychologist, family members, character witnesses.

"Had a visit from his mother the other day, such an elegant lady. Wanted me to tell you how sorry she is for what her son did."

Did I just hear her right? I can't be sure. So I ask her to please say that again, and she tells me that the rapist's mother sought her out. And since the mother could have said something that would help the case, it made sense to talk with her.

There's a howl beginning a slow boil in my throat. It's that mad-as-hell hornet anger again. I'm angry for his entering a plea of not guilty, for the DA Lena abandoning me, for this DA Megan taking over. And I'm angry for the rapist's mother's apology, as if her apology could somehow undo what he did to me, make it better. This DA Megan is speaking.

"She's concerned about you."

"What am I supposed to do with her concern?"

This DA Megan stares at me. She breathes in long, purposeful, says maybe we should start over. She tells me we'll proceed with the case, either to trial or a plea bargain. I have no idea what she means, what she's talking about, so I just ask. What's a plea bargain? She says it's when the defendant pleads to a set of charges we all agree to and we don't go to trial.

"Let's go to trial. I want to see him serve the maximum sentence."

This DA Megan eyes me. She extends that hand again, and I pull mine back, mumble a good-bye. I leave the office with a whole new sense of powerlessness. Even though this DA Megan seems nice enough, I don't like her meeting with the mother, her talking about a plea bargain option. I don't like any of it.

Why have I really been given a new lawyer in the middle of everything? Was I not worth it? Was the DA Lena a resource better placed elsewhere? And, why is this DA Megan so impressed by his mother? How could any of this possibly help me?

CHAPTER THIRTY-FOUR

Wednesday, April 26. Civil Suit.

The criminal court case seems to drag on and on. I don't know why. My life remains a fogged-up-frightened limbo-world. I lift weights and I keep rowing on my machine to nowhere. I'm dedicating myself to becoming a mini–Incredible Hulk minus the green part, because I have to be ready, ready at any time, to fight for my life again.

This DA Megan keeps saying that I'm free from danger. But I know he's out there. The order of protection won't stop him. He could be anywhere, so he's everywhere. Still I constantly look over my shoulder. Still I watch to make sure no one's following me. Most of my nights I just lie awake. And I wait for him. I wait for him to make me dead.

I'm still here.

After combing through law books and speaking to her political science professors about the options facing women who have been raped, Celia convinces me that I'll feel better if I do something proactive instead of just sitting around waiting to die, and maybe that something should be looking into how to pursue a civil suit against him. She tells me that apparently a court can award a crime victim money to cover the costs of therapy as well as pain and suffering for the years to come.

Celia's heard of a practicing feminist lawyer who teaches at Syracuse University's Law School part-time and handles civil suits. I say maybe I shouldn't go. Celia says come on, what harm could it do? You wouldn't have to pursue it, and maybe you could learn something useful about what's happening in your own case. Since I can find no solid evidence to dispute her point, I agree to make an appointment. She drives me there.

The lawyer's office is on the third floor of an ancient warehouse, gutted and refurbished to look chic and lofty inside with sleek, flaxen hardwoods, mod fixtures, slab tables, and we sit on wooden chairs that must be way too expensive to put butts on. The lawyer comes in and she's thin with short, dirty-blond–gray hair and a tunnel-tube skirt. She reaches across her desk to shake my hand, then Celia's.

She asks what she can do to help us. Celia looks to me to answer but heck if I know what to say, and so Celia jumps in, says we're here to learn more about how to pursue a civil suit. The lawyer smiles, eyes me, then Celia. She says she already understands quite a bit about my case because of the media coverage. But she also knows pieces about it that have not been publicized. She knows his lawyer quite well actually, she says. Without a doubt, he's the best lawyer in town, probably in this region of the country.

I hate her for saying this. But I tell myself I shouldn't be that surprised, because that's what money can buy, the best. Meanwhile I'm living in Lindsey's tiny attic for dirt-cheap rent, will have to work several summer jobs to cover my costs. Last week I ate mostly apples, the Red Delicious kind. Dad forgot to put sending money to help with my rent on his "to-do" list, and it's just easier not to bother him.

The lawyer asks how much money I'm thinking about, that she would take the case on contingency, that she'll get one-third of whatever the settlement is. But I haven't the flimsiest idea what she means by any of it. Celia jumps in. Fifty thousand dollars, she says. I haven't met this part of her before, a confidence that must come from many years of observing her father, a wealthy man responsible for many of New York State's highways, clinch a hard-fisted business deal. The lawyer snorts, pushes back against her seat. Well, that's quite a sum of money, my dear, she says. Then I jump in, say that no matter what we'll definitely demand an admission that he raped me, right? Gosh no, she says, laughing. That's not what a civil suit is about. But I don't understand. So I ask why I would want to pursue this sort of suit then. If it's not about him admitting it—when he was caught at the scene and he resisted arrest and he broke all those police bones—why would I bother doing this? For restitution, she says, to get money for my pain, my suffering. But I don't want his money, I tell her. I want him to give up part of his life—the way he took away mine. I'm thinking a limb might be nice, too—an arm, a leg, a something else—but I don't say these things. I seem to be sort of yelling now, and I've squirmed out of my seat and onto my feet, and I'm standing up and the lawyer has jumped up too and she's heads taller than me and she looks real hardy and definite. And I'm sure she takes absolutely no crud in the courtroom which, if I were the least bit interested in doing this civil thing, would make a major difference to me, but since I'm not, it really doesn't. Celia's sitting, rolling her inky eyeballs, motioning for me to plunk my butt back in my seat. But my legs. They won't move.

The lawyer huffs out, says that she doesn't know what will happen with the criminal trial, but it doesn't look very good. His family will spare no expense. They can move all of his trust funds away from him—which she's certain they did right after this happened. They could have a private investigator tailing me, prying into my history, my family, my academic record. They've surely already done all of this some time ago, she says, in preparation for trial.

I can see Sherlock Holmes—geeky tweed coat and magnifying glass—following me, and I realize that I wouldn't have even noticed him because I've only been watching out for the rapist, wondering when he would break that order of protection and kill me. I've been busy trying to avoid the revulsion, the forced tenderness in people's eyes. I've been trying to figure out how to just make it through each day. I flop back down onto the seat. There's so much I haven't known enough to know that I don't know. My breath's thin.

The lawyer adjusts the plunky stones on her necklace, sits down. She says it doesn't sound like this is a route I want to pursue. For a moment I envision holding all that green money I paid for with my body, my blood, my soul. It could mean never bothering Mom and Dad again. It could pay for food, for rent, maybe even graduate school one day.

Voice torrent-rushes out of my head. I won't do it, I say. I won't. She gets it, she says. She understands my decision. Of course, if I change my mind, don't hesitate to call. I shake her hand. Celia and I walk out. Celia says sorry that wasn't more helpful. I say thanks, but I just can't do that.

This whole thing's got me realizing just how unaware I am, got me wondering how my case would be different if he weren't a member of the family that runs Syracuse, if he weren't born with an inflated trust fund, if he didn't have the best stinking lawyer in town. But I won't ever know.

One thing is sure, though. The civil suit is not my way. I can't monetize what he did to me. This wasn't some sort of transaction, but a crime. That's the only definition of it that makes any sense to me, and I can't let that go. The criminal suit is where I need to concentrate my energies. If I'm ever going to feel better, if I'm ever going to have a chance of making sense of what's happened to me, he's going to have to be convicted of rape in court. Making this happen is what matters.

CHAPTER THIRTY-FIVE

Tuesday, May 9. Lindsey Graduates.

April's over. Sunshine has taken over the campus quad, warming the treetops, the thickening-wet air. When boys smile at me, I watch my sneakers fast-glide over the pavement, let Lindsey's knife stay closed in my mancoat pocket (a mancoat's always in season). Boys, no matter how nice-seeming, no matter how kind, just scare me now. I don't know what they could do or might be capable of.

Lindsey's marvelous family—the entire loud mishmash of sisters, brother, aunts, cousins—descends on our apartment to see her graduate. I want to be genuinely happy for her that she's moving on, leaving college for a life back in Boston, but I can't because I still need her something awful. I think I'll break apart when she leaves, but I try to act cooler than I am, nonchalant, like yeah-I'll-miss-you-sure-but-I-can-totally-handle-it. I know she doesn't believe me. I feel guilty for demanding all I have of Lind these last months, for desperate-depending on her so much. And whenever I think about her going, tears singe my eyes. Because what will I do with her gone? What can my life possibly be without her here in it?

Lindsey is gone and all of my work is done and I am left undeniably by myself—loneliness. I looked back on this semester today as I began to pack up this make-shift room, a stack of pages overflowing their folders (papers for classes) and a smaller stack of my own writing (crap). I was a machine—my moods, my feelings screwed down tightly by a nineteen-credit workload and friends with their own lives and problems I could listen to. But now everyone's left. And I'm still here, my heart pounding at night—Who is there? I am alone. I was alone that night too. I don't ever want to be alone again. I get so afraid, constantly waking, watching—Who is there?

Lindsey's life goes on without me. She gets engaged to her boyfriend, Jim. They plan to marry in the next year or so, and even though I like him so much—there's no guy out there nearly as good as him—I can't understand how she can commit her whole self, her whole life, to a guy. My mind can't understand making that serious decision so young. I can't really imagine making it period. It seems too trusting, too naive, too foolish. I have trouble coming off positive about her relationship. I also know that there's something wrong with that.

At bottom, I'm still really depending on friends to get me through. The only wise thing to do once Lindsey leaves is to move in with Celia. So we find an illegal third-floor apartment on the other side of town. It's far away from the neighborhood where it all happened. My new room is a smallish walk-in-type closet, its ceiling following the steep, peaky-outline of the roof. When I stand next to the walls I have to stoop my head, fold myself to three-quarter-size. I love it. It feels tons safer to sleep in a little den like this. There's just enough space for my old futon, no-name teddy bear, pink clock, lamp, and computer on its board supported by the book-filled milk crates. There's only one way in. I hire a locksmith to install a beefy lock system on the door.

CHAPTER THIRTY-SIX

I go back to New Hampshire for the summer. I get two jobs at the same mall, one at Ann Taylor and one at the Gap. I read many books. I write my thesis, even though I don't have to start working on it until fall—ten pages, then thirty, then fifty, then eighty. Much of the writing is poor. But it gives me a goal, a project, something to focus on. I try to make myself go outside, do something. I go for small hikes with Mom. I go for a tippy canoe ride with Dad. I go for a little bike ride with Dave. We don't talk much about what happened. Days move by, weeks. Every day I pin my hopes on his conviction. But I hear nothing about the line-up, the trial.

Sensing my mood, Mom springs for a family vacation to the Virgin Islands—her, me, my brother, and, of course, no Dad. She says she wants to rebuild our family, wants me to heal and relax before the trial. I'm glad to be going somewhere far, far away, somewhere hard for him to get to. But I'm feeling down and purposeless, and can't enjoy anything. My journal entries are blue-deviled and morose all summer.

CHAPTER THIRTY-SEVEN

Back in New Hampshire now, the phone rings. It's this DA Megan. Her voice is full and bubbly.

"Great news."

Finally! We're going to trial and he's going to be convicted of raping me. And maybe they found the knife too. If not those things, could be he's been mistaken for a buck by a bow hunter or whopped in the brain by a big-old wrecking ball.

"It's all over."

"What?"

"He agreed to the plea bargain."

"What plea bargain?"

"The details don't matter, Laura. What matters is that he'll serve jail time."

"Has he admitted raping me?"

"Well, no, he pled to first-degree burglary.'"

"I don't understand."

She starts talking very slowly to me now.

"Burglary and rape are considered the same level of felony. It doesn't matter which one he pled to as the top count. It's the same level of offense. He'll serve the same jail time."

"Shouldn't rape be the top charge?"

"Trust me, this is good news."

Maybe it is. Maybe I don't understand a thing.

I say thank you to her, though I don't why. And I try super-hard. I try to think about the good things—that he's been convicted, that he will serve jail time, that I won't have to go through the tough part of testifying at a trial.

But mainly I think about the bad things. He's been convicted on a lie. In pleading to burglary, the fact that he is a rapist, a person who threatened to murder someone, who was caught in the midst of trying to carry it out, is lost. And as a convicted burglar, his prison situation will most likely be far better than as a convicted rapist. While his sentence is four to twelve years, with good behavior, this DA Megan tells me, he could be out in one to two, even less.

It's over for the DA's office, done. But it's not over for me. Though I feel steadier because he's behind bars, he is no burglar. His conviction does not speak to any reality I know. It negates what happened to me completely, makes it look as if it never was.

There's nothing about this that really feels like vindication, like justice. But I understand it now. A rape survivor is just a witness. It was never anything like my call to make. It would have been a courtesy to consult me, nothing that should have been expected of this DA Megan. She was only responsible for informing me after the fact. Her job was to get a conviction. And she's done it.

But still. I just can't help it. I'm not satisfied with the result.

Thursday, July 6. Midnight.

Tonight of all nights I am most scared. If there might be any time he would want to kill me, would want to have it done with, it would be tonight. Tomorrow he confesses, confesses to being a burglar. He will acknowledge that he illegally entered an apartment, that someone was "injured" during the burglary. But he will not acknowledge what he did, say that he came that night to rape me. Though he was indicted on it, though it appears somewhere on the documents for the plea, he will not confess to what is true.

Thursday, August 3

I had a dream. A very old man in a wheelchair was wearing a blond wig and sunglasses, his face stretched tight. He was getting pushed around a supermarket by various women. He was following me, grinning. His grin frightened me. I knew he must be bald underneath, that his eyes were cinders. I knew what the wig and sunglasses were hiding.

CHAPTER THIRTY-EIGHT

Tuesday, August 29. Final Sentencing of the Burglar. First Day of Classes.

I'm back in Syracuse. Today he is being sentenced and my fall classes begin. On my way to class I stop at the convenience store, grab a copy of the *Syracuse Herald-Journal*. I stand outside on the corner with the paper. There it is, page A-1. "Lawyer's Son Sentenced 4 to 12 Years: Plea Bargain Ends Rape Case." For so many months I've imagined this article, been waiting for it. But the one I imagined, the one I'd been hoping on, had a different title, "Rapist Tried and Convicted."

The article begins with this sentence: "The son of a prominent local lawyer blamed alcohol for his troubles today as he was sentenced to prison for committing a burglary during which a young woman was brutally raped and beaten." The sentence is oddly constructed, revealing what happened without actually saying what happened. The next sentence might well have read: "He was there, she was raped. You put the pieces together."

Most of the article is about him, people saying what a wonderful person he is, what a tragedy it is that he drank too much and will have to serve jail time for burglary. The writer notes that during his court appearance "there was no admission of rape, although he was accused of beating and raping a woman while armed with a screwdriver." Instead, his lawyer calls him a "young man of character," a football player and captain of his lacrosse team in college, "a leader among students." The lawyer also says his client has a "very serious and deeply-rooted problem that was masked by his success as a student, by his success as an athlete, by his general kind and affable behavior and, after college, by his success as a business person."

The fact of my rape appears twice and only briefly in the article. The writer notes, "There was no mention of the victim in court today." And this DA Megan is quoted as saying "That's why he's doing 4 to 12. There was a victim. There was a very heinous crime committed."

Four to twelve years. At some point right after the plea was struck, this DA Megan told me what this really means—and I just can't forget what she said. In cases like mine it's often code for one to two.

My knees are weak. I'm something defeated. And I'm coming undone. The news story, what happened in that court room, the plea bargain. In all of them I'm just a trace, something erased, even if imperfectly, from the picture. My story was never told. My story will never be known. They're trying to scrub away what he did to me, make it like it never happened. I feel helpless, hopeless.

I mash that paper up, toss it in a trash can where it belongs. As I walk toward campus, I try to think about other things, like all of my great classes this semester—Senior Honors Seminar (for my thesis); Theories of Discourse (an English capstone); Women's Studies: Language, Culture, and Society; two graduate classes on the English Renaissance (my professors told me I'm ready for graduate-level studies); and Advanced Aerobics (okay, admittedly lame, but I'm hoping that the jumping-joviality of all those bodies might rub off on me a little).

And I tell myself other things to make myself feel better. I remind myself that there are many women who go through what I did, never see any sort of justice. Instead their perpetrators remain uncaught, unconvicted, their experiences oftentimes long-concealed and unacknowledged. Compared to all these women, I'm lucky. The man who did this to me will no longer be out there, free to stalk and kill me, free to rape other women. He will serve actual jail time.

I try hard to convince myself that even though a poor perpetrator would receive far more jail time for the same crimes, even though his pricey lawyer has managed to magically turn him from rapist into burglar, unlike many rape victims, I have an honest-to-goodness chance. While he is in jail, I can live something resembling a life. Maybe I can put together a few years of regular eating and sleeping. Maybe I can even begin graduate school before he's released.

But none of this works. The fact that he pled to first-degree burglary, the fact that the rape went unacknowledged, eats away at me. My mind keeps replaying that night, the grand jury testimony, the plea bargaining. I can't help it. I keep thinking that there ought to have been more, so much more, we could have done.

In the days to come, I quit smoking. My body works out furiously. It knows that it will need to be bigger, burlier when he gets out. If he comes after me once he's released, my body must be much more prepared than it was the last time to fight for its life. I may have as little as one year to accomplish this. So my body practices karate moves a lot, especially the ones meant to poke out eyes, rip off balls, smash up throats. My body lifts weights. It runs fast so it can get home quickly. It lifts weights again. The next time it sees him, it's doing the damage.

CHAPTER THIRTY-NINE

On Celia's advice I signed up for that women's studies class. I'm taking it with a philosophy professor named Dr. Linda Martín Alcoff. Celia keeps going on and on about her being an amazing feminist teacher and scholar. Celia insists I have to meet her before the class starts. I don't want to tick Celia off since we've just moved in together and that would start us off on the wrong foot. So I agree to go.

We're on the second floor of the H.B. Crouse Building, facing a row of offices. One door's slightly ajar, bright light shooting into the hallway. Celia knocks on it a bunch. A woman with a distinctly Southern accent calls out.

"Come in."

Celia goes in. I follow, peer over her shoulder. Books cover nearly every inch of the room from floor to ceiling—Nietzsche, Hegel, Marx, hooks, Friedan, Sartre, Anzaldua, Rich—and even though they're heaving off the walls, they're perfectly alphabetized. There's a computer on a desk with sinuous words on the screen. Beyond it there's a tiny picture window with a view out onto the quad. A striking woman with waves of ebony hair wearing a black leather miniskirt and suede top sits on a chair.

"This an okay time?"

"Sure. What's up, Celia?"

"This is my roommate, Laura. She's taking your women's studies class this semester. She spoke out about her rape at the Town Hall meeting last Spring."

Why is Celia blathering to my new professor about this? What is this woman going to think of me? I stare at Celia, wonder how I'm going to diplomatically tell her off when we get out of here. Dr. Alcoff's looking at me with opalescent eyes.

Her voice is steady, thoughtful.

"Sit."

She motions to two chairs nudged against the wall. We plonk ourselves on them. She asks me how I am. At first I'm sure I won't know what to say, but I start and I can't stop. I say I went to that Town Hall not planning to say anything then all of a sudden it was like I couldn't sit silent anymore, had to do something to make them see I was a person with a mind and a face and a voice, an actual real-life person who lived through this. She smiles. She speaks.

"I'm a survivor, too."

Now I understand. Celia brought me here because she knew. She also knew it was Dr. Alcoff's story to tell. It happened when she was just a little kid. After that, everything changed for her. She couldn't focus. She never wanted to be alone. She was afraid of all men. She couldn't study for classes. It's taken her many years to become the person she is. She says what I did took tons of courage, that it's important for people to hear what survivors have to say. She says she talks about it to individuals, to large groups of people. She goes on television, on the radio. She says she has to—people need to know about the debilitating effects it can have, have to fight against it. She says she talks about it more than some of her philosophy colleagues might like.

"But that's their problem."

A raped-girl like me. A raped-girl turned professor. A raped-girl professor who refuses to keep quiet about it.

I say that at the Town Hall they read all those statistics about me. I tell her that I didn't feel sad or numb anymore, just angry. I tell her that I said I'm not just some statistic, that I'm a person. She smiles, tilts back her chair, taps the air with her high heel. There's not a single thing about this woman that reeks of moldy-sour philosophy books.

I can't seem to close my mouth, so I tell her about my case, that the guy who raped me is the grandson of that man on the Syracuse University Board of Trustees.

"That's you?"

I waggle yes, and she tells me that she knows all about my case from the news, that I've made it through a lot. She says she remembers he was caught at the scene and she asks what's happening with the legal system. I tell her about his family's power, about him having the best lawyer around. I explain how it didn't go to trial, even though I was ready, how he took a plea bargain I never knew was on the table, how he was convicted of burglary. I watch her think. The air's on fire.

"Do you write about it?"

I tell her I do. I tell her about my journal. I say I have to write about it. Keep doing that, she tells me. Getting it out, talking about it, writing about it—it can save you. It saved her, she tells me. She says she wouldn't be here if she hadn't written about it, that she's known a lot of survivors who gave up their life's goals, who took their own lives. Some of the smartest, most talented women never finish their educations because they just can't handle what happened to them, she says.

She asks me if I'm getting any counseling, and I tell her I'm seeing a shrink but that it's not completely helpful and that I really wish that there was a support group on campus for survivors of sexual violence, that I think it'd help survivors to be able to talk with one another, other people who know what it's like. She eyes me.

"Start it. I'll help you."

"You will?"

She nods, grins. She says she's glad to meet me. I say I'm glad to meet her back, and I mean this in a major way, a way I don't have the first idea how to express. I'm so startled, so happy to meet a professor who is also a raped-girl, a survivor, who is vocal about it. A fog bell's banging through me, scattering the dank mists—and I know one thing, know it for sure. Nothing will be the same. Ever again. Everything is about to change.

Dr. Linda Martín Alcoff is my superhero in the flesh. And I'm actually taking a class with her. This Wonder Woman has no lasso of truth, no bulletproof bracelets. No preposterous, see-through plane. No gold tiara. No hideous, wedgy-producing one piece. She's a short-leather-skirt-wearing, Southern-accent-using, high-heel-wearing, rape-surviving, Latina feminist Marxist philosopher. Knowing she exists means everything to me. It means I'm not alone. It means maybe there really can and will be an after, something beyond all this. It means maybe my heart and my dreams of becoming a writer one day—things I've wondered whether I would ever be able to unearth again—may not be irrecoverable after all.

Dr. Linda Martín Alcoff *is*. And all of a sudden I can imagine being, too.

CHAPTER FORTY

Time speeds up during the fall. Having him behind bars is helping me to begin building my courage, to feel a tiny bit safer each day. I throw myself completely into my classes. My professors are telling me to consider graduate school. Even though I'm not altogether sure about it, I think that attending graduate school will help me to reach my goal of one day becoming a writer. My professors encourage me to apply to programs in English and cultural studies, and I send away for applications.

Though I love all of my classes, I adore Dr. Alcoff's classes most—the heavy load of feminist philosophy reading, the energetic class discussions, the challenging paper assignments. In response to one prompt, I write a long, wordy paper about problematic therapeutic models that have been used historically to treat survivors of sexual assault (like Sigmund Freud's) and troubling representations of survivors in the media. Based upon my beliefs in the potential value of survivor-created and driven support groups, I also include some brief arguments about the importance of survivors of sexual assault gaining power through speaking out about our own experiences. I'm a little embarrassed by the paper, not because of the subject matter—since Dr. Alcoff knows all about me and she's a survivor, too—but because of the argument's gaps. I know what and where they are, but I can't fix them. What I do know is that the argument I'm trying to make really matters to me. It's the first one I've ever made that feels like a great deal more than a compelling intellectual exercise. I care about it personally and emotionally, too. In my heart I know—I've stumbled on something that's truly important. It's the rough beginning of some sort of idea. If I only knew how to think beyond it, to get enough distance on it to see the whole of it, to envision it clearly, it could be something full and real.

When Dr. Alcoff turns my paper back, there's a blue "A+" on the top of the first page. I'm surprised that something of what I was trying to say has come across, in spite of the paper's many flaws. I'm thrilled that she liked it. On the last page, are the blue words: "This is phenomenal!"

I read that sentence several times, just to make sure my eyes haven't gone screwy. But that's what it really says. And next to those words are more blue scribbles. She asks whether I would be interested in developing this idea further, whether I might want to co-write an article with her, one that analyzes media representations of survivorship, examines when and where rape survivors are themselves taking control of the public discourses about it, publish the article in an academic journal. She tells me to take some time to think about it. There's no rush about getting back to her. But I don't need to think about it for one split second. I speak with her after class and I say "Are you serious?" and "Yes, yes, yes!" and "I'm so honored you asked me." I really don't have the first idea what this will entail—writing something with a professor—but I'm absolutely sure of one thing. Dr. Alcoff is giving me an amazing opportunity, something I'm fairly sure I don't deserve. Dr. Alcoff really sees me—she has since that first day we met—and all of my shuttered-shaky hopes, my mothballed dreams. She wants to help me to reach them. And now I'm not stumbling alone along on my path to becoming a writer. She's there with me.

In preparation for writing this article, Dr. Alcoff gives me a long list of important books to read, and I begin to make my way through them. There's Ellen Bass's *The Courage to Heal: A Guide for Women Survivors of Sexual Abuse*, probably the single most influential text ever published in the recovery movement for female survivors. There are memoirs like Truddi Chase's *When Rabbit Howls* (one of the first to focus on ritualized child sexual abuse, dissociation, and the development of alternative identities) and Elly Danica's *Don't: A Woman's Word* (a groundbreaking alternative to traditional narratives that uses a fragmented, outline format and unusual, strategic textual silences to tell a survivor's story). There are feminist theoretical treatments like Liz Kelly's *Surviving Sexual Violence*, a foundational text based on interviews with female survivors that examines how they fight against, live with, and ultimately survive their experiences. There are books about philosophical theory and history. While I have read some of Michel Foucault's *The History of Sexuality* and *The Archaeology of Knowledge and the Discourse on Language* for classes, she asks that I reread them again, carefully, this time taking especially detailed notes about how Foucault describes "the confession" and defines "discourse." And she suggests that I find more books to bolster my argument about sexual assault survivors and psychoanalysis. So I read texts like Jeffrey Moussaieff Masson's *A Dark Science: Women, Sexuality and Psychiatry in the Nineteenth Century*, a collection of crucial articles documenting how sexual abuse was systematically denied by psychoanalysts using really disturbing diagnoses (boys and girls who suffered child sex abuse, for example, were termed "prematurely perverted.")

It feels really good—no, kind of great—to have this academic work to do, even better to read things that are actually helping me to make sense of my experiences. And while I'm reading all of these books, we also start meeting regularly to talk about the article. We discuss the troubling cultural representations of survivors. We've seen them on television talk programs, morning televisions shows, soap operas, dramatic television series, and in film. In order to get a better handle on the patterns we're observing, we gather videotaped versions and transcripts. We watch *Sally Jesse, Donahue, Geraldo Rivera,* and *Oprah.* We watch *Good Morning America* and *The Today Show.* We watch *General Hospital* and *The Accused.*

And in the many days, weeks, and months to come we spend hours upon hours together hovering over a computer keyboard in Dr. Alcoff's office, drafting an essay that weaves our two minds together—mine the untrained, emboldened mind of a college girl; hers the seasoned, diplomatic mind of a university professor. She smiles, watches my two index fingers chopping away at the keyboard. Then she takes over. I watch her two digits flit lightning-fast across all those letters. I smile back at her. All this time I thought I was alone, hid the embarrassing fact that I'm unable to type correctly like all those smart people do. But it turns out we share this secret too. And one more time, I know. I'm not alone.

As we work, Dr. Alcoff teaches me. Through her example I begin to learn what it means to write like a writer, to think like a scholar. She doesn't tell me "this is how it's done," give me some poof-magic formula, the specific components of what a strong academic article should be. Instead, over and over again, Dr. Alcoff teaches me through the act of writing itself, by example. She shows me. She does it so thoroughly, so consistently, so kindly, that within a few weeks of working together it's her voice I hear in my head as I work on this article, as I write my papers for class, as I compose anything. This is a different kind of teaching than I have ever experienced before. Dr. Alcoff's not treating me like an undergraduate student with a good idea. She's treating me like a peer, a colleague. I know I don't deserve this kind of treatment, that I haven't earned it yet. But the fact that she gives it to me unconditionally—her deep respect, her camaraderie, even her deference—makes me begin to have a confidence in my own mind that I've never, ever had before. She believes in me and, because she does, I begin to believe in myself. This bit of confidence makes me capable of a level of thinking that is altogether new to me.

I watch closely, observe Dr. Alcoff's thoughts turn, how her mind reasons. And, in time, I start to learn how to think like this, too. After a while, who says what becomes more blurry, gets harder and harder to discern. Our thoughts begin to complete one another, and our conversations begin to sound something like this.

This is a solid start. But it doesn't feel quite right. Yep, it's not there yet. It feels stretched, wooden. Know what you mean. It has to be clearer, needs a more decisive thesis statement. Yes, we shouldn't be afraid to state it outright, you know, like we mean it. After all, this is ours. This is our argument.

I like this example. To fully substantiate this assertion, though, we're going to need more like this. What about relevant texts that have been published in the last year? Let's hit all of the major journals, read every relevant article we can get our hands on. Research time!

Now, here. Imagine what our detractors might say. Let's anticipate it before it ever comes, acknowledge it, and refute it. Right, right. We know what you're going to say, but we say this. We know what you'll say to that, but we say this. Gracious, genial, but still, we got you!

Do you feel that, that gap, that little leap between this paragraph and that one? Yeah, yeah. It's a jump in logic. We can't lose the reader, let her fall through that crack there. Got to fill that one in, patch it over. A smoother transition? How about this phrasing? Definitely getting there. But that's not quite right yet. Words . . . ummm. Try this instead. Still, not quite . . . oh, wait. This, what about this? Yes, yes! You think? Completely. That's it. Now that works. That really works!

As we compose the essay together, we begin to think about all of the survivors who are not students, not professors. And we decide that this project can't just be an academic thing. We don't want to talk only to people in universities. It's crucial that we reach people outside the academy as well. Though it needs to appear in a scholarly journal, we'll have to publish other, less jargon-y versions for popular audiences, too.

Our words blend, expand, contract. They fuse together, form different shapes and routes. In time our words become a full working draft. We revise it, rethink it, add to it, subtract from it. It becomes something coherent, meaningful. We polish it. We rework it again. And, after a while, it starts to sparkle.

My words, Dr. Alcoff's words, our words together—I see them all there on the pages. Dr. Alcoff didn't turn my head away from the most horrifying experience of my life, the thing that broke me. Instead, she helped me to look at it for what it was, taught me to find positive ways to integrate it into my future, to make something with beauty and wholeness that might allow me to live beyond it. Dr. Alcoff set me on a course, held my hand, gave me lift. She's given me the sort of gift I'll never be able to reciprocate, the kind that restores someone's spirit. But she knew that, and gave it just the same.

CHAPTER FORTY-ONE

Throughout the fall semester I write very sparely in my journal. Most of my writing is happening in other places—composing the article with Dr. Alcoff, writing for my classes, writing my thesis, and drafting documents on behalf of survivors' rights on campus. When I do write in my journal, it's often in note form, little chicken scratches about books I'm reading outside of classes, lists of texts I want to read, thoughts about the process of writing itself. But in and amid the various notes sometimes, there are entries.

Tuesday, October 24

> *I am strong. I am. But my dreams still suck. I don't remember most of them anymore. What I do recall are shattered pieces—a hit here, a punch there, the occasional blood-spattered floor. I'm going to be okay if I can just hang in, hang on.*

Sunday, November 19–Monday, November 20

> *One year gone. I will not sleep tonight. I cannot imagine ever sleeping again on this night. My throat's*

clasped. My wrists hurt, as if bound. My back aches. It's as
if I've been thrown back into that night all over again.

One year has passed. Am I getting better yet?

I CAN . . . *walk down the street in the daylight by*
myself, be alone in the shower or in my bed with my body,
sleep a little more during the night, concentrate on my
school work better, write on and on forever.

I CAN'T . . . *ever turn off the lights, sleep through any*
night without waking up seven or eight times, imagine
ever dating a guy (though I wish I could), keep myself from
startling at strange noises, go anywhere at night alone
without running there, like someone is chasing me.

Sometimes it occurs to me that I should find out exactly where in the state of New York he's been imprisoned. I have a fear that he might be released. I have an impression that it could happen anytime. I know his sentence is four to twelve years, but no one has ever explained to me what that really means. Is it really just one to two? Three to five? The full twelve? I want to check on this, but I never can seem to make myself do it. It's thinking about him, and nothing good ever comes from that.

CHAPTER FORTY-TWO

During the spring semester I take English Honors (credit hours to complete my thesis), Continental Philosophy (not a requirement for my majors but too insanely cool not to take), Texts of the Third World (senior capstone), and Theories of Gender and Race (another graduate class). It's a lighter course load than usual. But my writing commitments in each class are significant. And I'm engaged in more and more political work on campus on behalf of survivors of sexual violence.

With the help of two other very deeply committed and politically active student survivors, I create the first campus support group for survivors of sexual assault at Syracuse University. Dr. Alcoff helps us to do it. Our group begins small. We meet in a tiny room in the basement of Hendricks Chapel and we share our experiences with each other, encourage each other. The members' stories are terrifying, their courageousness astounding. The group is run by a doctoral student in psychiatry who is herself a survivor of childhood molestation. And each week more and more survivors mysteriously arrive. More and more people join us.

A freshman with a slight build, fine-type features, shows up, for months sits silent. Then one day she begins talking. We listen as she describes how she was raped repeatedly by her cousin for twelve years. It's only since she's heard the rest of our stories that she's begun to hold him accountable in her own mind, not blame it all on something her nine-year-old self did or said. Eventually she decides that she's going to confront her molester, to call what he did to her rape, incest. She tells her parents, her siblings. They rally around her. Together—as a group—they take him on. And once they do this, she witnesses something she never imagined. The monster who stole her childhood is frightened of her. She tells him to never come near her again. And, so far, he hasn't.

A librarian with the flaming red hair and translucent skin appears. I've handed her many teetering stacks of books across a desk, thought I saw something in her eyes that told me we were the same kind. When she arrives at our little group, smiles break out over both our faces. She tells us that when she was little she was awkward, bookish. She wanted desperately to be accepted by other kids, not be teased by them relentlessly. And around her twelfth birthday the neighborhood boys started to befriend her, invited her to play baseball and hockey with them. She finally felt like she belonged, like she was part of something, not just a freaky outsider. One day a whole group of neighborhood boys and girls made plans to meet at an abandoned house. But when she showed up, she was the only girl there. When she tried to run, the boys caught her, held her down, gang raped her, threatened her life if she ever told, left her bleeding and bruised on the floor. She was so scared after this that she had trouble leaving her house for fear that they'd do it again. She's never told anyone what happened, worried they'd for sure say it was her fault, that she never should have gone there. Even her own husband doesn't know. She's worried if she tells him he might leave her. But when she does, he just holds her for a long time, until her sobs go sniffle, and he says he loves her and knowing what happened won't change that love. He's not going to leave her—now or ever.

And one man, a university athlete, comes to our group. He says he saw the signs posted in the dorms, that there should be campus support groups for male survivors, too. His big brown eyes tear up. His long, muscular body buckles. He was just seven years old. His parents were busy working four jobs just to keep dinner on the table for him and his six brothers and sisters. His parents needed a safe place the kids could go after school and dropped them at a sports program. One of the male counselors molested him, told him if he ever spoke about it, he would hurt his siblings. He's never told his family about what happened. But he knows he's not alone. He knows other guys—they're gay, straight, bisexual, transgender—who have been through this too. Everyone's so afraid to talk about it, he says, worried their masculinity's going to be questioned. But he's done with that crap. If no one talks, if no one presses charges, it will never, ever stop. These men in positions of power will keep hurting children. So he's going to keep talking about it. He really doesn't give a flying fuck what anyone thinks.

In the months to come, because of his courage and the courage of other male survivors like him, new groups for male survivors form on the Syracuse University campus. And the difficulties male survivors experience become a far greater part of everyone's consciousness.

More and more survivors show up each week. Soon there's the pretty cheerleader who was assaulted by her boyfriend's best friend while he was away in South Africa. There's the woman whose female partner was molested when she was young and needs help dealing with her partner's anger. There's the sorority girl who was raped while serving as an au pair for a family in Scotland.

I look around the room and feel better than I did. I'm so glad that we are sharing our dark shadows with one another like this. I'm amazed that we're all alive. We made it through our nightmares alone. But now we've found one another. And together we will make it through what happens from here.

As I move to and from my classes each week, my path passes some of theirs. Sometimes we greet each other with waves, hellos, huge bear-embraces. Other times only the diamond glint in our eyes registers each others' presence. But seeing each other around, knowing what we know about each other, somehow this makes new things seem possible. We—the group—are an invisible network sparking alive just underneath the university campus's skin. We live with rape. Maybe we live beyond it. And soon we three co-founders and Dr. Alcoff begin to hear from other survivors on university campuses around the country who want to use our little group as a model for their own.

In the midst of applying to graduate programs, writing my thesis, composing the article with Dr. Alcoff, and founding the support group, during the spring I make concerted, calculated efforts at frivolity—buy a pretty dress for no good reason, get blue nail polish manicures. I also make awkward, tentative attempts at dating again. This is the first time I've really considered having a boyfriend since Geoff and I were together. I feel damaged. And mostly it seems forced. But I try. I find that I'm newly attracted to thin, small men with kind hearts, ponytails, and impressive vocabularies. In my heart I know why. They appear less physically threatening. And because they're smart, I'm hoping maybe they're far less capable of brute, unthinking violence, too.

By the end of Spring semester I'm accepted to a number of good graduate programs in cultural studies and English. I'm offered fellowships, teaching assistantships, research positions. My ever-greater addiction to writing and reading has enabled me to get perfect grades, be accepted into all those nerdy honors societies with the strange Greek letters in their titles.

The world seems better than it has in a long time. I feel like things are really starting to look up, like I'm becoming stronger and stronger, and that this new life I'm building might be the beginning of something beautiful. I tell myself that I do have the chance to make my dreams come true after all. I tell myself that my life is coming around to what it was supposed to be.

After a lot of thinking and talking it over with my adviser, Dr. Yingling, my other professors, and Dr. Alcoff, I accept a place in a cultural studies graduate program in Wisconsin. Even though leaving Syracuse University seems strange, I know my time here is done. I must be gone from Syracuse before he is released from prison into this city. And I'm ready to take my next steps.

I am twenty-one. In three months I will begin my doctoral degree.

CHAPTER FORTY-THREE

It's graduation day! Mom, Aunt Anne, Gram, Dave, and even Dad are all here with me. Though Mom and Dad won't look at each other or sit in the same row and Mom's talking manic-excited and Dad's more quiet than usual, neither of them are bickering or being mean. I'm really happy about this, and I'm grateful that they are both here.

Not wanting to walk across that stage, to be seen by anyone who might know the rapist, I'm not down there with my punch-drunk friends. Instead, I'm sitting way up in the stands, gazing around at the domed arena. I'm proud of myself, but I feel like I'm in enemy territory, too. The rapist's family's money helped build this stadium. I tell myself not to think too much about this, but the name of their company is all over the place. I'm wearing a black cardboard hat, a gold tassel. I'm graduating with Honors, summa cum laude, Phi Beta Kappa, and I'm being recognized for that fellowship.

Gram's sitting right here next to me. I've never talked with her about it. When Mom told her about the rape Gram cried and cried, told her never to speak of it again, and for sure not to tell Grandpa, who is home in Florida fighting colon cancer. Gram's crying now, too, but these are different tears—balmy, smiling-happy ones. She brushes them from her cheek with an off-white embroidered and laced kerchief.

I hear my name sing out, echo in a surging wave against the stadium walls, flow back to me. I hold Gram's hand tight, stand up. The reader mentions the fellowship, tries to pick me out of the high-tiding sea of black. But he can't find me because I'm way up here, and he sure looks silly and antlike way down moving his head all around. When he says my name again, we all start laughing. He pauses. Not finding my body this time, he crimps his lips, moves on to the next person on his list whose last name begins with a G.

I've made it! I've made it through the rape, its aftermath. I've done well in school and I've been rewarded for it. I'm proud of myself, of what I've been able to accomplish. I'm beginning to actually believe in myself. And now I'm going to graduate school. I'm getting better. Everything is better. I can do this.

After graduation my family helps me pack. I schlep my things back to Mom's house in New Hampshire for the summer. For a few days, I miss the survivor groups, but after a while, the thought of them starts making me uncomfortable. I start to think that I'd be happier not talking about the past that much, turning my attention to the present or the future. I feel like I have run out of things to say about the past, anyway—like I've repeated the general story of the assault enough and repeating it more isn't helping.

I concentrate on other things. I work several jobs (hostess, shop girl, book store clerk). But during my off hours I'm mostly living for being outside, running as fast as I can down our dirt road past the red-weathered barns, broken-down pickups and pecking chickens, through the center of town with its one-room library, two-room schoolhouse, Town Hall, Congregational Church, past Uncle Sam's childhood home, along the crashing cascades, up the hill hemmed in by white pines and fir. Or lazing under a peach tree, bumbling through hefty books by Spivak, Derrida, and Žižek. Or railing around muddy trails on my mountain bike, daydreaming about graduate school and devouring those hundreds of pages each night, whipping up those thirty-page papers. Nothing in this world could possibly sound better.

And it occurs to me that I haven't felt this hopeful since—well, for a long while. From my perspective on the summer lawn of my mother's house, things look pretty good. When Lindsey calls to ask me how things are, I tell her I'm fine. When she asks again, I feel a shadow creeping over me, sense myself getting defensive. I'm okay, I say, but I can't talk now. I have to go. I have reading I have to do.

I put the phone down and will myself back to my book. When Lindsey's voice slides back into my head, I choke it. I don't want to look backward anymore. I only want to think about the future in Wisconsin. I concentrate on imagining what I will be like when I'm there.

PART
TWO

CHAPTER FORTY-FOUR

What I was like in Wisconsin wasn't good. Six months after graduating from Syracuse—it was actually November 20, two years to the day from the rape—I found myself huddled in my apartment, unshowered for days, startling at small noises, my heart drumming with fear, my mind flashing images of horror whenever I closed my eyes: my battered face, the Grand Jury, the yearbook and his eyes, the bloody hair, the phone cord. I had completely fallen apart.

This crisis had been developing for weeks. At first I began to notice a disturbing return of the gappy, memory-less feeling that I'd had immediately after the rape. I was going to classes apparently. But I couldn't remember anything at all about them. My insomnia had progressively returned as had my fear of going anywhere in the dark. At the beginning of the semester I was able to run down the dim hallway to do my laundry. But by October I was unable to make myself go there at all. I stopped washing my clothes. By early November I'd stopped washing my arms, thighs, and toes too. By the middle of November, I was barely able to acknowledge the existence of my body, let alone look at it or touch it. Time was doing mystifying, unnatural things. Sometimes time was ahead of itself, sometimes behind, sometimes standing still. Whatever time was, it was disappearing, and I was starting to stink. And so I found myself, on the night of November 20, in this terrible condition.

The next day I was fortunate to get an emergency appointment with a psychologist. I told her about my concerns, described the rape and what I thought it had done to me. My eyes were taking in the big boxes of bandages on the shelves, the buzzy-fluttering fluorescent light above. When I finished and looked at her, she was crying. For a few minutes I watched tears brook down her cheeks, watched her dry them. Then she did something that unnerved me even more. She looked at me, eyes bugged-out and unblinking, and she asked me for more details.

Was the perpetrator caught? I said yes. The police had caught him while he was raping me. Was he *convicted* of the rape? I wasn't quite sure how to answer that. I knew that he had pled to first-degree burglary. But I didn't know what that really meant in terms of the rape charge itself, I told her. She looked slightly puzzled, asked whether the perpetrator was in prison. I said I thought he was, was pretty sure, somewhere in New York. But I really couldn't say what sort of prison. And I couldn't be completely sure if he was even still there: I'd been told by the DA's office, I thought I remembered, that even though he had been sentenced for four to twelve years, he would likely get out much earlier than this, that he could be released any time. I really didn't know how his sentence worked, I confessed. I felt a little embarrassed by that, but I had had my reasons for not wanting to look into it.

The psychologist asked if the perpetrator knew me in any way. I choked a moment, recalled the policeman telling me that he had claimed to be my boyfriend, that he could have been stalking me, that he might have known the layout of my apartment. No, I said, I'd never met him before. So it was a random assault? I wasn't sure how to answer her. He had been looking for my room, the police believed. They suggested that it might not have been random, that he might have been after me in particular. But what this really meant, I just didn't know, I told her.

Then she asked me how he had managed to break in. I remembered hearing the police saying something about him shattering the glass on the back door, unlocking it, using a hoe to prop it open. I recalled them saying that he had broken the chain lock on the back door to our apartment, that our bolt lock wasn't locked. But beyond these things, I had no idea, I said.

Here's what I did know. My roommate Sal had most likely barricaded herself in her room next door. The psychologist wanted to know. Had he tried to get into her room? Based on what Sal told me that night, I said that I didn't think so. But I really didn't know for sure. Did Sal call the police? No, Sal remained in her room, I answered. Do you know why? I couldn't say. As I responded to the psychologist's questions, I realized how little I really understood Sal's actions and feelings.

Then she asked for more details about that night, anything I could recall. I told her I remembered seeing Cathy, too, that she'd been the one who had gone downstairs, told the neighbors to call the cops. Beyond these things, I recalled mainly images—the pink clock, the chandelier, the ambulance, the hospital. I remembered, but didn't tell her, about the shower at Lindsey's.

And she didn't stop there either. The psychologist wanted to know more. What happened over the next few days? I thought a moment, and told her that I wasn't altogether sure. I did know that I spent much of that time at my friend Lindsey's. Did you really talk to anyone, anyone else, about exactly what happened that night? The police, I said. Anyone else, she asked? Did I ever really talk about it with anyone else? Not just to say it had happened or to provide a few details, but really talk about it? I thought about the last counselor I saw back in Syracuse and I realized that we never really discussed the things this psychologist was asking me about. We spoke mainly just about the assault itself and my emotional responses to it. I told her that I couldn't for-sure remember doing so. I recalled phoning my parents, that these calls had been short. But how I had coped in the first few weeks and months I wasn't altogether sure. Looking back at that time from the perspective of two years later, I couldn't remember many details.

She asked what else I *could* remember. During the long moment that followed, a sense of hot, oily panic grew in me. I didn't have anything else to say. There was this bewildering experience in my room that I could remember starkly. But it seemed that that enclosed perspective was the main thing that I knew. I could remember the violence of the experience itself, but that didn't mean that I understood it. At all. I had these vivid memories of being raped, but almost no perspective on it other than that. I simply couldn't put together an intelligible account of any of the details surrounding the event or of what had happened after. Two years had passed and I had to acknowledge that I comprehended what had happened to me not one bit better than I did while it was happening. I had frequently *relived* the experience, it seemed, but I could not say that I *understood* very much about it.

Then she asked how the rape had affected the other people who were in the apartment that night. I told her that I really didn't know since I'd never spoken with them about it. And just hearing these words fall out of my mouth felt strange, altogether not right. I never saw Cathy again after that evening. And I saw Sal, who had been one of my closest friends up until that night, a few times after that and only very briefly. As I told this psychologist these things, I realized that I had many questions I'd never asked of my roommates, things I wanted and needed to ask them. What did they see and hear that night? Did they recall anything in particular about the event that might illuminate what had happened? How had that night shaped their lives? And I also realized that, while Lindsey and I still remained good friends, I knew only in the very vaguest of ways how my rape, how caring for me in its aftermath, had impacted her.

The fact that I had no answers for this psychologist's questions upset me more than anything so far. I didn't have real knowledge about other people's experiences around this event. And, even more strange, I didn't know my own story, didn't even know its pieces well enough to coherently describe it to myself or others. How could this be the case, I asked her? How could something I alone experienced—something that had so altered the course of my own life—have so many holes and gaps, so much confusion?

How could I have so many unanswered questions about it? These were my experiences, and yet I seemed peculiarly incapable of understanding them fully or relaying them in any meaningful, genuinely graspable and cohesive way. If anyone had a right to be able to know what really happened that night, shouldn't it be me?

The psychologist said that, yes, ideally it would work that way, that I would be able to retrieve each and every one of my memories. While survivors of violence oftentimes have the ability to access very detailed memories about the trauma itself, she told me, it's not unusual for them to have far fewer memories of what happened before as well as after the primary traumatic events. This struck me as unfair and I said so. She agreed that it was, but explained that this was just how traumatic memory worked. It would be almost impossible for any survivor of trauma to have a full account because, in order to survive the trauma, she likely had to resort to other coping mechanisms, like dissociation.

She went on to tell me that when someone is severely traumatized by what's happening at the moment, the person often has no other choice but to go somewhere else, to vacate his or her body. She explained that some clinical studies had shown that those who experience dissociation may both have more difficulty processing the event in treatment and be more likely to develop posttraumatic stress disorder (PTSD). I told her about pieces of me—little wisps, feathery scraps and shreds—taking flight, about my leaving that room and feeling like I was actually up in the streetlight instead of in the room being beaten. Like that, she said. Just like that.

Then the psychologist told me something else. The many memory gaps I had had since the rape, she said, were not at all unexpected, didn't mark me as especially non-adaptive or unusual. Quite a few people who suffer grave, difficult traumas are often afflicted with many of the very same things that had been plaguing me. All of my trouble sleeping, my loss of memories, my feelings of being in danger all of the time—this was what PTSD looked like, she said. She also told me that the symptoms for PTSD often come and go throughout a person's life, that they can disrupt one's life completely for periods of time. And she said that clinicians generally found that PTSD symptoms were more severe in people when their trauma was especially intense (such as when close to death), when they were the direct victims of the trauma, and when they experienced little control over what happened. As she went through the many symptoms, the various reasons for why PTSD would affect someone so much, I knew without a doubt—this psychologist was describing my experiences. She was describing me.

At the end of our hour, she encouraged me to come back, to see her later that week. But I told her I didn't know what I was going to do, and I left.

That night, back in my little Wisconsin apartment, I made a decision. I didn't know it then, but it was perhaps the biggest one of my life. I couldn't continue to exist this way. In order to really live my life, I resolved to make some radical changes in my current situation, to embark on a quest of sorts—to try as best I could to solve the mysteries of my own past.

The first thing I had to do was leave Wisconsin as soon as the semester was over. Being there just wasn't working. My PTSD symptoms were making the basics of daily living nearly impossible. Instead, I was going to have to do what felt counterintuitive, even outright dangerous. I needed to go back to the place I had chosen to leave behind both physically and mentally—Syracuse, that scary place where it had all happened. It would only be through going back there, I realized, that I could have any real chance of restoring some of what I'd lost.

The second thing I would need to do was to learn everything I could about what really occurred that night. Only then did I have any chance of reclaiming who I had been, something of the college girl I once was. I would have to research what happened to me as if I was studying someone else's life, writing someone else's biography. And, as paradoxical as it sounded, I would have to rely on things other than my own memories in order to remember what had happened to me.

I'd begin by discovering those many things I had never known, I determined—the forensic and legal aspects of my case. Researching them might shed light on the events of that night. And I'd have to look fully at the gaps in my memory that I couldn't fill, too, the memories I simply didn't have. Perhaps other people who had been there had memories that could help me to make better sense of some of these missing pieces. Hard though it might be for me to go back to Syracuse, living there would likely also enable me to learn crucial information about the perpetrator and his sentence. Perhaps I would even find the strength to begin to keep real tabs on his whereabouts.

The third thing I had to do was to face the fact that even all of this looking into things—the learning of the facts—might not ever be enough on its own. These were not just memories, not just experiences, not just truths to be discovered. I was going to have to write about, around, and through these things in order to reconstruct myself. It was time to work toward making something more coherent out of what had happened, to write something more than journal entries or even academic articles.

Eventually I was going to have to find a way to tell my story. Making narrative out of this chaos, I understood, was about to become a central focus in my life's work. I'd continue my graduate studies at Syracuse, concentrating some of my work on the subject of rape itself and how it is treated in public discourses like law, literature, and TV. And since I ultimately wanted to create a narrative about my own experiences—to tell my story—I determined to start a comprehensive study of the major storytelling genre itself, the memoir.

Each of these three goals would take time, I knew this. Not weeks or months, but many years. And I knew my plans were in danger of being full-out derailed in various ways, too, by practical considerations.

If I did somehow manage to accomplish these goals, the payoff might be well worth it. I'd have a chance of being able to better live with what had happened to me and, to whatever degree it might be possible, weave this experience into the fabric of my life. And I'd have a chance of doing something else, too—writing a story. This would have to not just be the story of what happened to me, what I experienced, my own transparent memoir. It would be a memoir that also exposed gaps and fissures in my traumatic memory, somehow negotiating the divide between those gaps and my desire

[175]

to have coherence. It would be a memoir that acknowledged and exposed the limits of storytelling and memoir-writing themselves in adequately relaying traumatic experiences.

Having a story that made sense to me in these ways would be no small thing.

CHAPTER FORTY-FIVE

I did leave Wisconsin. Before I moved back to Syracuse, enrolled in the doctoral program at the university and began teaching freshmen writing, I would complete all of the necessary paperwork to ensure that my name, address, and phone number appeared in no university or public documents. In effect, I tried to stage my public disappearance while still remaining present. I couldn't have the rapist or anyone who might know him realizing that I was back in the city. Once in Syracuse, I reentered the sexual assault support group and the activist communities but now as a graduate student and with more distance between myself and what had happened to me. In some important ways being back felt good—I had friends there, professors who knew me, a community of other people also committed to educating people about sexual violence.

In the next few years I would study all of those subjects I'd hoped to and planned to study. I was feeling my way toward the kind of career I thought I wanted—studying feminist theory, rhetorical and literary criticism, literature, and cultural studies—but always with one eye on my other goal, too. I needed to continue to confront what had happened to me, not just lose myself in academic work. Early on I discovered that I loved teaching, especially working with students who were transitioning from high school into college. In time my passion for teaching writing would cause me to want to study writing students themselves, especially those who had been culturally marginalized. I wanted to find ways to provide them with the support systems they needed to make it through college, to feel empowered, to find their own voices despite adversity, much as I was still struggling to do. After several years teaching in a writing program aimed at "at risk" students (first generation, racial and ethnic "minority," and in economic need), this student group fully captured me. My dissertation would focus on those students who are often shunted into developmental writing classes, Basic Writers, exploring how to harness the verbal and social skills they already possessed to teach them to become effective students as well as to keep them in college.

It was also during my first few semesters back in Syracuse that something completely unexpected happened. I found myself in a seminar on Kenneth Burke and Georges Bataille, scribbling furiously in my notebook, trying to discern exactly what Burke meant by the word "consubstantiality." When I looked up, Steven, a quiet, tall, blonde, blue-eyed, graduate student wearing a mountaineering jacket, was gazing intently at my feet. I caught his eye, he turned red, stared down at the table. It was then that I eyed his feet. He too was wearing heavy leather hiking boots, scratched and weathered from years of use. And I wondered. Where—to what mystical and exciting locations—had his boots taken him? What had he seen there?

Though I tried not to, I found myself watching him from then on. Steve was handsome, possessed a razor-sharp intellect, had an easy, warm way with people. He was studying American literature, cared deeply about environmental and working-class issues. He had also spent his childhood playing for hours in the woods (like me), had spent a good chunk of his life hiking trails in the fog and wind (me too), had been stranded on a mountain peak out West, hunkered down in a tent during a blinding snowstorm for three days (well, not for me, I thought, but it sure sounded exciting). He was a truly good cook—and having any kind of cook in my life was a step up. Given my history, a romantic relationship was the last thing on my mind. But I had never met anyone like Steve before. He was truly extraordinary—confident but not at all arrogant, hilarious yet very introspective, adventurous yet incredibly intellectually disciplined.

At first I was afraid to tell him about myself, certain that learning what had happened to me would make me lose him. When I finally summoned the courage, he just paused and looked at me. Without much obvious emotion, he said that I never should have had to go through something like that. But I could tell that the story disturbed him. After I told him a few details about my assault, he did something that very few people had done: he kept the subject alive. He wanted to know all sorts of things, but especially how this experience had affected me, not just at that moment of terror, which was where I usually focused, but also afterward, in the time between then and now. I told him that I was still figuring that part out, still trying to make some peace with it all, that it had made me more skittish about the idea of men, sexuality, and relationships, that I guessed I would be dealing with it for a long time. He said that this made total sense.

And that wasn't the end of it: from that day onward, the rape became an acknowledged part of our lives rather than something dredged up only to be submerged again. Unlike most people I had tried to talk to, Steve didn't flinch or cry, didn't make his own emotions an issue, didn't show signs of waiting for the subject to pass. He did tell me when what I said about things didn't line up for him, when the gaps and skips in my own account made things confusing.

In other words, he was trying to see the whole picture, too: what had happened, how I'd tried to move on from it, what needed to be done next. I knew that it was rapidly becoming something in his life, and at times I felt guilty about that. In the weeks to come, Steve would tell me that he'd been having "revenge dreams," in which he savagely beat the rapist, caught breaking into my apartment again, to death. He was visualizing his anger more concretely than I dared to do myself. While in a way I regretted bringing him into all this, it was good, really good, not to feel alone. Someone else was making this thing a part of his life, for the simple reason that it was a part of mine.

Between my activist work, my teaching, my classes, and my new relationship, I was becoming more happy and confident. Increasingly I tried to see myself through different eyes. I was much more than a raped-girl trapped by what had been done to me. I could see that my whole life was moving in a great direction. Steve got me outdoors more. In our first few months together, we backpacked and snowshoed through the Adirondacks in the dead of winter, canoed our way through claustrophobia-inducing mosquito clouds in the Boundary Waters of Minnesota, climbed and camped in the forested wildernesses in the high peaks of Montana. We did everything together. I had never felt this way about someone before—impressed by each and every new thing I discovered about him, continually buoyed by his passion for learning, his curiosity about and appreciation for life.

Our trips together reminded me of other things too—that I possessed considerable physical and emotional strength, that it had seen me through trauma, and it had been there all the while. Since the rape, I hadn't really believed that a relationship like this could ever be a possibility. But here it was right in front of me.

CHAPTER FORTY-SIX

Stronger now, I was finally ready to face some of the things I hadn't had the courage to look into before. I was ready to learn more about what had happened to me. I'd never sought out any of the forensic information, the legal documents, the various witness depositions, though I knew that they had to exist somewhere. I hadn't had much involvement in the decision to reach a plea bargain. Instead, like all rape victims, as a witness for the state, I didn't have much of a say in whether the case went to trial. Why exactly it never had gone to trial, what the plea bargain meant in all its details, I didn't fully know.

I contacted the DA's Office, telling them that I was the victim of that crime a few years ago, that I was back in Syracuse completing my doctoral studies, and wanted to find out more about my case. They were very helpful, especially the assistant district attorney, Rob Nichols, who handled Victim Services. He told me that they had quite a bit of information and invited me to his office downtown to see it. Steve came with me. I was very glad for this. I didn't really know what I might find, but I knew I wanted him with me when I found it. When we arrived there, the ADA

Rob brought out a bunch of file folders overflowing with all of the materials pertaining to my case. We could read most of them, make copies of them for my records, he assured us. But there were a few I would never be able to see, things like a psychiatric evaluation the DA's Office had done on the perpetrator in preparation for trial, his medical reports, pictures of him after being arrested. The ADA Rob pulled those documents from the files, then left us to go through the rest on our own.

Steve grabbed my hand, I took a breath, and together we opened that first folder. Steve sighed. There she was, the college girl, in a series of photos that must have been taken at the hospital that night. She was dressed in a gown, legs out in front of her like a ghoulish, ball-jointed doll. She was on an examination table, shock, desperation, fear, numbness in her one partially open eye. I could sense Steve's intensity ratcheting up. I had forgotten that there might be photos. Her picture, my picture, was followed by many others, images of my arms and legs, gashed, bruised, cut, each of my doughy, puffed-up eyes, my busted nose, my bloodied lips. Steve fidgeted uncomfortably in his chair. These things were hard to look at.

We moved on through the pile, though. There were copies of letters and handwritten notes composed by the DA Lena before she was pulled from my case, evidence of the preparations for trial. My fingers traced dozens upon dozens of old paper edges. After a few minutes I came upon this next document, a piece of paper I didn't know existed. But, of course, I thought, it had to exist. It was a list of all of the items taken into custody from the crime scene. I could feel Steve's hand on my shoulder, his warm breath on my ear. He was reading it with me. It looked like this.

```
Property Record

Itemization of Property

1. Leather Jacket "Adventure Bound" (from kitchen)
2. Base Ball cap "BT Equipment Co." (from bedroom)
3. Phillips Head Screwdriver Fuller #807 (from
suspect)
```

```
4. Putty knife (from bedroom)
5. Philips Head Screwdriver "USA" (from bedroom)
6. White plastic cord (from bedroom)
```

The leather jacket whose smell I can't make myself forget. The baseball cap that I thought was milkweed silk or stockings. The two screwdrivers. He might have used them to break in. He might have jabbed one against my throat, told me it was a knife. A putty knife. The only actual knife that would ever be found at the scene. Maybe this was the knife that was not a knife.

There were pages upon pages of other documents, too, like this one Steve pulled out.

```
Item(s) for Examination        Only One Item Per
Line

1. one yellow striped shirt
2. one pair of gray pants
3. one pair of white underpants

Item(s) for Examination        Only One Item Per
Line

1. one white top
2. one pair of white sweat pants
3. one pair white socks

Items for Examination          Only One Item Per
Line

1. one mint bedsheet
```

His clothes. My clothes. My sheet. All those items iced up in time.

I turned the page over, put it in the pile to be copied, flipped to the next one.

```
Make: Pontiac
Model: Firebird
Color(s): White
Date and Time: 20 Nov 88
Nature of Incident: Poss Used in a Crime
Location recovered or towed from: 2500 Ostrom Street
Key in Switch: Yes
Doors Locked: No
Windows Closed: Yes
Radio in Car: Yes
```

I had never given much thought to how he actually got there, arrived at the scene of the crime. I guess if I had thought about it, I'd have imagined him walking. In a college town, everything's so packed-in close together. Walk in, walk out, it'd be way harder to link him to the crime. But he had driven. "Adventure bound," he had pulled to the curb outside my apartment in his white Pontiac Firebird. How long had he sat there? How long did it take him to determine which door he would choose, how he would break in? Steve was thinking the same things, and said that it seemed to him as if the rapist expected to return to his car in short order. After all, those doors weren't locked and on that cold November night and into the early morning he left his keys dangling from the ignition. I looked at Steve and nodded, feeling as if I were only half there. Seeing these little details sent me careening back to the horror of those hours. To me, the state of the recovered car was consistent with premeditation, with an act that had been planned. Do you get in your car and drive to a location without forethought? And why leave your keys in the ignition unless you're figuring on fleeing quickly? I turned to Steve, told him how the policeman at the scene had said something about the fact that my rape could have been a planned thing, how it was beginning to look that way to me, too.

The next document Steve removed was the injury report for the three police officers who were at the scene.

```
Department of Police
Syracuse, New York
Accident/Personal Injury Report

Injury Sustained: Several cracks in the bones of
left fifth digit
Injury Sustained: Right arm and elbow, cannot be
straightened
Injury Sustained: Dislocated left, fifth digit
```

My eyes simmered a while on that page, too, thinking just how close he was to escaping, how close I was to never knowing who had raped and almost killed me, to never seeing any justice for the crime committed against me. I was sorry the officers had been hurt, I kept thinking. But I was grateful that they hadn't let this keep them from capturing the rapist.

I plucked out the next document, a series of extra-long legal-sized pages stapled together. The first group of words were written in an oddly beautiful, old-fashioned calligraphy—the kind I tried (and completely failed) to master as a kid, my fancy pens mainly leaving behind tiny pools of gloopy ink.

```
County Court
Onondaga County

The People
vs.
XXXXXX

The Grand Jury of the County of Onondaga by this
incident accuse Him of the crime of rape in the
first degree in violation of Section 130.35 (1) of
the Penal Law of the State of New York committed as
follows:
     The said man on or about the 20th day of
November nineteen hundred and eighty-eight at the
```

city of Syracuse in this county, engaged in sexual intercourse with a female known to him by forcible compulsion.

Second Count

And the aforesaid Grand Jury by this indictment further accuse the defendant of the crime of attempted sodomy in the first degree in violation of 100.00/130.50 (1) of the Penal Law of the State of New York committed as follows:

That on or about the 20th day of November, 1988, at the City of Syracuse, in this county, the defendant attempted to engage in deviate sexual intercourse with a female person known to him, by forcible compulsion, to wit: defendant attempted to engage in penis to anus intercourse with the victim.

Third Count

And the aforesaid Grand Jury by this indictment further accuse the defendant of the crime of sexual abuse in the first degree in violation of 130.65 (1) of the Penal Law of the State of New York committed as follows:

That on or about the 20th day of November, 1988, at the City of Syracuse, in this county, the defendant subjected a female person known to him to sexual conduct by forcible compulsion, to wit: Defendant engaged in hand to vagina and penis to anus contact with the victim.

Fourth Count

And the aforesaid Grand Jury by this indictment further accuse the defendant of the crime of assault in the second degree in violation of the 120.05 (6)

[186]

of the Penal Law of the State of New York committed
as follows:

That on or about the 20th day of November,
1988, at the City of Syracuse, in this county, the
defendant in the course of and in furtherance of
the commission of the felony of rape in the first
degree, attempted sodomy in the first degree and
sexual abuse in the first degree, caused physical
injury to a female person known to him, who was not
a participant in the felony, to wit: facial cuts and
swelling, leg and neck abrasions.

Fifth Count

And the aforesaid Grand Jury by this indictment
further accuse the defendant of the crime of
unlawful imprisonment in the first degree in
violation of 135.10 of the Penal Law of the State of
New York committed as follows:

That on or about the 20th day of November,
1988, at the City of Syracuse, in this county, the
defendant restrained a female person known to him
under circumstances which exposed her to a risk of
serious physical injury, to wit: bound her wrists
together and held a screwdriver against her neck and
threatened her repeatedly.

Sixth Count

And the aforesaid Grand Jury by this indictment
further accuse the defendant of the crime of
burglary in the first degree in violation of 140.30
(3) of the Penal Law of the State of New York
committed as follows:

That on or about the 20th day of November,
1988, at the City of Syracuse, in this county, the
defendant knowingly entered or remained unlawfully

[187]

in the dwelling of a female person known to him at
2500 Ostrom Street with intent to commit a crime
therein, and when in effecting entry, or while in
the dwelling or in immediate flight therefrom, he or
another participant in the crime used or threatened
the immediate use of a dangerous instrument, to wit:
a screwdriver.

Seventh Count

And the aforesaid Grand Jury by this indictment
further accuse the defendant of the crime of
burglary in the first degree in violation of 140.30
(2) of the Penal Law of the State of New York
committed as follows:

That on or about the 20th day of November,
1988, at the City of Syracuse, in this country, the
defendant knowingly entered or remained unlawfully
in the dwelling of a female person known to him at
2500 Ostrom Street with intent to commit a crime
therein, and when in effecting entry or while in
the dwelling or in immediate flight therefrom,
he or another participant in the crime caused
physical injury to that female person, who was not
a participant in the crime, to wit: facial cuts and
swelling and leg and neck abrasions.

Eighth Count

And the aforesaid Grand Jury by this indictment
further accuse the defendant of the crime of the
crime of assault in the second degree in violation
of 120.05 (3) of the Penal Law of the State of New
York committed as follows:

That on or about the 20th day of November,
1988, at the City of Syracuse, in this country, the

defendant, with intent to prevent a police officer
from performing a lawful duty, caused physical
injury to such police officer, to wit: Syracuse
Police Officer James Warbucks, who suffered a broken
finger on his right hand.

Ninth Count

And the aforesaid Grand Jury by this indictment
further accuse the defendant of the crime of the
crime of assault in the second degree in violation
of 120.05 (3) of the Penal Law of the State of New
York committed as follows:

That on or about the 20th day of November,
1988, at the City of Syracuse, in this country,
the defendant, with intent to prevent a police
officer from performing a lawful duty, caused
physical injury to such police officer, to wit:
Syracuse Police Captain Richard Pull, who suffered a
dislocated finger on his left hand.

Tenth Count

And the aforesaid Grand Jury by this indictment
further accuse the defendant of the crime of assault
in the second degree in violation of 120.05 of the
Penal Law of the State of New York committed as
follows:

That on or about the 20th day of November,
1988, at the City of Syracuse, in this country, the
defendant, with intent to prevent a police officer
from performing a lawful duty, caused physical
injury to such police officer, to wit: Syracuse
Police Officer Rhonda Bialosky, who bruised her
right elbow.

Eleventh Count

And the aforesaid Grand Jury by this indictment
further accuse the defendant of the crime of
criminal possession of a weapon in the fourth degree
in violation of 265.01(2) of the Penal Law of the
State of New York committed as follows:
    That on or about the 20th day of November,
1988, at the City of Syracuse, in this country, the
defendant possessed a dangerous instrument: to wit,
a screwdriver, intending to use the same unlawfully
against a female person known to him.

Twelfth Count

And the aforesaid Grand Jury by this indictment
further accuse the defendant of the crime of
resisting arrest in violation of 205.30 of the Penal
Law of the State of New York committed as follows:
    That on or about the 20th day of November,
1988, at the City of Syracuse, in this country, the
defendant intentionally prevented or attempted to
prevent three police officers, namely Captain Pull
and Officers Warbucks and Bialosky, of the Syracuse
Police Department from effecting an authorized
arrest of himself.

The Grand Jury's findings. They were strangely worded things
and, at times while reading them I felt like I was reading some
wacky mixture of Pig Latin and Middle English. But they were leg-
ible in spite of that. The Grand Jury had ruled in mid-January that
there was enough evidence to proceed to trial. I remembered hearing that result. But most of the rest of that year was a big blank to
me in terms of what had been happening in the courts. Why had
it taken so long, I wondered—the better part of a year (until late
that next August, apparently)—before the case had been settled?
I'd sometimes imagined people sitting in offices playing Tiddly

Winks, thumb wrestling. But what really had been going on during all those months when I heard virtually nothing from the DA's office?

It was then that I came upon another set of pages I'd never seen before. Unlike the Grand Jury documents, though, they were not strangely worded. But removed from their context, both their reason for being and their import were completely lost on me. We read them over and over again—but we just couldn't make any sense out of them. Two doctoral candidates in English and here we both were, stymied by language.

So I opened the ADA Rob's office door, asked if I could talk with him about a few things. He followed me back into the room, and when I showed him the documents, he explained that they were letters between the DA's office and the perpetrator's lawyer. But what were the letters about? Rob explained. When the perpetrator was caught at the scene and the police were arresting him, he had apparently said these words: "There's no problem here. This is my girlfriend. We're just having a fight." I recalled the Tall Tree policeman—Captain Richard Pull—asking about this that night/early morning. Rob told us that the rapist's lawyer wanted to claim that these words could not be used in the criminal case against him because he had not yet been read his Miranda rights (a warning issued to suspects while in police custody that is aimed at preserving the use of their statements in court). The letters were concerning a number of hearings that were held to determine whether what he said would be admissible in a trial.

Hearing this, I felt snuffed out. I hadn't ever been told of any of this. I'd heard nothing from the DA's office for months that year, while all of this had been going on. Probably no one wanted to bother me with legal details, Rob explained. But here it was, a significant part of the story—my story—I had missed. The police statements to the Grand Jury contested his lawyer's claim: they testified that he was already effectively in custody and so had forfeited such rights, that he had voluntarily made these statements, that they should be considered evidence for use in the criminal trial.

Under these transcripts, we found the judge's decision on the matter. Because of the nature of the situation, the crime, and the arrest, the question of when Miranda rights were given was declared moot. As I looked at this ruling I stifled a small yippee. This had been a tiny win. The judge had denied his lawyer's request to have the statements thrown out: the statements could be used as evidence.

Had we gone to trial, it would have been far harder for his lawyer to make the case he was trying to make—that his client raped me during an alcohol-induced blackout. After all, right after the assault he was cognizant enough to make up a series of lies to cover his actions. Like the car keys and the tools, this was evidence that could be used against the perpetrator. Not surprisingly, shortly after the judge's ruling, his lawyer had a sudden desire to plead the case.

Rob stayed with us as we removed the last set of documents in that folder: these detailed the plea bargain that had been rapidly struck after the judge's decision. The first page read "PLEAD GUILTY to BURGLARY 1st (in satisfaction)." But the second document stapled to it listed a bunch of other charges—"RAPE 1st (1 CT), ATT SOD 1st (1 CT), SEX ABUSE (1st (1 CT), ASSAULT 2nd (4 CTS), BURGLARY 1st (2 CTS), UNLAW. IMPRIS 1st (1 CT), CPW 4th (1 CT), RESISTING ARREST (1 CT)." Once again here we were—two people whose lives had been dedicated to the study of language—and we were beyond stumped. So we asked Rob to explain these documents, too. He told us that pleading to the burglary charge "in satisfaction" meant that all of the other charges listed were effectively merged and subsumed underneath it. He went on to say that this meant the perpetrator would not have to plead guilty to each charge in court in front of witnesses and that burglary would always be the first charge that appeared on his record. A plea like this might mean that he would be treated less like typical sex offenders, that he might have more job prospects once released, too.

Some of the boiling-over outrage I'd felt on first hearing of the plea returned. If future employers didn't know about the rape, he might be treated like a common burglar (a person of questionable judgment but not a violent criminal) rather than as a rapist. In effect, the public perception of his crime might amount to the equivalent of someone lifting a stereo. Because of this plea, this man would get to live the rest of his life as if he were a burglar, not a rapist. To my mind, a rapist's ability to plead to burglary "in satisfaction" was, in effect, a clever loophole in the law that allowed rapists to appear like burglars, to cloak and disguise their other, more violent offenses.

I could feel my breakfast thick and rising in my throat. This was a public as well as a personal outrage. Like the man who had raped me, all of the rapists whose lawyers used this plea strategy successfully would slide through the system without ever having to account for the true nature of their crimes.

But the real and true situation, the full insidiousness of the plea-bargain strategy for sexual offenders became more and more clear to me over the course of several years, as I witnessed the passage of important laws meant to protect the public from sexual predators. In 1990 the Clery Act (known also as the Crime Awareness and Campus Security Act) was put into law. Once this was in place, all university campuses receiving federal student aid had to warn their students about convicted sexual offenders' whereabouts. I was especially happy with another provision of this act: for the first time universities were legally compelled to publicly disclose statistics about crime on campus. Now people on college campuses would know exactly how sexual violence was impacting their communities.

By 1994, the Jacob Wetterling Crimes Against Children and Sexually Violent Offender Registration Act (Federal 1994 Omnibus Crime Bill) arrived. Now all states had to "track sex offenders by confirming their place of residence annually for ten years after their release into the community or quarterly for the rest of their lives if the sex offender was convicted of a violent sex crime."[1] And soon absolutely crucial amendments would bolster the power of these laws. Megan's Law made information about sex offenders more accessible to states while The Pam Lychner Sexual Offender Tracking and Identification Act included provisions about what FBI and state agencies must do when a sex offender moves across state lines.[2] Other important laws and amendments would follow, too, further protecting people from predators. The Campus Sex

Crimes Prevention Act (2002) demanded that convicted sex offenders tell colleges and universities (where they were working or going to school) about their offenses. And local police had to be made aware as well.[3]

Then the much-needed Adam Walsh Child Protection and Safety Act (2006) extended the reach of earlier laws to include Indian reservations and other places, and it created a new Office of Sex Offender Sentencing, Monitoring, Apprehending, Registering, and Tracking (SMART Office) within the Department of Justice. With these important changes, I was thrilled to see that law enforcement would have far greater power to police the actions of all sexual criminals. Many states, however, have yet to fully comply with and put into practice the Walsh Act guidelines.[4]

Thankfully these many acts have done a great deal to track the whereabouts of those convicted of sexual offenses. However, if a rapist pleads to a burglary charge "in satisfaction" in a criminal case (whether back in the late 1980s or today), he never has to have his name placed in a sex offender registry, never has to inform a state that he's relocated there. Unlike other convicted sex offenders, he moves around the country freely, remaining relatively unmonitored and putting the public at high risk. So in addition to being personally insulting to me, the rapist's burglary plea was really also an affront to public safety altogether, even though his sentence was the same as if he'd been convicted of the rape.

One has to wonder whether such pleas have resulted in additional crimes. Most researchers believe that since sex crimes are underreported at very high levels, recidivism rates generated from rearrest reports are inconclusive and vastly underestimate actual reoffenses. As a result, increasingly researchers are suggesting that other, more complex measurement devices must be used. However, in longitudinal studies that do take undetected sexual offenses into consideration, it is estimated that approximately 88 percent of sex offenders are recidivists.[5] That's no small number. And we have no reason to believe that a rapist who plea bargains to a lesser crime "in satisfaction" and is therefore not registered or monitored after release is any less likely to reoffend.

Many years later this problem in the law remains, and state legislatures are in the process of considering bills meant to solve it. If such laws passed, instead of being able to plead to a lesser crime in full satisfaction of all charges, no defendant charged with offenses of a sexual nature would be allowed to plead to lesser, nonsexual charges "in satisfaction."[6] The purpose behind such laws is to make sure that sex offenders would no longer be able to mask their rapes with burglary convictions and would instead have to register as sex offenders.

But thus far no such bills have been made law. The reasons for this are complicated. Some prosecutors fear that removing their ability to plea bargain would actually result in more perpetrators of sexual crimes remaining free. Though I had been more than willing to testify in criminal court, in many rape cases victims are not. A victim may know the assailant. Or, a victim may be too traumatized to face that person. In the absence of victim testimony, obtaining a conviction for sexual crimes is extremely difficult. One of the few options available to prosecutors in such cases—other than simply failing to obtain a conviction at all—is to allow defendants to plead guilty to lesser charges and serve jail time without the stigma of registering as sexual offenders. For these and other reasons the loophole in the law remains to this very day and more than likely will for many years to come.

Although none of the laws I've just mentioned were yet in effect as Steve and I pored over the stack of documents in the DA's office, that day marked the beginning of an education, of a practice of keeping tabs on such things. But we'd both had enough, after reading the plea document, for that one day. We left the ADA Rob's office with a stack of copied materials already reviewed, and another stack I'd had copied for careful study in the coming months.

CHAPTER FORTY-SEVEN

For a number of weeks I thought a great deal about what we had learned at the DA's Office, specifically the potential import of the burglary plea bargain. This was, I had to admit, a somewhat worse reality than I had allowed myself to imagine. In point of fact, it blew some serious chunks. The language of that old *Syracuse Herald* article about his sentencing, in which his lawyer described him as a "young man of character" who had made a reckless mistake of burglarizing a home, kept coming back to me. I suddenly had a lot of new questions I really needed answered. What in fact was his current status? Exactly what kind of prison was he in?

Once again I asked for the ADA Rob's help and, after some phone calls, he tracked down exactly where the perpetrator was. He was serving time in the Wende Correctional Facility in Alden, New York, in the western part of the state. This was an old county jail that had been converted into a maximum security prison. We learned that they had drug and alcohol treatment programs and housed mainly first-time offenders. Along with the typical Health Facilities and Work Program Buildings, prisoners there received some perks that weren't at all typical of maximum security prisons at that time—an auditorium for recreational activities and televisions in their cells. Hearing all of these things, I once again wondered whether his money and family's connections had enabled him to receive preferential treatment. It certainly appeared as if the burglary rather than rape conviction had played a role.

Rob also told me that I could find out more information about the rapist's status by speaking with his case worker. A few days later he tracked down the man's phone number. The idea of calling his case worker frightened me. After all, even if he didn't mean to do it, what if this case worker said something that revealed where I was living to the rapist? By contacting the case worker, wouldn't I be putting myself in further jeopardy? Still, I had to take the risk. I needed to learn whatever I could.

The phone call with the case worker was disturbingly revealing. I'd been reluctant to make the call myself, and Steve's attempt had failed, too, because as my boyfriend he had no legal status in the case. So my mother made the initial inquiries, phoning the case worker we were looking for. After establishing the name of the inmate, she told him that her daughter was still in Syracuse, in the area where the inmate would eventually be released, and that we wished to be as informed as possible of the inmate's status.

The case worker, puzzled, stopped her mid-explanation. He asked her who she was, and what connection she had to the inmate. She told him my name, that I was the victim in the case, the one he had raped. There was a longish silence. Finally, he cleared his throat and began speaking again. And what he said was this: According to his records, this prisoner was in for burglary, not rape. Rape was not something he had heard about.

Days later I received a phone call from him. He apologized, said that he had read through the prisoner's entire file now and knew the truth. He went on to say that he and the rest of the prison staff had absolutely no idea about all of these other charges. They were buried deep in the file. The only thing they had seen—the only thing that the regular prison paperwork made in any way obvious—was the top count to which he had pled: burglary.

Since no one knew he was a rapist, he hadn't received any sort of sex offender treatment or counseling. The case worker assured me that this would change. Then the case worker told me something else. This guy was no model prisoner. And he wasn't a likely candidate for early parole.

Within the year the rapist would be transferred to a different prison in the eastern part of the state, the Great Meadow Correctional Facility, also maximum security. But this prison housed people who had committed multiple felonies, served sentences multiple times. It would be a tougher prisoner population, a place, it seemed to me at least, more fitting of someone convicted of his crimes.

Learning all of these things about his status—especially the fact that because of the plea he had been treated more like a burglar than a rapist within the prison system—started me on another process I would engage in for many years. With the ADA Rob's help, I began to more fully exercise my rights as a victim. When he told me that I could submit a Victim Impact Statement to the Parole Board each year he came up for parole, that it might shape the board's decisions, I began to draft documents. These were my early attempts to tell my story in a more coherent, public way, though they served fairly narrow rhetorical purposes. Each year I would write my letter, revise it until I got the language as right as I could, place it carefully in an envelope with a stamp, send it to a group of strangers who were considering him for release. I would tell them what he had done to me. I would share my hopes and plans for my life, explain that I was living in Syracuse, the place where his family resided, the place where he would go once released. And every year I would await their verdict, learn the answer to my question: How much longer could I remain safely in Syracuse?

And that's how things went for a few years. With each passing year, there was a greater likelihood that the rapist would be released. It scared me. Each year I would contemplate abandoning my doctoral studies, leaving the area. And each year I would breathe a huge sigh of relief—the Parole Board had once again denied his release. During these years I worked as hard as I could. The sooner I finished my schooling, I knew, the sooner I could leave Syracuse and the safer I would be. During these years my relationship with

Steve grew stronger, too. We knew we belonged with one another. One day while we were out hiking Steve surprised me, got down on one knee, and pulled out a sapphire ring with tiny, glinting diamonds. In that moment it was like he was handing me a bucket full of stars he'd special-picked from the heavens himself. I had no doubt about my answer. It was a yes, a resounding yes. A year later we were married at my Aunt Anne's farm in Pennsylvania. We spent our honeymoon camping, backpacking, and mountain biking our way across the West—wending our way through the Dakotas, Montana and Wyoming, Idaho and Utah, Colorado and Arizona, then beyond. We were beginning to build a life together.

In the end, the perpetrator would serve eight years in prison. Steve and I accepted professorial positions at a university across the country. Just days before the rapist's release, we were defending our dissertations, packing a rickety U-Haul truck with everything we owned, our hundreds upon hundreds of books, our salt water fish and corals, our dinged-up mountain bikes. And by the time the rapist was released, we were nowhere near Syracuse anymore. Instead, we were driving, azure-bright sky stretching for miles in front of us, filled with thankfulness that we'd been able to leave just in time.

CHAPTER FORTY-EIGHT

As I reflect back on it, if writing those Parole Board letters each year was in part empowering, it also made me fearful, as did many of the things I had to do to cope with my history. Although my PTSD symptoms progressively receded with each step I made toward shaping a way of living with the rape, I remained wary of giving the experience too much of a foothold in my life. Throughout this process I came to realize that part of what scared me was the awful PTSD itself: What if those months of lost time and depression were something I could trigger again?

I already knew from my work with survivor groups that sexual assault and abuse is frighteningly common. Most studies of U.S. populations place the likelihood that a female throughout the United States may end up being a victim of some kind of sexual assault or abuse at about a one in four.[1] For men, the estimate is about one in six.[2] Most of these human beings will suffer in horrible ways long beyond the minutes and hours of the actual assaults. According to the National Center for PTSD, ninety-four percent of all victims of sexual abuse will experience some form of PTSD in the months and years immediately following their assaults. It is estimated that about one-third of victims will continue to experience these symptoms for many years after the abusive events.[3]

According to the Mayo Clinic, "posttraumatic stress disorder symptoms are generally grouped into three types: intrusive memories, avoidance and numbing, and increased anxiety or emotional arousal (hyperarousal)." Intrusive memories can involve "flashbacks, or reliving the traumatic event for minutes or even days at a time, and having upsetting dreams about the traumatic event." Avoidance and emotional numbing can encompass "trying to avoid thinking or talking about the traumatic event, feeling emotionally numb, avoiding activities you once enjoyed, hopelessness about the future, memory problems, trouble concentrating, and difficulty maintaining close relationships." Finally, avoidance and emotional numbing may entail "irritability or anger, overwhelming guilt or shame, self-destructive behavior, such as drinking too much, trouble sleeping, being easily startled or frightened, and hearing or seeing things that aren't there."[4] And many of these symptoms of PTSD are also among the few coping mechanisms available to trauma survivors, making PTSD all the more difficult to eradicate. Inevitably, as more veterans of war return home and more trauma survivors of all kinds begin to speak out, these issues will become increasingly visible and need to be addressed even more directly in our culture.

In *Traumatic Stress: The Effects of Overwhelming Experience on Mind, Body, and Society,* recognized by many as the key text that takes on the interpersonal, biological, and psychological issues associated with trauma, Bessel Van Der Kolk and Alexander C. McFarlane write that PTSD can be particularly difficult to treat long-term even for those who do get help. For the trauma survivor, "the past is relived with an immediate sensory and emotional intensity that makes victims feel as if the event were occurring all over again."[5] In studying veterans, the National Center for PTSD has found that neurochemical changes in the brain caused by PTSD may make people more vulnerable to long-term health issues such as chronic pain, hypertension, as well as other infectious and immunological disorders. And, according Dr. Kay Jankowski at The National Center for PTSD, some studies have shown correlations between PTSD and "physician diagnosed disorders including cancer, ischemic heart disease, and chronic lung disease."[6]

While avoiding talking or thinking about the traumatic event is among the major symptoms of PTSD, psychiatrists have long believed that the trauma survivor's ability to tell his or her story is absolutely essential to living beyond the trauma. Though "the talking cure" was a term adopted initially by Sigmund Freud to describe one of the key features of psychoanalysis, now it is a phrase used widely to refer to many forms of helpful therapy that involve sharing one's story. Only through sharing the experiences can the survivor begin to gain some measure of control over what happened, as well as find agency and a way to live with painful memories.[7] As Kim Etherington notes in *Trauma, the Body, and Tranformation: A Narrative Inquiry*, telling one's story is what creates a "possibility for change and a better future. In telling our stories we are also reaffirming and re-educating ourselves, our experiences and our lives as well as creating new stories."[8]

Most contemporary therapeutic models support the notion that recovery is a reconstructive process and that trauma survivors ourselves need to be its primary authors and arbiters. One key step to recovery involves telling the story in depth, transforming difficult memories so that they can be integrated into the survivor's life. The construction of a narrative that draws on the past as well as brings it into the present and future, the thinking goes, enables the survivor to not only understand what happened but also to more fully process her or his reactions and feelings around it. It also helps traumatic memories to become what Bessel Van Der Kolk and Rita Fisler term "declarative" or "explicit memories" (memories that usually entail "conscious awareness of facts or events that have happened to the individual"), enabling the survivor to recognize that events were bad at that time but not live in and with them in the present.[9]

My own recovery process, like that of most survivors of trauma, roughly followed the three stages of recovery that Judith Herman outlines in *Trauma and Recovery*, one of the most significant books ever published about how to best care for survivors of trauma. The stages include "establishing safety, reconstructing the trauma story, and restoring the connection between survivors and their community."[10] Now, as I look back on all those years, I have no doubt that narrating my own story helped me to make sense of what happened and gradually lessened my PTSD symptoms. Painful and difficult though talking about it in therapy was right after the assault, I know that this aided me in beginning to put what were a series of disjointed sensory experiences existing outside of language into words. Only then could I start sorting through them and begin the long process of recovering my own sense of self, reaching back through time to restore some of who I had been prior to the rape's occurrence. This would help me to see that I had some power after all—the power of my own voice—and that I could exercise it. I recall talking about my rape in small ways at first, to friends. In time, though, sometimes in spite of myself (as was the case with the Town Hall meeting), I found myself speaking to larger and larger groups of people. Narrating what had happened to me in the presence of others helped me to lift the experiences outside of my individual, isolated world and bring them out into larger, communal spaces. Only then was I able to start reframing and revising my story. In the perpetrator's version I had been pure victim. I was not even human, let alone someone capable of action or agency. But in my own version I could, step by step, become not only a person again but a survivor, someone who had lived through it, would live with it, and someday would live beyond it.

Soon I had urgent things to say about the issue of sexual violence, too, and started to speak out about what had happened to me in thoughtful, measured, and politically calculated ways that I myself could control. Who I was and what had happened to me became woven into a social fabric of larger political and therapeutic communities such as student activists and the survivor groups I'd founded on campus. My experiences became intertwined with other people's traumatic experiences, with the larger spheres of social justice. And then I began to understand and incorporate what had happened to me into other important areas of my life, building new narratives around my career goals and personal relationships. I was able to create forward-thinking versions in which I could be a writer and a scholar, not someone whose life effectively ended when she was raped. And in my own story, I could be a girlfriend and a partner, a wife, a friend, a professor, not someone who was stuck-in-trauma unlovable or forever damaged.

CHAPTER FORTY-NINE

Storytelling can be important therapeutically for survivors. But often this is simply not enough. While therapists, lawyers, and the media did represent my rape, when they did so, especially early on, it felt like another affront, as if what they said somehow silenced me or denied me. Various social and cultural institutions tend to want to "handle" survivor discourse—to mediate and co-opt it for purposes that are not always in the best interests of the survivor, seeking to redefine what survivors have to say in terms that will not threaten the status quo or require sociopolitical change. And so, in my academic work, I wanted to look at the subject of survivor narratives from philosophical, socio-critical, and political perspectives. How and when were survivors' narratives being used by others to fulfill their own, oftentimes dubious, goals? In what ways were the real stories of survivors being silenced, their political power diminished? How and when were survivors' own narratives being used in empowering ways? And in what situations were survivor stories able to deflect and reroute these attempts to thwart us?

The article I wrote with Dr. Alcoff eventually appeared in the scholarly journal *Signs: A Journal of Women and Culture.* Using French philosopher Michel Foucault's definition of "discourse" as our analytic framework, we argued that survivor discourses, if not recuperated, may have great power—the ability to undermine traditional power hierarchies, to build identities for survivors, and to challenge the cultural foundations that make sexual violence possible in the first place.

Drawing upon our scholarly, academic training and its vocabulary, we wrote that:

> Michel Foucault argued that speech is not a medium or tool through which power struggles occur but an important site and object of conflict itself.[1] He also claimed that bringing things into the realm of discourse, as the confessional structures brought bodily pleasures into discourse and thus "created" sexuality, is not always or even generally a progressive or liberatory strategy, and can contribute to the containment and domination of embodied subjectivities. These claims are at odds with each other or at least point in different directions. The first suggests that movements of social change should focus on the arena of speech as a central locus of power. Speaking out *in and of itself* enacts transformations in subjectivities and power relations. But the second claim warns that the tactic of bringing things into the realm of discourse works also to inscribe them into hegemonic structures and to produce docile, self-monitoring bodies who willingly submit themselves to (and thus help to create and legitimate) authoritative experts.

In other words, although we saw how important it is for survivors to speak out for themselves, we also recognized that survivors' speech may become the focus of an effort to exert social controls over the more threatening features of what survivors have to say. Survivors of sexual assault can be in a unique position to critique, for example, our society's investments in male power or the objectification of women's bodies, and this kind of social critique can be expected to meet with resistance.

This kind of effort to co-opt survivor discourse was especially interesting to us when we found it operating in mass media. In the *Signs* essay, we went on to describe that while survivor groups have historically depended on viewing speaking out as a form of empowerment, many television talk shows and other media forms utilize survivors' speech for their own purposes, to create shock value or to further the effects of sadistic voyeurism (perhaps to boost ratings). When they do this, talk shows work in concert with the history of psychiatry which has, at moments, depended on blaming victims or determining that an expert mediator be present for survivors to make sense of our own experiences. This has too often led to the undermining of survivor discourses and stories rather than the transgression of dominant ones.

We made a point of including ourselves in our analyses, too, explaining our reasons for this collaboration, our connections, our common experiences. We wanted this essay—while not a traditional memoir or account of our experiences—to show the empowering nature of survivor narrative, but we also recognized that this was an unusual move in the academic disciplines in which we were working. We were choosing to speak out within a scholarly context that had traditionally been resistant to if not outright dismissive of "personal experience," especially this type. But this was a risk we were willing to take, and so we wrote:

> Our motivation to reflect on these issues emerges from a need to reflect on our own practices. We are two women who share three traits: we are survivors, we work within (and sometimes against) post-modernist theories, and we have been active in the movement of survivors for empowerment and liberation. We have also been affected by the institutionally enforced distancing and dissonance between what gets thought of as "theory" and "personal life," which splits the individual along parallel paths which can never meet. This paper is an attempt to rethink and repair this dissonance and to begin weaving these

paths—and their commitments, interests and experiences—together.

In the essay we analyzed many extremely troubling representations of survivor discourse. When rape is being talked about in public forums, we contended, it's not usually for the benefit of survivors, and it's often not survivors of rape doing most of the talking. We examined a variety of television shows in which survivors were asked to sit in front of an audience, told to tell their stories. On such shows, we found, survivors are frequently made to speak about the violent act itself, questioned about details surrounding it, and forced to defend their experiences. One example we cited actually featured a Syracuse University student who went on a morning television show and tried to talk about how patriarchal, sexist attitudes can perpetuate various forms of sexual violence. In this specific case, as in others we analyzed, the people who were able to ask questions and shape the discourse, the people who were able to interpret this survivor's experiences, were not in fact themselves survivors, but rather show hosts, audience members, and experts. Survivors had little to no control over their own narratives.

We argued that there are some transgressive examples out there, however. And one of the main ones appeared on *The Oprah Winfrey Show*. Oprah was among the first to ever talk about her experiences as a survivor publicly on national television. While this can happen today through other means—Facebook, YouTube, and Twitter—on her television show many years ago Oprah paved the way for many other survivors to speak out and to challenge the traditional discursive arrangements.

> The most transgressive moments have occurred on TV talk shows when the splits between victim and audience and between recorder of experience and interpreter of experience are obstructed. This has occurred not surprisingly on "The Oprah Winfrey Show" when Winfrey has referred to her own history as a survivor and thus subverted her ability to be a more objective and dispassionate observer of the victims on the stage. Because of her own

identification with survivors, Winfrey rarely allows them to be put in the position of having to defend the truth of their stories or their own actions. And when the focus is on child sexual abuse, Winfrey does not always defer to an expert but presents herself as a survivor/expert, still working through and theorizing her own experience.

There was one episode on Oprah's show that we analyzed in detail since it beautifully illustrated the disruptive power of survivor-produced discourse. During this show, Oprah invited dozens upon dozens of other survivors to join her on a brightly lit stage.

One particularly transgressive segment of "The Oprah Winfrey Show" stands out: nearly (or possibly all) the entire audience of about two hundred women were themselves survivors and a wide-ranging "horizontal" group discussion took place with little deferral to the designated expert.[2] This show had the most potential to thwart the efforts to contain and recuperate the disruptive potential of survivor discourse precisely because it could not be contained or segregated within a separate, less threatening realm: there was too much of it for any one expert to effectively handle and the victim-expert split could not be maintained . . . For at least one brief moment on television, survivors were the subjects of their own lives.

Survivors streamed over the stage, blurring the lines between audience and performer, survivor and expert. The survivors both made sense of their own experiences and controlled the discourse about their experiences. Survivors were themselves the recognized experts.

In time, other versions of our article appeared in mainstream publications, too. In time survivors from around the world—people both inside and outside of university settings—began to contact us, sharing how much our essay meant to them, how it made them feel like someone else out there understood and helped them to not feel so alone. Spanish, German, and other translations of our essay popped up in other journals, in edited collections, too.

I treasured the experience of writing this article. It was my first published self-representation of what I'd been through, the first time I shared something of what I'd experienced—in writing— with a wide audience. Through its publication and reception my own experiences were validated and recognized. And, in writing this piece, we overtly affirmed the importance of survivors' owner- ship of narrative, whether for therapeutic purposes or for socio- critical ones. In doing so, we exposed exactly why it would be important for many survivors not to let the journalistic, medical, and legal treatments of our experiences be the only ones available. Survivors had things to say and ways of saying them that no one else possessed, and we alone had a right to tell our own stories in the ways that we wanted them told.

Looking back on it, I think that the article presented our own form of disruptive survivor discourse. We were able to adopt roles as experts of our own experiences, interpret them, and offer sug- gestions for how other survivors might do the same. In our way, we were working against cultural, philosophical, and psychiatric attempts to control the kinds of things that can be said about rape, to control our accounts of what we had ourselves been through. We were openly challenging the academy's attempts to do so as well. By insisting on saying things that academic writers typically didn't say—and doing so within the language of the academy—we were, even if only temporarily, shifting the terms of the debate and demanding that we and other survivors like us be heard.

CHAPTER FIFTY

While writing this article was a crucial step, I knew that it was just a beginning. Even in graduate school I'd tried to draft a more extended treatment of my story, a memoir of the rape and its impact on me. But every time I worked on it, I felt blocked, as if the only memories I had to report were the frightening ones I also feared. The larger truth of my experience—whatever that was—seemed always to be overshadowed by a sense of sheer *victimage*, forged in the violence of the act itself and codified by the legal system. Even during my early years working as an assistant professor, I continued to avoid looking at the remaining files from my initial research visit to the DA's office: although that trip had been useful in many ways, I couldn't help but feel depressed as I imagined opening the folder of unreviewed documents and seeing myself reduced, in page after page, to my legal status as "victim" of the crime. Looking at these documents, I also feared, might lead me to worry more about the fact that he was out, perhaps even result in a return of PTSD symptoms like nightmares and trouble sleeping. Plus there were plenty of good things to focus on instead. I was working on book projects. I was creating and teaching new classes. And Steve and I were traveling a lot in our free time. When we weren't doing those things, we were on our mountain bikes, going hiking, as well as renovating our new home.

By the time I did finally return to the files, I'd received tenure and my job life was secure. It was time to write my story, I knew, and I would need to learn whatever else might be there to learn. Now I was ready.

The first document I pulled out of the folder was my deposition, taken by the policeman right after the events of that night. My pulse quickened a bit, knowing that this was as close to an "originary" account of the rape as I was ever likely to have. This was my first attempt to actually write my story on pages of paper in the police station years ago. In its halting way it captures what happened to my twenty-year-old self, some of what I experienced, some of my perceptions.

It's not exactly an original, however, and in some ways it's another disappointing reduction. Even that first account, what I scrawled on that paper, was typed up by someone else and then destroyed. My original language was probably altered a bit to fit into a formulaic structure that would serve the legal system's needs. A victim's deposition is a crime narrative with distinct rhetorical purposes, to convey what happened to whom and when, and my deposition mainly conveys the meaning of my rape as located in a series of violences done to me, failing to capture much else about the event or its aftermath.

This new, typed version contains creative typos, including one that I found particularly uncanny. It illustrates what I have come to see as the central problem for anyone trying to do something useful with the memory of a traumatic experience.

On November 20, 1988 at approximately 3:00 am I was asleep in my bedroom at the above location. At this point I heard some xxxx noise in my room and I woke up When I woke up I saw a male standing in front of my bed I noticed that this male had his pants down and he had something over his face. At this time this male was attempting to put his fingers down my

throat and he did put his fingers down my throat.
AFter doing this the male put something sharp up
against my throat and stated approx 5 or 6 times you
better do what I tell you or I will kill you.

At this time the male made me lie on my stomach
with my face down on the bed. He then told me to
put my hands and arms along my side. He then stated
now with your right hand he told me to take my pants
off. I told him three times that I wouldn't pull my
pants down While this was going on this male kept
his hands on my throat After I told him I wouldn t
take my pants off this male took them off himself.
After taking my pants off this male started feeling
the area around my vagina and ass.After doing this
for awhile the male attempted to penetrate me
anally. He was unable to fully penetrate me anally
but I could still feel his penis up against my anal
Then this male made me get on my knees.

After I got on my knees this male took something
out of his pocket I thought it was a rope and he
tied my hands together When he pulled the rope out
of his pocket I believed he was going to strangle me
with it.Once this male put what I thought was a rope
on my hands I looked down at my hands and relized
that it was not a rope but a telephone cord I would
like to state during this xxxx WHOLE time this male
had his fingers down my throat.At one time during
this part of the incident I felt I was going to
throw up and when this occurred the male removed his
fingers and I let out a scream.

At this time the male put his hand over my mouth
and said you are going to be quiet and I told him
yes I do not want to fight you anymore. At this
point the male started to remove his hand from my
xxxxxx mouth and when he did I screamed again When I
screamed this male punchdd me in the mouth with his
fist and stuck his fingers down my throat

When this occurred this male was behind me and when he had his fingers down my throat I could feel his penis penetrate my vagina from behind.While this male was attempting to have sexual intercourse with me he was having problems keeping his penis inside my vagina.At this time I also began to kick this male and I also turned around and looked at this male.The male didn't have anything over his face At this time when I saw this male I could see that he was a white male. wearing a leather jacket he had a wide face and light colored hair.At this time this white male put his fingers down my throat again.

After a few minutes I could hear noises coming from the hallawy outside of my bedroom door At this time I saw my bedroom door crash open and saw some police officers rush into my bedroom When the police came into the room this white male kept saying this is my girlfriend,we are having a fight.When he was saying this he was attempting to get away At this time the police and this white left my room and I got up and went to my roommates bedroom When I was in this room I could hear some loud noises coming from the kitchen area.

I was then interviewed briefly my police at the apartment and was asked if I knew this person and in fact was this white male my boyfriend.I stated to the police that this white male was not my boyfriend I didn t know this person and have not seen him before.

I would like to state that during the whole incident the white male who attacked me punched me numerous times across the face he slapped me in the legs he constantly kept putting his fingers down my throat he held a sharp object against my throat and he numerously stated to me taht he was going to kill me. he was going to slit my throat, strangle me,and

break my back. During this whole ordeal I was in
fear of my life.

I would like to state that I did not allow this
Because of the beating I took I have pain in my
face I have a swollen mouth, my throat area hurts
my neck hurts and my leg hurts. I have recieved a
scrape to my leg and neck that was caused by this
white male.

I would like to state that I did not allow this
white male into my apartment I was forced to have
sex with this white male and I do not know this
white male

I was told by Inv F Pull that this white male s
name is XXXXX and I stated after hearing this that I
still don t know this person

I would like to prosecute this person for
assaulting me breaking into my house and forcible
having sex with to the fullest

This statement is the whole thruth

"The whole thruth": I had to laugh when I first read that, so many years after it was originally typed. It seemed to mock the very goal I'd set myself—to try to come to grips with my own experiences, to try to arrive at a useful, livable understanding of it, to get at the whole truth of its meaning for me. Right at the very beginning of my attempts to tell my own full story there was this typo, as if I couldn't even spell "truth," much less arrive at it.

Since then, though, I've come to realize that maybe I was thinking of truth in the wrong way. Given the problems of memory, it would be necessary for me to stop thinking of my goal as some absolute, reliable account of experience, but rather as something approximate and not entirely derived from my own personal experiences and memories alone. I spent more years reading scholarship about remembering and forgetting, truth, and the memoir genre. Through this process—as well as through considering my own experiences in light of this research—I came to some insights about these issues.

Memory is dynamic and ever-changing, never just some static thing. It's always being reconsidered, revised, and rewritten. We might like memory—and the genre of memoir that purports to convey one's memories truthfully—to be straightforwardly representational and transparent. But, try as we might, memory provides no literal versions of the past that we can access. Our identities and memories are constantly being molded and altered by our desire to make meaning as well as subject to the whims of perspective, context, history, time, and culture.[1]

Survivors of violence—be it in warfare, sexual assault, or other deeply difficult situations—face far greater problems in relaying our memories than any other writers seeking to tell their stories. We have the added concern of trying to relay traumatic experiences around which our memories themselves are necessarily fragmented and scattered. Since our memories alone cannot be relied on to produce anything like a full picture of what occurred, we almost have no other choice: we have to take our readers into those gaps with us.

And traumatic memory is more complex still. It flies in the face of the easy equation people like to make between "truth" and "the facts."[2] When dealing with traumatic memory, finding the truth oftentimes isn't about accessing precise details or statements. Instead, trauma survivors who want to get to the heart of what has happened to us find truth not always in facts or evidence alone. We find truth in remembering the events, something that always entails acknowledging all we don't know (the missing moments, the lacy Swiss cheesiness of memory.) And we find truth in recalling exactly how we experienced the events themselves (not just what happened but what was heard, smelled, tasted, felt.) As Edward Casey contends in *Remembering: A Phenomenological Study*, "Truth resides not in statements that may accompany the remembering, or in items of evidence, but *in the remembering itself*—in its relation to the past with which it is reconnecting, whatever the precise evidence or expression in words may be."[3]

In his history of the memoir genre, Ben Yagoda writes that "there is an inherent and irresolvable conflict between the capabilities of memories and the demands of narrative. The latter demands the specifics; the former is really bad at them."[4] Here survivors of trauma find ourselves in a trickier spot than most. Since our memories are made up of many jagged missing pieces, the truths we convey cannot rest on some false sense of memory's infallibility. Trauma survivors' narratives must often interrogate the very nature of memories themselves, frequently calling them into question.

Many trauma survivors hope to write our stories. But given our particularly complex relationships to memory and truth, how are we to do this? The memoir genre, for example, is understandably still dominated by a view of personal experiences as authentic and transparently true. As G. Thomas Couser indicates in his analysis of the genre, memoir derives its identity in part from its "distinctive ethical dimension," particularly its "fidelity to the truth and consideration for the rights and interests of others."[5] As a result, as Couser asserts, the genre has supported the publication of but a few postmodern and metaphorical memoirs, pointing to Dave Eggers's *Heartbreaking Work of Staggering Genius* and Lauren Slater's *Lying* as specific examples. These are texts that expose the inner-workings of the genre and/or call attention to multiple constructions of truth. And, in recent years, this has led to a situation in which writers who have not adhered to these understandings of memory, truth, and experience, have come under some scrutiny (examples range from James Frey[6] to David Shields).[7] At the same time, however, because of the very nature of traumatic memories and experiences, most trauma survivors cannot help but produce texts that do not fit this mold, sometimes having no other option than to create texts that are postmodern, metaphorical, or nontraditional to some degree. Even when we may not make the overt choice to do so, trauma survivors necessarily construct narratives that challenge the very demarcations between truth and falsehood, nonfiction and fiction, on which the memoir genre has been based historically.[8] As Leigh Gilmore writes in *The Limits of Autobiography: Trauma and Testimony*, "texts that are concerned with self-representation and trauma offer a strong case for seeing that in the very condition of autobiography (and not the obstacles it offers for us to overcome) there is no transparent language of identity despite the demand to produce one."[9]

It's precisely for all of these reasons that I believe trauma narratives have a particularly crucial role to play. Our stories are necessarily always about slippages, about what we know as much as what we don't know. Our writings reinforce the fact that personal narratives should not just be understood as products but also as processes. They are unusual creatures—tangible, material examples of an act of remembering that's always developing, changing, and ongoing, that's really never finally over.[10] And trauma survivors' stories undermine the publishing industry's deep desire to present personal narratives (such as memoirs) as finished products to their readers, instead announcing over and over again—this is no done thing.

Trauma survivors' stories are primarily works about the complex process of learning new things (discovery and investigation), acknowledging that it's what we create and build as a result of our experiences that is perhaps most important.[11] As a result, truthful narratives based on traumatic memory often have to showcase the fact that our written accounts are never just lived things. They are things that are very much constructed and sometimes long after the fact. They are things that are constantly being made and remade, in the ever-changing present.[12]

In *Inventing the Truth: The Art and Craft of Memoir* William Zinsser contends that writers of personal narrative "arrive at a truth that is theirs alone, not quite like that of anybody who was present at the same events" or there is "multiple ownership of the same past."[13] Since each individual's truth is unique, the thinking goes, each person's telling of a given story will necessarily be different. While trauma survivors' narratives certainly share this trait, they are unlike other forms in one major way: At heart, our narratives are never really about just one person's story. Since traumas are experienced communally, our stories are always shared ones, impacting (and continually revising) every other life and story they touch. Oftentimes, too, the construction of trauma narratives themselves is not possible without communal involvement.

Survivors may need other people's angles on the events in order to piece our own stories together.

It was this final realization that would lead me to make my next decision. I knew as much as I could about my own experiences of that night. But I had more to discover. I needed to dig into those files of copied materials again and, for the first time, read the depositions of my two former roommates, Sal and Cathy, things that I'd never been able to make myself look at.

Eventually there was another step I would have to take, too, of course. I would also have to get in touch with them and with Lindsey. Lindsey and I still kept in regular contact. But I knew that this experience had been extremely hard on her and we'd settled, over the years, on a relationship in which these matters were not spoken about much. I worried that asking her about it all again might strain our friendship.

Contacting Sal and Cathy would be even harder. I'd never spoken with either of them about that night—about what it was like for them, about what they saw, about what they knew. Sal had stayed in her room during my assault. Maybe she slept through it all. But maybe she hadn't. After all, there was some evidence to suggest that Sal had barricaded herself in her room with her furniture. I'd seen Sal just a few times in the years immediately following that night. It hadn't felt good. Our talk had been forced, awkward, superficial. Neither one of us was going to mention it.

And Cathy had likely saved my life, somehow found the strength to run downstairs and call the police. But the last time I saw her was some twenty years ago. My face was bloody, my nose was smashed, and only one of my eyes really worked. She was handing me a pair of her sweatpants, her sweatshirt. We'd never spoken or seen one another again.

Thinking about it, I realized that for years I'd harbored the notion that I was somehow responsible for bringing something ugly into their lives. I'd always assumed that they would be no happier to be reminded of the event than I was. And I didn't know whether they would even be willing to speak with me. But I knew this much. I was going to have to try.

CHAPTER FIFTY-ONE

I began with Lindsey. Those many years ago a twenty-one-year-old Lindsey had done something remarkable for me—had become the main caregiver to me in my most debilitated state. As others tiptoed away out of confusion, fear, disgust, or self-preservation, Lindsey moved toward me and took me in. Back then I hadn't the first idea what I needed or how to ask for it. But Lindsey saw what it was, and gave it freely when she could. Lindsey was the person most responsible for the fact that I was able to make it through that time and create any kind of life beyond it.

We remained close friends after she graduated from Syracuse and moved back to the Boston area. She married her college sweetheart, Jim, and they had two children. When Lindsey found time between her daughter's ballet lessons and her son's guitar performances, she was running marathons like a demon-lady, performing in local dinner theater productions and improvisation troops, singing in a rock 'n' roll band, and writing plays. Once her children were well into their school years, Lindsey began studying the

Alexander Technique and became a teacher who trained other performers. She began to wear her dark hair in a spiky, pixie cut. Sprightly and energetic, Lindsey was the kind of mother who might have been mistaken for one of the older kids.

Over the years Lindsey and I had spoken a bit, here and there, about my assault, but now I asked her to have a series of focused conversations. I asked her, essentially, to tell me everything she remembered about that year, to tell me the story of what had happened from her own perspective. I knew we had many similar memories. Lindsey recalled many things—receiving the phone call from Cathy, coming to the emergency room, witnessing me give my statement, and seeing my pictures taken. Lindsey remembered that milkshake, the shower, listening to my phone conversations with my parents. But there were also things that Lindsey remembered that I could not recall. She wasn't afraid to talk, either, and in this way we filled in some of the gaps in my memory from those minutes and hours after the rape when I'd lost time entirely.

In many ways Lindsey seemed to know more of the practicalities of my life in the days after the rape than I did. I'd never known, for example, how any of my things had ended up at Lindsey's apartment the day after the rape. Years later, Lindsey told me that she had done it: after she'd taken me to her place from the police station, she went to my apartment and got my things herself, including the journal where I would make my first attempts to keep track of time, of what was happening to me.

She had tried to talk to me, Lindsey recalled, to tell me that everything would be okay. She'd be back in less than half an hour and her female roommate was at home upstairs. I wasn't alone. I would be safe. But, I barely acknowledged her. Slumped on the floor, my lips bleeding, I seemed to be staring at the wall with my good eye. Lindsey leaned down and hugged me before locking her front door behind her.

Lindsey's heart was gallop-racing out of her chest as she drove toward my apartment. Once she got there, for a long few minutes she just sat outside in her car, her hands shaking on the steering wheel, her mind scattered, staring at the house, unable to catch her breath. It was hard to look at it for long. The thing felt cadaverous, like it'd been overrun by phantoms. But she made herself do it, Lindsey told me. She snagged an old duffle bag from the backseat, slammed the car door behind her. As she stood on the sidewalk, nausea came at her in pounding waves. Her veins were adrenaline-filled, pulsing. She kept telling herself, It's all over, okay? Calm the heck down. It's done now. He's gone. Nothing in there can hurt you. But, Lindsey remembered, it was hard to make herself believe it.

Lindsey forced herself to make that long walk up the front stairs, to unlock the door with my keys, to climb the stairs to the second floor. Her knees shook as she thought about the fact that his feet had run down them just hours before her, that he had nearly escaped. Then Lindsey carefully opened the upstairs door to my apartment. The air was sharp and stale. Lindsey recalled stopping in the hallway, afraid: his paint footprints led to my bedroom door. Like he'd turned to vapor, she thought, gone invisible. Or like he was still in there, like he never left. But he was gone, in custody, she reminded herself again, and the footprints were just a terrible residue, something left over from his presence.

Once in my room, Lindsey glanced at the futon, at the clothes strewn on the floor, at the pink clock ripped from the wall. It was a bitter cold in there. My God, Lindsey remembered thinking. This isn't her room anymore. It's something else. It was then, Lindsey told me, that she first realized she was crying.

The police hadn't found the knife, she knew. I had kept talking about that on the way home. So Lindsey decided that she was going to find it. She searched each of my dresser drawers. She opened my closet, felt in every pocket, searched around each shoe on the floor. Lindsey looked under my futon, my dresser, my desk with the milk crates. But Lindsey didn't find the knife. Eventually she gave up. She grabbed my notebooks, my homework, my journal, my books, my clothing, stuffed them into the duffle bag.

Her head began to clear then. If she couldn't find the knife, maybe she could find something else, anything that would explain what had happened here, answer the question why, nail this guy and keep him in jail for a long, long time. Lindsey recalled opening Sal's bedroom door. Loose charcoal sketches of rotund bodies papered her floor. Her bed was unmade, her furniture out of place. Then Lindsey sprinted to Cathy's room. Her bed was unmade too. Otherwise, her room was neat, as usual. There were no signs of anything amiss. Lindsey ran back to the kitchen, looking around for clues. But she could find none there either.

It was then, Lindsey told me, that she started to feel faint, light-headed. The place was so creepy and she was worried that I would wonder where she was, what was taking her so long. So Lindsey picked up the duffle, charged out of the apartment, relocked on her way out. The whole way home she had trouble getting a grip on the steering wheel, seeing the road through her tears. When she pulled into the driveway, she paused a moment and composed herself, then got out of the car, unlocked the door, stepped inside. I was still sitting in a heap on the floor, my eye staring at the wall, exactly as she had left me. Seeing me there like that, Lindsey told me, she wasn't sure what to do next. But she knew I was going to need a shower and I'd need fresh clothes. Now I had those clothes.

How my stuff got to Lindsey's is just one of a host of details that I never knew about, and initially that's the sort of thing I thought I was trying to find out. But what really struck me as I listened to Lindsey talk wasn't so much the gratification of filling in missing information. Instead, I was focused on the extent to which this story had been Lindsey's, too. This crisis had crashed suddenly into her life. This must have been an incredibly wrenching experience for Lindsey—to see what she was seeing, to do the things she had to do. And how frightening it must have been to walk into the scene of a crime alone to get my things, to come back home after that, and see me still sitting there on the floor.

There had to be lots of really difficult moments like this for Lindsey, I knew. I was pretty sure that the shower I took right after I was assaulted would be one of them as well. How did Lindsey feel, helping me bathe, seeing my blood, my injuries? And what ran through her mind as she continued to witness just how incapable I was of caring for myself, just how detached I was?

As Lindsey remembered it, she told me that I had to take a shower over and over. But I just kept mumbling that I couldn't do it, wouldn't do it. When she asked me why, I didn't seem capable of speaking much, let alone explaining my reasons to her. Lindsey knew it had to be done, though, and after a while she decided that, even though I might scream or break down, she would have to insist. When she did, however, I didn't scream or break down. I didn't really agree to do it either. Instead, it was more like I just stopped resisting. This sort of giving up was a trait that Lindsey hadn't seen in me before, one that hadn't been a part of me before that night. And seeing this change really concerned her. It also gave Lindsey insights into my experiences in my bedroom, she told me, that truly scared her.

Lindsey settled on trying not to think too much, keeping busy, she recalled. She helped me stand and walk into the bathroom, told me to take my clothes off. But I didn't seem able to move, just stood there like a department store window mannequin. I was no longer capable of caring for myself and, in that moment, Lindsey realized this fully. Trying not to worry about this, she turned her attention toward helping me take them off. Seeing me naked like that, bruised, bloodied, and vulnerable, Lindsey described, was disturbing. The extent of my emotional injuries was already daunting, but now she saw physical ones, too. As much as she could, though, Lindsey tried to push those thoughts away, turned on the shower, helped me get in. Water crashed down on my body, on her arms.

Lindsey remembered trying to focus only on what had to be done. The most important thing was for me to get cleaned up. Lindsey grabbed a bar of soap, handed it to me. I looked at it in my hand like I wasn't sure what it was, what to do with it. So Lindsey talked me through each step. She watched as I slowly washed my own body. For Lindsey, I came to understand, this was a particularly disconcerting memory. Even as Lindsey told it to me so many years later, there was shiver in her voice. As I washed, Lindsey said, she caught sight of my eyes. It wasn't me looking back at her. It was as if someone strange to her was looking out from behind my eyes. And seeing this, Lindsey had to wonder. Would she even be able to help me?

As these thoughts flew at her, Lindsey watched me wash the blood off my body. Then I stopped, stood completely still, as if I'd once again forgotten what to do. So Lindsey picked up the shampoo, she recalled, poured some through my hair, lathered it up. I was making sounds, she remembered, bizarre grunting noises. Hoping I would stop, she moved quickly, rinsed my hair under the shower water. Lindsey knew there was a lot of blood mixed in with those suds. But she determined not to look at it so she wouldn't have to think too much about it. Still, she saw the white suds mixing with blood, forming a strange pink.

Hearing Lindsey's memories, I couldn't help but be aware of the differences in our accounts of what happened. In my version, Lindsey washed me, but in Lindsey's version I washed myself. In my version, I laughed as she washed my hair, but in her version the noises I made sounded nothing at all like laughter. Such discrepancies between our accounts might have bothered me at one time, and I might have felt a need to find the one real version, concerned that both of us couldn't possibly be right. But, for me, the fact that these differences existed between our two versions was no longer that relevant. She was doing for me nearly everything I couldn't do myself. In a way, her hands were mine for a while during those days, and both our memories confirm that.

Interviewing Lindsey, the hardest thing to come to grips with was the fact that in many of those moments when Lindsey was making me feel taken care of, she herself felt anything but safe or secure. Instead, she was extremely worried, frightened, and lonely—feelings that I didn't perceive in her at all at the time, and that didn't become a full part of the story for me until years later.

If that first day was frightening, I came to understand, it must have been terrifying for Lindsey to see my altered state persist for several days, and to realize that my parents weren't rushing in to take over and relieve her of these responsibilities. But Lindsey stayed with me and did her best to keep me emotionally alive. When after a few days she drove me to her parents' house, for example, she was feeling anxious, angry, fearful, and sad, trying not to let it show. Much of the time Lindsey wasn't watching the road, she recalled. She was observing me as I peered out of my one good eye at the gray landscape, trees, dilapidated houses.

Lindsey could feel that she was losing me, and she didn't know what to do. So she did what came naturally. She went through every silly face in her repertoire, told every bad joke she knew. And she even got me laughing a little, Lindsey recalled. But that laughter was short-lived. I was wincing a lot, my lips bloated and oozing. Even with everything she tried, Lindsey told me, it seemed like I was fading away from her, my eyes without light or life, fixed. She was running out of ideas, fighting back tears. She slammed on the gas hard after that. Get her home, she remembered thinking. God, please get us both home.

A female cop pulled us over, having clocked us doing ninety in a sixty-miles-an-hour zone. Lindsey recalled looking the officer square in the eye. She wasn't at all sure what she was going to say, so what flew out of her own mouth surprised her. Lindsey said that she knew she was speeding, but she had to because her friend had been hurt real bad and she needed to get her home. The officer looked from Lindsey's own wet eyes to my puffed, bloodied ones, told Lindsey to get back on that road, to drive as fast as she needed to drive. Lindsey nodded at the officer and rolled away, continuing to go thirty miles over the speed limit.

There are lots of stories like these that I learned about during my talks with Lindsey. Although she doesn't tell them this way, they are really stories about Lindsey's amazing determination to save me in those days. Though it was clear that everything that was falling to her during that time carried a risk to her, right away Lindsey had made a life-altering decision—to fully commit herself to caring for me in whatever ways she could, to endure the days with me, but also to move toward me and embrace my life and what it had become. And so she became the one, the one who would get me into the shower, who would dial numbers for me, who would for months escort me to and from places after dark.

All this did take a toll on her that I never found out about until our discussions years later. In the months directly following the assault, she experienced severe panic attacks. Not wanting to worry me, Lindsey began secretly seeing a therapist at the very same time that she was picking me up from my own appointments. This therapist didn't do her any favors either, told her that she didn't have any right or reason to be anxious, upset, sad, or angry because she wasn't the one who was raped. As a result, for several years Lindsey felt tremendous guilt for having any suffering of her own and tried to ignore her feelings as much as she could. Eventually, though, Lindsey found a new therapist who enabled her to grieve and feel anger about the fact that my rape had changed her life irreparably. And over the years Lindsey's panic attacks dissipated, then disappeared, my assault and its aftermath becoming something she thought about less and less frequently. By the time I began asking her to let me interview her about those times, she was no longer rocked by the memories. But I could tell that this had taken a great deal of time, and effort.

It would have been so much easier for Lindsey to have kept some distance from me back then. This is what most people, young or old, would have done. It probably would have been much safer emotionally. You can let someone borrow your clothes or you can go to a crime scene and get her own clothes for her. You can point someone to your shower or you can make sure she gets in there, gets the blood off. You can buy someone a bus ticket to get home or you can drive her yourself, break the speed limit, and argue with a cop to get her there. You can assume someone else, someone in a better position than you, will be there to help, or you can make sure to be there yourself. You can let someone crash on a couch for a few days, or you can see her fear and let her into your own bed, keeping quiet when she thrashes you in her sleep like you are an attacker.

And this is what I learned in my interviews with Lindsey. What had happened to me in the weeks after the rape had happened to her too. In those days, I think it's fair to say that Lindsey risked herself to save me, doing the harder things I needed done.

CHAPTER FIFTY-TWO

I decided to contact Sal next. Aside from one or two awkward encounters, we hadn't been in touch for many years. I had liked her as a roommate, but after a heavy night like that night, when she had barricaded herself in her room, returning to any kind of casual friendship seemed somehow impossible. For years, my thoughts about Sal were dominated by certain detailed memories of that night—in particular, of pushing against her blocked bedroom door. I had an especially keen memory of the relief I'd felt when I realized that Sal hadn't also been attacked, but I could clearly remember, too, her failure to meet my gaze when I asked her questions.

Most of the time, when I thought of Sal barricaded in that room, so close to mine, it was with sympathy. I had never really established what had happened for her that night, but certain pieces were obvious enough: she'd heard something happening in the house, and whatever she'd heard had convinced her that her own life was in danger, so much so that she had fortified her door. She must have been incredibly frightened.

But I still had questions. There were a few details that I was eager to learn. When had she first sensed that something was amiss? At what point had she decided to barricade her room? What had she heard and felt? What thoughts had run through her mind as she waited?

I was sure that I wanted to be as prepared as possible when I spoke with Sal, to already know all I could about her perceptions right after the events of that night. So I found that old file folder from the DA's Office and I pulled out a police report I'd never looked at, the one describing what Sal witnessed. These words leapt out at me from that page.

```
The witness was awakened by the sound of someone
screaming and wrestling . . . sounds were coming
from the bedroom of the victim . . . the witness
heard what sounded like someone running . . . saw
someone flash a flashlight through a crack in her
bedroom door . . . yelled out "WHO IS THERE?" . . .
heard a male voice say "IT'S THE POLICE, ARE YOU
OK?" . . . spoke with the uniformed officers . . . a
scream came from the bedroom . . . officers forced
entry . . . white male who she did not know came
running out of the victim's bedroom . . . started
to fight with the police and broke free and ran
into the kitchen . . . the victim walked out of her
bedroom . . . victim's face was swollen, and bruised
. . . naked from the waist down . . . asked the
witness to untie her hands . . . they remained until
the police returned . . . witness went with the
victim to CIM ER while the victim was being treated.
```

Reading that document tossed me backward in time. I recalled those moments—running into Sal's room, asking her to take the cord off my wrists, her untying me.

But this report shed no real light on my questions. And it raised new ones, too. This document suggested that the police went to Sal's room before they came to mine. But did Sal talk to the police officers through her closed door (indicating that she'd moved the furniture during my rape), or did she open it (revealing that she'd moved the furniture after the police arrived)? In addition, there was this puzzling last sentence "witness went with the victim to CIM ER while the victim was being treated." I had no recollection of Sal being with me in the ambulance or at the ER. But had she been? It was time to talk with Sal.

Finding Sal wasn't as difficult as I'd imagined. I Googled Sal's name, was immediately directed to several of her web pages. The first site was wallpapered with colorful, abstract art, likely one of Sal's own pieces. Another click and I discovered that after graduate school Sal had formed a series of web companies, taught art in New York City. Sal had exhibited her work around the world. With another click, I found myself on Sal's university web page. Sal had become an assistant professor at a university, was publishing essays about artistic authorship, digital art, and consumerism as well as teaching classes about visual culture and technologies of place. At the top of the page was her picture. In this black-and-white image Sal looked much like she did years ago. Her shoulder-length blond hair was windblown, slightly wild. She wasn't smiling and there was a faraway look in her eyes, as if she were envisioning her next big project. Sal's school address and work phone number appeared on that page, too.

Seeing Sal there I felt a mixture of joy and guardedness. And I felt pride, too. Sal had become who she wanted to be those many years ago, and I was happy for her. Still, I wasn't ready to call her yet. So I clicked on Sal's e-mail address, sat in front of my blank screen thinking up what to write. I typed in something like this: "Hey, Sal. Is this you? If it is, e-mail me back. I'd like to learn what you're up to, catch up a bit. Best wishes, Laura." As I hit send, I wondered. Could that message have sounded any more stupid?

Hours later a return message popped up on my screen. It was indeed Sal and, yes, she'd like to catch up, too. Sal sent along her cell phone number and over e-mail we set up a time to talk. In the days that elapsed between our various e-mails and this phone call I found myself feeling vaguely off, edgy. I wasn't sure what to expect of our conversation. Would Sal find it hard to talk with me about that night—even refuse to go there? And, if Sal was willing to talk with me about it, how would I bring up the subject of her furniture?

When that scheduled time came, Sal and I began by talking about what had been going on in each others' lives. Sal's life sounded jam packed. She was trying to keep up with her many art projects plus her writing and teaching. In the last several years Sal had also met and married a kind man, a film director, and they'd had a boy together. It was a lot to juggle. Early on in our conversation, her talk was fast and her attention seemed divided even as we spoke.

After some time had passed in this way, I asked Sal to talk about what she remembered of that night. I was completely unprepared for her answer. She told me that she recalled very little, that she wouldn't be able to provide me with many details about her own experiences. She had huge lapses in memory around the events. For her, most of that night was what she called a "cavernous void." And even though Sal had spent many years wishing she could fill things in, she just couldn't remember much. When Sal thought about that night it was mainly in terms of emotions like paralyzing fear and deep sadness. As I listened, I was having a strong emotion of my own—despair. If Sal's memory was this sketchy, she likely wouldn't be able to answer basic questions, let alone harder ones. I would never learn what really happened or know what to believe about Sal.

Then Sal proceeded to tell me what she could recall. As she told it to me, she interrupted herself frequently to comment and reflect on her memories. I caught myself smiling as she did this. The highly intelligent, analytic parts of Sal I so loved and admired back in college were alive as ever.

Sal came home late that night after working in the art studio, she remembered. She was exhausted and hungry. Cathy and I were already asleep in bed. The clock read just around midnight as she stood in the kitchen eating a bowl of cereal. Then she got ready for bed, went to her room, fell asleep. Hours later she was awoken. There were no particular sounds that woke her up initially, Sal explained to me. But she was uncomfortable, restless. Her breathing felt oddly constricted and she had what she described as a "strange, terrible feeling" that she couldn't understand.

At this point in our conversation, Sal interrupted herself to comment on what she'd just said. And I would never have anticipated what she said next. Sal's words could just as easily have come out of my own mouth as hers: Whenever she remembered these things, time became confused. It twisted, changed, turned liquid. For Sal, clocks couldn't make sense out of this kind of time. She didn't feel as though she understood what had happened when. I told Sal that I felt that way too, how time sped up for me, slowed down, stopped, even went backward.

It was only after she was awake that she thought she heard something. It was an odd, muffled sound. Brushing off sleep, Sal tried to make sense of it. She couldn't tell where it was coming from. Thinking that something might have been happening on the street below, Sal jumped from her bed, looked out the window. There was no one out on the street. It was quiet. All Sal could see out there was a bright streetlight (the same one I was watching just feet away from her in my bedroom.) Then, wondering if the noise might be coming from my room, Sal put her ear to the wall that connected us. She listened, but she couldn't hear anything. So Sal went back to her bed, sat up for a few moments. Sal told me that she tried to rationalize what she'd heard. Maybe she was so tired from working in the studio all those hours that she was imagining things, she told herself. She must have dreamed it.

Then Sal stopped herself again to reflect on everything she'd told me thus far. She said that it was during this last part that time acted especially strange. It was like time slowed way, way down, as if Sal experienced hours of indecision about what she'd heard. But she knows that it had to have been minutes.

Sal went on with her story. Not hearing anything else, she tried to shake it all off then, attempted to go back to sleep. For a while she drifted in and out. Then suddenly she was jolted awake. Someone was running down the hallway. She remembered thinking. Someone had broken into the house. Fear spread over her, took her hostage. She simply could not move. Sal felt incapable of doing anything to defend herself and she couldn't stop trembling.

At this point, Sal interrupted her story again. She told me that those were the things she could say for sure. From there her memories became a lot more hazy. Sal recalled the police being there. She remembered me, partially naked, my face bludgeoned, coming into her room. She had a memory of untying my hands. But the rest of Sal's memories of that night are what she described as "out of order and outside of time." Sal thought she might have been in the ambulance with me, but she's not certain if that really happened or not. She was pretty sure that she was in the emergency unit for a little while but doesn't know where she went from there. And Sal recalled being taken to the police station, though she has no idea when or how she got there. The last thing Sal recollected from that night, she explained, was sitting with a policeman and giving her statement.

But there was one thing that Sal was absolutely certain about, she told me. One image from that night was forever seared into her mind and she still thought about it often—seeing the rapist. Sal wasn't quite sure exactly when this happened. But she recalled watching the police hook his shirt collar, push his face against a wall near our living room. And what Sal heard him say, she told me, has always stuck with her. He was yelling, "That's my girlfriend. It's no big deal. She's just upset."

It was at this point in our conversation that Sal's voice cut off completely. The line went silent. I waited. Then her voice came back, full of storming growl, a fury I would never have expected. She was so angry. What the rapist said still disturbed her a great deal. The fact that he would do what he did to me and then try to make up a lie to get away with it absolutely incensed her. It was the clearest part of the whole thing to her.

What had happened to Sal after that night? Her story was uncannily similar to my own. She moved in with a girlfriend. For many months Sal was so afraid at night—experiencing flashbacks and nightmares—that she had to sleep in her friend's bed, just like I did with Lindsey. For years after that night, she remained very angry about what happened, she told me. She has never slept well since then. She couldn't trust men the way she had before. It took her ten years—ten—to begin dating again. When she did begin dating, the rape—my rape—was a big issue still: it was crucial, she said, that anyone she dated understand exactly what she'd been through. And while she did eventually find understanding in the man she'd ended up marrying, she believed that what happened that night impacted all of her relationships with men and likely always would.

As I listened to Sal describe how this event had changed her, I was mesmerized. It was remarkable just how similar Sal's and my own responses to this event were. Sal exhibited all of the classic symptoms of PTSD. She had horrible memories of the event such as nightmares and flashbacks, expended energy not reflecting on it, found herself having trouble expressing her thoughts and feelings around the event, and experienced many of the same symptoms such as getting panicked-jittery, feeling generally angry, and having a tough time sleeping. All of these symptoms went on for years, and some were still with her.

But there was one huge difference between Sal's experiences and my own. And it wasn't the difference one might be most likely to focus on—the fact that I'd been raped that night and she hadn't. Instead, the key difference, I realized, was that I had been recognized as *the* victim of the crime and therefore received both medical and legal help. Sal, on the other hand, had not at all been recognized medically or legally as a victim of the crime. While she gave the police an account of what happened, it was not written up as a victim impact statement. There were few large cultural organizations or institutional programs in place to help someone like Sal through this process. This meant that over the years far fewer people had made a specific point of searching out PTSD symptoms in Sal or helping her with them. And, as a result, Sal still seemed to be coping with many of them.

It had never hit me quite this way before. Sal had remained an altogether unrecognized victim in this event. And this wasn't right. Sal was a victim of this event just like I was. It had ripped through her, changed her in ways she might not yet even understand. I felt a deep compassion for her. Sal was in a very hard place to be. I knew this because I'd been there, too, and still went back there on occasion.

[234]

It was at this point in our conversation that I really debated with myself. If I now believed that Sal was a victim, too, was it inappropriate to ask her about the furniture? I didn't want to traumatize Sal further. Still, I had to know the answer to my question, so I could finally put the issue to rest in my own mind. So I asked Sal the only way I knew how: Did she recall piling anything in front of her door to protect herself?

What she said next surprised me too. She didn't remember moving the furniture to block the door. She had only the very foggiest recollection of this part of the night. She did remember *thinking* to block her door. But, in Sal's memories, Sal had completely failed to do so. The way she recalled it, she was too scared to move her own body, let alone a dresser.

And yet, of course, she had done exactly that: she was alone in the room and the dresser was in front of the inside of the door. She simply couldn't remember. I'd never really learn the details.

Sal's voice cracked on the other end of that line as she spoke. She said that all these years she'd wished she could have done more to help me, that she was still angry with herself for being "a statue."

I'd imagined this apology a couple of times in the years in between, I had to admit. But hearing it, I realized that while this was a more heartfelt and genuine apology than any I'd received before in my life, it wasn't needed. It didn't matter exactly how long she'd been awake, what she did or didn't do. It just wasn't like that.

At some point in our talks, Sal asked me about what finally happened with the case. The last thing she'd heard from the DA's Office all those years ago was that it wouldn't be going to trial so she wouldn't have to appear in court. Sal never looked into it further, fearful of revisiting the incident. As a result, Sal had lived her entire adult life in a low-level state of fear. He was out there somewhere and he might try to find her and hurt her at any time, in any place. It was then that I told Sal what she'd never known. Though the case hadn't gone to trial, he had in fact served jail time—eight years of it. When Sal heard this, I could tell that she was deeply comforted, that her world had suddenly become lighter. But then I had to tell Sal the piece of the story that she hadn't known—he'd been out for some time since then. I heard her breath swing, snare.

My conversations with Sal taught me a great deal. The two of us have far more in common than either of us ever realized. Our stories were essentially the same—we were victims of a violent crime, tried to recover from it around loving people who had never been through anything like it themselves. We also shared a common set of physical and emotional responses to the event. We both experienced the symptoms of PTSD in remarkably similar ways. And in the years since the event we had both worked hard to achieve recognition in our chosen fields, at least partially cloaking ourselves in our careers as a coping strategy. Sal and I understood each other in a way that few other people in our lives ever could. The horror of our experiences had made Sal and I keep our distance from one another all of these years. But, as we were both starting to understand, we'd traveled parallel paths in the years since the assault.

After my last conversation with Sal, I kept thinking about how few "facts" the interviews had added to my story of that night. I had thought to fill in some missing pieces, to increase the reliability of my story. But that's not what I got at all, and it got me thinking again about why I was doing all of this, what could be accomplished by figuring out how to tell my story. Musing over Sal's history one night, I picked up John D'Agata and Jim Fingal's *The Lifespan of a Fact*, a book devoted to questioning the idea that facts alone are the mark of a "true" story. In their compelling dialogues, D'Agata and Fingal were redefining what the real goals of storytelling and other arts should be—not to make us comfortable or to tell us *the* truth, but rather, as they put it, to "break us open, to make us raw, to destabilize our understandings of ourselves and of our worlds so that we can experience both anew, with fresh eyes, and with therefore the possibility of recognizing something that we had not recognized before."[1] That's pretty much what had happened in my conversations with Sal. Our ideas about ourselves and our worlds had been forever altered. We'd been broken open to a reality we hadn't recognized before: although we'd seldom spoken, we'd both been living with many of the same horrors, facing many of the same attempts to cope in their aftermath. Sal and I had been fellow travelers all these years.

[236]

CHAPTER FIFTY-THREE

By the time I called Cathy, I'd been going after this story for many years—nearly twenty. But my investigation was soon coming to a close. My feelings about this were mixed, to say the least. The project had been with me a long time. It had been my own personal quest for sure. I'd hoped to learn about myself—to discover how I'd gone from the college girl I once was to the person I'd become, to learn how I could carry what had happened to me into the future. There was one last major figure involved in the rape who I hadn't talked to, my other roommate, Cathy. I hadn't seen her since that moment the night of the rape when she gave me her sweats to wear to the hospital. Everyone had dispersed from the apartment that night, never to return except to gather belongings: it was as if the house had suddenly been declared haunted and was promptly abandoned. Interviewing her would be my last opportunity to get information and understand the incident from a wider perspective. After this, I realized, there might be fewer and fewer opportunities to learn anything new.

Though I'd thought to find Cathy many times over the years, I'd always stopped myself. There were reasons for this. Since Cathy had been a relative stranger, someone who answered our ad for a roommate, up until that night I'd known very little about her past. From things she'd mentioned, I'd had the distinct sense that it hadn't been easy. But she'd never told me details and I'd been hesitant to pry. At some point after I'd seen Cathy for that last time on the night of my assault, though, I'd overheard one of the police officers talking to another officer who'd just arrived on the scene, telling the new arrival that Cathy had been the one to call the police. He described Cathy as pretty shaken up. And then he added this— "Her sister was murdered a few years ago, and when she heard a struggle going on, she thought it was happening all over again."

Cathy had already been the victim of a horrifyingly violent event before I'd ever met her. I couldn't begin to fathom the grief and loss that would come from losing a sibling. In effect, Cathy had been a victim of a violent crime a second time that night when she witnessed my near-murder. Though I didn't know the circumstances around her sister's death, I realized that this event would likely have brought up many issues for Cathy. She'd been forced to endure what no twenty-year-old college student should—she'd been a victim of violent trauma twice within a matter of a few short years. Cathy would need a lot of time to heal from all of these events, to find ways to live her life, to put these things in the past, I'd reasoned. If I did contact her, wouldn't I just be reminding her of all she hoped to forget?

I had to admit, though, I'd stopped myself for less noble reasons, too. While I'd thanked Cathy that night, I'd long felt that she deserved far more than that from me. Though she had taken a relatively small action—gone downstairs and made a phone call—its consequences for me were very significant. Cathy very likely saved my life. And I wasn't sure how to begin to thank her for that.

I had the sense that I'd mishandled all of this. But I worried that anything I could say would seem horribly overdue, insufficient. Still, I told myself, I had to do this. As with Sal, before I tried to locate Cathy, I pulled out the police report describing what Cathy had witnessed, and I read it. Again, phrases flew up in front of me like haunted house skeletons.

The witness (Cathy) was asleep in her bedroom . . .
got out of bed and went over to the victim's bedroom
to listen . . . heard a male voice from inside the
room . . . could hear the victim breathing heavily
as she was hyperventilating . . . heard the male
say "BE QUIET I GOT A KNIFE TO YOUR THROAT AND
I'LL SLIT YOUR THROAT IF YOU DON'T SHUT UP" to the
victim . . . ran downstairs and had the downstairs
tenants call the police . . . went outside to wait
for the police . . . police arrived . . . she told
them what was going on, that the victim was being
hurt and that someone was holding a knife to the
victim's throat . . . police went into the house and
she could hear more screaming . . . the police came
out . . . they had a white male with them and they
put him into a police car. I asked if the witness
knew this white male and she stated that she didn't
and has never seen him before . . . that the rear
door latch was broken off the door . . . she also
noticed a leather jacket that does not belong in the
apartment.

After reading that report, it occurred to me that there was
another reason that I'd avoided talking to Cathy for so long. More
than anyone else, she'd actually heard what was happening to me
and had understood it. While I had started trying to confront my
experience soon after the rape, certain moments of the assault had
remained very difficult to think about without triggering terrifying flashbacks. And thinking of Cathy, listening at my door while I
was being beaten and abused inside, brought me very close to the
worst moments of that night. Talking to her was probably something I *couldn't* have done until a great deal of time had passed. I
had had to work on other things first.

Unlike Sal who I found relatively quickly, it took many months
for me to even discover where Cathy had once worked. It was like
Cathy had done her very best to vanish, to poof-disappear, as if

I only had thin, vague shadows to follow. It would take several more months to track down Cathy's married name, to compile a full list of everyone across the country who shared that name, and to search out their phone numbers. Then I began calling. All of these Cathys were nice, accommodating. But none of them were the right one. I was down to my last phone number. If this turned out not to be Cathy, it was time to give up. With quaking fingers and a lead sinker heart, I dialed the number.

It was the real Cathy who answered. Her voice sounded just like it did those many years ago, sweet and melodic, unpretentious, genuine. I took a deep breath, said my name, and waited. There was no response. In those long, quiet moments, I wondered. Was it possible that Cathy simply didn't remember me? That seemed quite unlikely. We experienced something not easily forgotten. Was it possible that Cathy was angry with me, just trying to think of a way to hang up? That seemed unlikely too. Cathy was too generous a person, too thoughtful and kind for that. Soon Cathy's voice came back, full of laughter, saying she couldn't believe it was me, how long had it been, and how on earth was I anyway? As Cathy spoke I could almost see her, her broad smile and pale light-blond hair, seated on an armchair in her living room. There had to be quaint-country curtains, rich wood end tables, family pictures on the mantle. I heard a baby's soft cooing sounds nearby.

During our conversations that followed, I discovered what Cathy had been doing since that moment when I thanked her and accepted her sweatpants those many years ago. This was Cathy's story.

After that night, Cathy was confused, severely traumatized. She wasn't sure where to go. Cathy couldn't live in the apartment anymore but she couldn't find another one on such short notice either. So Cathy contacted her former sorority house, told her sorority sisters the situation. They took her in, invited her to stay in one of their spare rooms. Things were rough for Cathy the rest of that fall and into the spring. She never slept. She had constant nightmares. She suffered from periodic bouts of anxiety, fear, and sadness. She was always restless, anxious. Everywhere Cathy went she was sure he was behind her. Cathy became convinced that he knew who she was, what she looked like, that he had seen her standing on the porch watching. She feared that when he got out on bail or out of rehab he would try to kill her. While Cathy knew this wasn't likely, that he probably didn't know what she looked like or who she was, she couldn't keep herself from thinking this.

Tremendously difficult though it was to remain in Syracuse, Cathy was determined not to abandon what she'd started. It was important. She had to finish her undergraduate degree. The moment Cathy was done, though, she packed up her belongings and left Syracuse never to return, moving to be closer to her family on the other side of the country. Over the next number of years, Cathy would take jobs doing accounting work for companies and counseling patients at weight loss support centers.

But the traumatic events and the associated symptoms of PTSD Cathy had experienced were always with her, Cathy explained. She was not only desperately trying to cope with the aftermath of surviving that night as Sal and I were. That night had triggered something else for Cathy—painful-petrifying memories of her older sister's murder. Though Cathy had not witnessed the murder itself, she told me, she was all too aware of exactly how her beautiful sister—her role model, the person she most looked up to—had died. She'd been brutally stabbed fourteen times by a jealous ex-boyfriend.

In time these two traumatic events began to carve away at her, leading to what Cathy described as a "breakdown." She couldn't sleep. She couldn't eat. She couldn't see the sense in anything anymore. Cathy simply couldn't function. She would find herself "balled up" in her room and "crying for hours." The world had emptied and collapsed, gone gray. People, particularly men, could never be trusted.

Over time, though, she found ways to slowly work through things. With therapy and the passing of time, she was able to integrate her experiences more fully into the rest of her life story. They became something not separate from Cathy—anomalous experiences and responses—but rather an essential part of who she understood herself to be. Her religious faith and church community also helped her to gain tremendous strength, purpose, and hope in the face of these devastating events. In time, Cathy met a great man, too. It took time for her to consider dating him. But they fell in love and, eventually, they got married. She helped her husband with his small business part-time. But mainly Cathy's life was filled with one job, being a stay-at-home Mom. And she just loved it. They had one child, were thinking about trying to have more.

Despite my fears, Cathy was actually eager to talk with me about that night. She had many things to tell me, she said, things she'd always wanted me to know. And I was anxious to learn what they were. But I knew that I had to do something else first. And so I did. I told Cathy that I felt embarrassed and guilty for how long it had taken me to call her, that I was sorry that I'd never thanked her properly for what she'd done for me.

Cathy paused a while, then spoke. I had thanked her that night, she told me. She didn't need or want any more thanks than that. Cathy's graciousness and empathy enveloped me. I felt tears moving down my face. Of course she hadn't been sitting around all of these years waiting for my thank-you, annoyed that it never seemed to arrive. She'd fully accepted the one I gave her those many years ago. And, holding back a round of heaving sobs, I thanked her for this too. Cathy went on to tell me that she was grateful that I had contacted her, that she believed it was her fault as much as my own for our remaining out of touch. She too had avoided contacting me. She too didn't want to upset me or remind me about what had happened. And she too had some fear about looking closely at that time in our lives.

Then she began to tell me what she recalled about that night. As Cathy fell asleep she heard our downstairs neighbors—two men and one woman—having a gathering with friends. Early in the morning she woke to the sound of breaking glass. Someone downstairs must have dropped a bottle, she told herself. She tried to get back to sleep, dozing on and off. Suddenly she was jolted awake. She heard screaming. It was too real for her to have dreamed it. Not sure where it was coming from, Cathy got out of bed, ran to the wall to my room and listened. I screamed again. These weren't the vague, fuzzy kinds of sounds you make during a bad dream, she remembered. They were very, very different. Something was terribly wrong.

Cathy quietly opened her door to the hallway, walked to the closed door to my bedroom. She stood there a few moments, her hand resting lightly on the doorknob. Then she took a deep breath, turned the handle.

Her hand froze like that. She heard an unfamiliar male voice coming from my room. The voice said that he had a knife and was going to kill me. In the background Cathy could hear me hyperventilating, small snippets of my voice coming through. As Cathy described it to me, she'd never heard anyone's voice sound that way before. Cathy knew I was terrified.

Then something strange happened. Cathy never told the police about it at the time. It seemed too odd to mention, and Cathy thought no one would believe her if she did. An image flashed as if on my door and stayed there before her. It was her murdered sister's face. Cathy started shaking, crying, let go of the door knob, raised both hands, and backed away.

She decided that she had to get help. She ran to the phone in our apartment, picked it up, began to dial. Then she stopped herself. He might hear her. She had to get out of there, use a different phone. As quietly as she could, Cathy made her way down the front stairs, opened then closed the door to our apartment. She pounded on our downstairs neighbors' door.

The two men answered. They were cleaning up after their party. Breathless, bawling, Cathy rushed past them into their living room. She was speaking but the men couldn't understand her, kept telling her to slow way down. Cathy managed to convey the words "murder" and "Laura" and "call 911." But 911 wasn't yet available in Syracuse, so they didn't know what she meant. But one of them got on the phone, spoke to an operator, asked to be connected directly to the police department, then gave the phone back to Cathy. Still Cathy couldn't speak. She was too in shock, afraid, shuttering. So the man grabbed the phone back from her, blurted out our address, told them to come quickly, that someone had been hurt. The police said they would get there right away.

The three of them stood in that living room and waited, Cathy recalled. Through sobs she explained what she had heard coming from my room. The two men looked at each other. Just a ceiling separated us. They told Cathy that they were going the hell up there. They were going to save me. Cathy tried to talk them out of it, explained to them that the man sounded very violent, to let the police handle it. But the idea of waiting was just too much. The two men rushed out of their apartment, went into ours, ran up the stairs. They crossed into the living room, the dining room, ran up to my door.

They stopped. They could hear the man's voice, too. This was a dangerous person. If they ran in there, there was a very strong chance that they wouldn't be able to take him down, that they would both get hurt badly, that he would escape. The two of them looked at one another and together made a tough decision. The police would have to handle this. They backed away from my door, ran downstairs. Then they stood on the icy-frigid front porch with Cathy and waited for the police to show up. Minutes later, as she remembered it, the police arrived.

The officers jumped out of their vehicles, led Cathy and the neighbors over to a porch on a house across the street, told them to stand there and wait. Cathy watched as the police rushed in. It was almost as if in slow motion, she recalled. She could see them through the windows upstairs, running into the living room, toward Sal's door. Cathy prayed that Sal hadn't been hurt too, that she was okay, that she hadn't been awake and frightened, that she'd slept through it all.

Cathy waited on that porch across the street for what seemed like forever. She was numb, unable to comprehend what had just occurred. Once the police disappeared from view in the upstairs windows, she had no idea what was going on inside the house. She was trembling, sick to her stomach, which "felt like an empty pit." Time seemed to stretch out like Cape Cod salt water taffy then. It felt like she was waiting for a very long time, she told me. Eventually the police marched out of the house, a strange man in handcuffs with them. He was kicking, screaming, flailing around. He looked like he might have been crazy or on drugs or both. As Cathy watched, one thing struck her, she remembered. It was odd how impeccably dressed he was. Then she heard his voice. Cathy wanted so badly to run off that porch, out of the shadows, to punch his lying mouth. But she knew she couldn't. He yelled it over and over again, Cathy told me, as if he'd been saying it his whole life. "I'm innocent. I'm innocent."

While those parts of Cathy's account were very clear, other details were more murky. The police told Cathy that they found beer bottles on the back stairs where he'd broken in. But Cathy wasn't certain if the police officers ever learned whether these bottles were his or not. Cathy wondered exactly when he broke the glass on the downstairs door. Maybe that was the same glass she'd heard break earlier in the night, but she couldn't be sure. Cathy told me that the police mentioned something about him taking things from our landlord's basement, about him having used them against me. But she'd never been clear on what the rapist brought along with him, what he might have taken from downstairs.

These were Cathy's experiences, things that she alone saw and knew: hearing him threaten my life, seeing her sister's face on my door, telling the men who lived downstairs what was happening and calling the police, watching our neighbors try to help me and then change their minds, standing by as the police rushed in, seeing them emerge with the rapist in handcuffs.

As with Sal, until Cathy and I talked, she never knew what had become of the case. Like Sal, Cathy had wanted to avoid thinking about it too much. Though Cathy was also glad to hear that he'd been arrested and had served jail time, she very quickly asked about when he'd been released. She knew how these things worked. And his incarceration didn't change many things for her, she explained. She would never get over her fear of men who are strangers. She would always lock every door and window, check each lock carefully multiple times. She would always be far more attuned to and sensitive about her surroundings than the rest of her friends. Cathy would always be much more deeply affected by representations of violence in the media than others she knew.

As Cathy continued to speak, something else began to dawn on me. Cathy held a complex understanding about the effects of these two traumatic events in her life—both her sister's murder and my assault. On the one hand, Cathy was describing how random these horrifying experiences seemed. These were senseless, violent acts that defied meaning or comprehension. I could hear the deep sadness and sense of futility in Cathy's voice. On some basic level, these events made Cathy feel like the world was screamingly out of control, like there was no way to make sense of any of it, and that therefore there were few ways to anticipate it or take proactive actions in relationship to it. The fundamental upshot was that traumas were unstoppable, their effects never really over, done.

Simultaneously, though, Cathy held another viewpoint that struck me as genuinely optimistic. She spoke about her decision to leave our apartment and call the police. Cathy hadn't been operating in the realm of conscious thought. Something else was happening. Cathy was "in overdrive," propelled by instinct. Her body knew something had to be done and just did it. She'd been in the right place at the right time to be able to save me. While she many times stated that she wished she could have done more to stop him from hurting me, she acknowledged that she also felt a sense of victory. She had in fact done something. Though she characterized it as a small example of agency, it also sounded like it had been an important one for her personally in her own healing. She'd been unable to do anything to save her older sister. But she had been able to help me. In other words, though Cathy saw herself as a victim of this trauma and all of the horrors associated with that, she also saw something positive and valuable in the story. Cathy had been a victim who had successfully challenged victimhood, even if in a minor way. And that seemed like the right way to look at things to me, too. For me, for Sal, for herself, she absolutely had.

And that was my last interview. By this point, I'd revisited this period of my life in the fullest way I knew how. I'd conducted research, spoken with many people. But what exactly did it add up to?

Several things had emerged from all of these interviews for me. I was more sure now than ever about the degree to which this story defied the strictures of traditional narrative. What happened wasn't ever going to be made sense of in terms of one linear set of perfectly comprehensible events. There were many perspectives, many key moments, many potential plots and possibilities for how to construct them, to tell them. What lingered with me instead were the myriad, pervasive, and ongoing effects that these events had had on so many people's lives. There would be no tying up all the loose ends neatly, shutting down the subject finally and for good. Instead, whatever peace was to be had could come only from the realization that this kind of closure was a false goal.

Instead of a linear story, instead of closure, what I'm left with are a few compelling images that, taken together, for me, now stand in for that kind of story. Over the years, several of these images have taken their place alongside the more frightening ones that had dominated my recollections. In the earliest phases of the project, what I found compelling was the image of myself as the college girl, the idea of who she had been, the image of her sleeping peacefully that last night before the rape. In a way, many of my attempts to understand my experience had really been focused on this girl and the possibility of restoring in my own life something of what she had been. There was, too, the image of Lindsey shampooing my bloodied hair, a picture that will always evoke her voluntary and self-sacrificial choice to care for me, to be involved. With Sal the idea was one of involuntary self-protection in the face of terrifying danger, the image of her furniture piled against the door.

I had a resonant image of Cathy too now—her standing inches from my bedroom door, hearing my muffled screams, her hand trembling as she reaches for the knob.

What does this image of Cathy mean to me? When I told Steve about my interview with Cathy and my image of her at the door, all he could focus on at first was the fact that she *hadn't* opened the door, hadn't stopped the rape right then. He could understand *why* she hadn't turned the knob—with or without her vision of her sister on the door to warn her, it was a dangerous situation. But it was hard, he said, to know about those minutes lost before salvation came, the minutes between her decision to turn away from the door and the arrival of the police.

That is a hard thought, for sure, I said, but then I had to add that this wasn't the main idea I associated with the image of Cathy at the door. He looked puzzled, so I explained. For all of the years that had passed since the rape, one of the toughest aspects of the entire thing had been the *singular* nature of my experience. While many other people had surely had sympathy for me, had perhaps even tried to imagine what had happened to me, they didn't share the experience and would never remember it. I was the only person, I believed, who could actually remember the rape itself. Unless I counted the perpetrator, and that was an even lonelier thought.

And so, I said, when Cathy talked about her moment of crisis at the door, the thought that struck me more than any other was that I hadn't been alone in those terrible moments. Cathy was there with me. Although I felt a true camaraderie with the many other survivors who had told me their stories, what I shared with them were analogous but not identical experiences. For twenty years I'd believed that I would always carry this specific bewildering memory entirely by myself. But now I had learned that another person, a living witness, had been aware about much of what was happening to me in real time, in the very moments it was happening. My trauma was known by another person—Cathy. Though we certainly had different memories that were uniquely our own, on some basic level we also shared some of the same key memories. In effect, Cathy had heard him threaten my life. She had heard me fighting him for it. Cathy was with me.

One of the best things to come out of my interview with Cathy were a few moments that we spent talking about the many positive developments we'd seen in our lives over the years. Cathy said that, after what she'd been through with her sister and with me, for a while she'd had real trouble imagining a life with a husband and children. And she'd thought that there would never be days when she didn't think about these terrible events, when they didn't take over her nights. But she had plenty of beautiful days and even some nights now. I smiled as I listened to Cathy, and I told her just how much she deserved each and every last one of them, how glad I was for her.

And Cathy asked me more questions, too. After what I'd gone through, she'd been fairly sure I would never be able to trust men again, never be able to have a relationship. For years she'd imagined me permanently damaged, my dreams of a loving partnership and becoming a writer forever lost. I told her that I'd had those same fears. But I'd had a wonderful life with Steve for many years now. In him I'd found someone I would love forever, who I could trust completely. And I too had many days and nights when I didn't think about that night or its aftermath, when life was more about soul-enriching things like trying to garden in the impossibly rocky Flagstaff soils, like trail running through the air-stealing San Francisco mountains, like spending hours silly-laughing with dear friends. Cathy was so happy for me, too, she said. Then she asked me about my family life. She'd remembered a few details about my parents' divorce, how it had been a rough split, and she'd long thought about how hard it might be for them to help me. I explained just how much Lindsey had done in those months right after my assault and how, in the later months and years, my parents came through, too, did what they could to help me in spite of the deep pain they were experiencing, how we'd worked through that time in our lives, how today our relationships were stronger.

And Cathy asked about my career, too. Given all I'd been through, how exactly had I come to reach my goals, to make my dreams of becoming a professor and a writer come true? I told her about how important writing about my life had been to me throughout the ordeal. I told her about my first journals after the rape, when I could hardly remember the minutes and hours passing—my earliest drafts of an experience that I was still writing about, still trying to understand. I told her about Dr. Alcoff and her encouragement, about what I'd been doing to try to flesh out my gappy story.

Cathy said that the fact that I had stayed the course and finished my PhD shouldn't have surprised her.

"You were always such a darn bookworm," she laughed. "You always had your nose stuck in Shakespeare, Dante, or Frost."

I had to admit, I was a bookworm then, I said—but (can you

believe it?) even more of one now. That set Cathy off giggling because she had to admit that she couldn't.

Cathy mentioning Frost reminded me of that poem "Birches," and so I told her about it. Reading that poem had bothered me so much early on, I explained, because it seemed to suggest that permanent damage after trauma was an inevitability, that there were things from which one could never recover. I recited the lines I'd never forgotten to her, those ones about trees bent over after an ice storm: "They never right themselves. You may see their trunks arching in the woods / Years afterwards, trailing their leaves on the ground." Cathy found the description graceful though sad. And I had to acknowledge that I did, too. But now, I told her, I doubted the accuracy—or at least the necessity—of Frost's metaphor.

"I've thought a lot about what we've both been through, of course," I said. "It's years later and, sure, it hasn't been easy, hasn't happened all at once or in a straight line. And we will never again be who we once were. But things *have* gotten progressively better. Our lives have moved on, gone forward. We were hurt, devastated by those things. But along the way we also found real gratitude, brightness and joy. We have rewarding lives now, too."

"That's true," she said. "We really do."

Sometimes those birches do right themselves.

CHAPTER FIFTY-FOUR

There's no research left to do, no one central to the story with whom I have yet to speak. But there's one last thing I need to do—to come back here, to see this house. We're just passing through Syracuse, taking a quick detour from a trip East in our camper. All through my time in graduate school, I avoided this neighborhood. When I returned to the university as a young assistant professor a few years later to give a talk, I didn't make a point of driving down this street either. Just the idea of seeing the house, of facing it, still scared me a little then. But it doesn't anymore.

During these many years I've been searching memories and conducting research in an effort to flesh out my story, to find whatever missing pieces might fill in the gaps in my understanding. On some basic level, my project was conceived in the days right after the rape, when I first despaired about the bewildered, stunned, forgetful person I had suddenly been turned into. Would I ever, I wondered, be able to slip back through the curtain to that "before" moment, to reclaim some pieces of my former self—the college girl—to recapture some of who I had been? I'm back here for much the same reason, I suppose. I'm looking for her.

There's nothing about the house that hints at its terrible past. It looks like most of the other structures on this street inhabited by college students—two levels, a porch slouching off the front of the second floor. There's a wine bottle with candle drippings caking its sides, a frayed hammock slung from eyebolts, a string of flapping Tibetan prayer flags. A bright-shiny new Volkswagen Beetle sits in the driveway.

As I walk the old stairs to the door, each step is in my muscle memory, all the times I've done this before. I glance through the downstairs apartment windows. A desk's piled high with text-books. There's one for a sociology class, I think, and maybe one for organic chemistry. In the desk corner is a jar jammed with pens, scattered barrettes and hair ties next to it. If I squint I can just make out bookshelves against the far wall, a few stray plates, utensils, and glasses pressed alongside the book spines. A pink sweat-shirt, pocket book, and iPod have been hastily tossed across an old couch, and there's a mess of flip-flops, sneakers, and heels by the front door. As I look at these things, I'm surprised at how familiar all this seems, at just how easy it is for me to imagine sliding into this life, living here, again. It doesn't seem so long ago that I was a college girl just like one of these.

I press, listen as the sound of the old doorbell buzzes through the house. And I wait and wait. But no one answers. I guess no one's home. The students who live here probably walk to campus or ride their bikes. It's just as well. I'm not altogether sure how I would explain my presence here anyway. I walk back down the stairs, gaze back at the house. The differences are clearer to me now. The house has been repainted—the salmon color I remember long since replaced by blue. The crackled driveway's been repaved. The bushes and trees have sprung up feet taller. I can barely recognize most of them. The streetlight out the window's no longer there. I try to recall exactly where it was, where it might have hung. But somehow it's difficult to pinpoint its placement now.

I will never know the whole story. We writers of memoirs—but especially trauma memoirs—never can. But I do know more of it now, and I know the extent to which it really was a part of lots of other people's stories, too. I can no longer conjure the names or recall the faces of my downstairs neighbors. Leaning against our truck in front of the house, I try to imagine the courage it took for those two men to run toward danger to save me, the feelings of despair, fear, and anger that must have washed over them as they realized that they couldn't. These men are still out there.

There are those police officers. I try to imagine the strength it took for them to rush into that apartment, not knowing what they might be facing. I think about what the officers might have felt as the rapist broke free of them, as they chased him down, finally caught him, as he broke their bones trying to escape. I think about what the officers saw, what they thought when they looked at my face, spoke with Sal and with Cathy about their experiences. Those officers are still out there.

It's a wide circle of victims, in the end. There are all of our families, our parents and our siblings. There are our friends and colleagues. There are our partners and children. And beyond them there are lawyers, medical professionals, counselors. The list goes on and on.

I move to the side of the house now. The partially glass back door's gone, too, replaced by a solid wood one. I stride back to the sidewalk, around the other side of the house, look up. There's my old bedroom window. On one side of it is Sally's. On the other is Cathy's. Spider lines shimmer their way through the bushes in front of me. And for a few moments I allow myself to imagine her—imagine the college girl who was me in there studying. Imagine the college girl eating. Imagine the college girl jabber-talking on the phone.

When I look down at my watch, twenty minutes are gone. We aren't staying. It's time to get back on the road. Steve starts the engine as I begin to walk back toward the camper. Our Doberman Max leaps into the back to make room for me, his tail wiggling as he vanishes behind the seats. I get in, close the door. As we sway down the street, the house shrinks in the rearview mirror.

I watch the light glint off my old window, see the curtain ripple.

I catch myself thinking as the house recedes, go back, she could still be there, that college girl.

But no, I realize, as we turn the corner and the house disappears.

She's gone.

NOTES

Acknowledgments
1. See Vonnegut, 1.

Chapter Two
1. See Pirandello.
2. See Crane, 21.

Chapter Three
1. In 1983 Farrah Fawcett replaced Susan Sarandon as Marjorie in an Off-Broadway version of *Extremities*. In 1986 Fawcett would star in the film version. She received a Golden Globe Nomination for her performance in the category Best Performance by an Actress in a Motion Picture-Drama in 1987. Posters for the film featured a black-and-white image of Fawcett's face broken up by red-edged boxes and the words "Vulnerable and alone. The perfect victim . . . or so he thought. What she did to survive is nothing compared to what she'll do to get even." Mastrosimone's important tale—a story of brutal

violence and revenge—continues to evoke powerful performances both on stage and in film.

2. See Mastrosimone, 6.
3. Ovid's *Metamorphoses* tells the story of Philomela, the princess of Athens, who is violated by King Tereus. She tells him "I will proclaim it . . . Tell everybody; if you shut me here, / I will move the very woods and rocks to pity." After this, Tereus removes Philomela's tongue, making it literally impossible for her to tell others about the rape. However, Philomela finds other ways. As Ovid writes, "Sharpness of wit, and cunning comes in trouble. / She had a loom to work with, and with purple / On a white background, wove her story in" (147–48). When Tereus tries to capture Philomela, the Gods turn her into a nightingale, allowing her to both avoid capture as well as to sing about her tragedy. This myth has been employed in many texts, including Aristotle's *Poetics*, Shakespeare's *A Midsummer Night's Dream*, and T. S. Eliot's *The Wasteland*.
4. See Moore, 49–50.
5. See Vonnegut, 26.

Chapter Twenty-Nine

1. See Cheever, 603–12.

Chapter Forty-Six

1. See the SMART (Office of Sex Offender Sentencing, Monitoring, Apprehending, Registering, and Tracking) website at http://www.ojp.usdoj.gov/smart/legislation.htm. In addition, copies of the actual laws can be accessed here.
2. See http://www.ojp.usdoj.gov/smart/legislation.htm.
3. During the last few years the Department of Education's Office for Civil Rights has provided some additional rules for how Title IX should be put into practice. To summarize the "Dear Colleague" letter, all students should have their grievances addressed in exactly the same ways and all departments need to make this knowledge public. In addition, schools have to make substantial efforts to help victims of sexual violence such as offering counseling services and altering their living

situations. And, importantly, while the Federal Educational Records Privacy Act of 1974 (FERPA) does not typically allow disclosure of students' records, under such Title IX provisions universities have the right to share these records when and if a student has violated university policies and/or if doing so will further protect other students. For more information, see http://www.whitehouse.gov/sites/default/files/dear_colleague_sexual_violence.pdf and http://www2.ed.gov/documents/press-releases/title-ix-enforcement.pdf. It is troubling, however, that just as educational institutions and major governmental programs are directly challenging rape myths, these myths seem to be resurfacing elsewhere with a vengeance. Consider, for example, Rep. Todd Akin's (Missouri) comment during the 2012 election cycle that women are not physically able to become pregnant after "legitimate rape" or Richard Mourdock's (Indiana) statement that no abortions should be granted in the case of rape because God intended these pregnancies to occur. See Rheana Murray's article at http://www.nydailynews.com/news/politics/rape-remarks-sink-gop-senate-hopefuls-article-1.1198170.

4. For further information, see the Jacob Wetterling Resource Center's pages on the history of legislation at http://www.jwrc.org/KeepKidsSafe/SexualOffenders101/LegislationBackground/tabid/106/Default.aspx.> See also "Legislative History" at http://www.kidslivesafe.com/learning-center/legislative-history.

5. For an analysis of the problems of inconsistency in study measurements of recidivism, see Hanson and Morton-Bourgon, 1–21. For a longitudinal study examining sex offender reoffense rates, see Langevin, et al., 531–52.

6. For one such example, see Open: New York Senate Government at http://open.nysenate.gov/legislation/bill/S2000-2011.

Chapter Forty-Eight

1. This statistic comes from the website One in Four which provides superb resources for both female and male survivors. See http://www.oneinfour.ie/. See also RAINN and National Sexual

Violence Resource Center. It's important to mention another significant form of PTSD here as well. "Complex PTSD" (C-PTSD), a term introduced by Judith Herman in *Trauma and Recovery*, importantly describes severe, multi-faceted reactions to protracted, continuous forms of trauma. Summarizing Herman, the National Center for PTSD cites examples such as "concentration camps, prisoner of war camps, prostitution brothels, long-term domestic violence, long-term child physical abuse, long-term child sexual abuse, and organized child exploitation rings." In addition, those who suffer from C-PTSD may experience problems with "emotional regulation (may include persistent sadness, suicidal thoughts, explosive anger, or inhibited anger), consciousness [includes forgetting traumatic events, reliving traumatic events, or having episodes in which one feels detached from one's mental processes or body (dissociation)], self-perception (may include helplessness, shame, guilt, stigma, and a sense of being completely different from other human beings), distorted perceptions of the perpetrator (examples include attributing total power to the perpetrator, becoming preoccupied with the relationship to the perpetrator, or preoccupied with revenge), relations with others, (examples include isolation, distrust, or a repeated search for a rescuer), and one's system of meanings (may include a loss of sustaining faith or a sense of hopelessness and despair)." See http://www.ptsd.va.gov/professional/pages/complex-ptsd.asp. For a more thorough treatment, see Herman, 121.

2. This statistic comes from the website 1in6 for Men. See http://1in6.org/. I also recommend MaleSurvivor. Both sites offer excellent resources as well as support specifically for male survivors. Importantly, organizations such as SNAP (Survivors' Network of Those Abused by Priests) offer support systems for both male and female survivors who have suffered sexual abuse by members of the clergy. See http://www.snap-network.org/. For an analysis of sexual violence and athletics, see Moushey and Dvorchak.

3. This statistic comes from http://www.ptsd.va.gov/public/pages/sexual-assault-females.asp. See also the National Institute of Mental Health at http://nimh.nih.gov/health/publications/post-traumatic-stress-disorder-ptsd/what-are-the-symptoms-of-ptsd.shtml and the National Center for PTSD at http://www.ptsd.va.gov/public/pages/what-is-ptsd.asp.

4. See "Post-traumatic Stress Disorder (PTSD)" at http://www.mayoclinic.com/health/post-traumatic-stress-disorder/DS00246/DSECTION=symptoms. Also see Nancy Zielinski's "Facts and Figures of PTSD in the Military" at http://www.examiner.com/article/facts-and-figures-of-ptsd-the-military. For more information on PTSD symptoms, consult The National Institute of Health.

5. See Van Der Kolk, McFarlane, and Weisaeth, 8. See also Chu.

6. This information can be found at http://www.ptsd.va.gov/professional/pages/ptsd-physical-health.asp. In addition, The National Center for PTSD website overseen by the U.S. Department of Veteran Affairs contains a wealth of resources about the connections between PTSD and other health issues. See also Finley; Milliken, Auchterlonie, and Hoge, 2141–48; Vasterling et al., 519–29; Lapierre, Schwegler, LaBauve, 933–43; and Tanielian and Jaycox. For an important analysis of veterans, PTSD, and high suicide rates, see Kristof. This article notes that "for every soldier killed on the battlefield this year, about 25 veterans are dying by their own hands," that "at least one in five veterans from Afghanistan and Iraq" has PTSD symptoms, and that "veterans kill themselves at a rate of one every eighty minutes." And, according to Jeff Ousley with the Veterans United Network, "less than half of soldiers with PTSD seek treatment." See http://www.veteransunited.com/network/soldiers-continue-to-struggle-with-public-perception-of-ptsd/.

7. LaCapra contends that trauma survivors' narratives are often necessarily "nonlinear," enabling "trauma to register in language and its hesitations, indirections, pauses, and silences" and asserts that "narrative at its best helps one not to change

the past through a dubious rewriting of history but to work through post traumatic symptoms in the present in a manner that opens possible futures." See LaCapra, 121–122.

8. See Etherington, 35.
9. See Van Der Kolk and Fisler, 505–25.
10. See Herman, 3. Herman's more detailed overview of the stages of recovery can be found on pages 133–236.

Chapter Forty-Nine

1. Foucault, "The Discourse on Language," 216.
2. See *The Oprah Winfrey Show* that aired on April 14, 1988.

Chapter Fifty

1. Along with the other texts cited in this chapter, these books about philosophy, trauma narratives, creative nonfiction, and the science of recollection have greatly informed my thoughts about memory: Erll, *Memory in Culture*; Hampl, *I Could Tell You Stories: Sojourns in the Land of Memory*; Murdock, *Unreliable Truth: On Memoir and Memory*; Radstone and Schwarz, *Memory: Histories, Theories, Debates*; Rossington and Whitehead, *Theories of Memory: A Reader*; Scott, *The Time of Memory*; Smith and Schaffer, *Human Rights and Narratives Lives: The Ethics of Recognition*; Smith and Watson, *Reading Autobiography: A Guide for Interpreting Life Narratives*; and Whitehead, *Memory: The New Critical Idiom*.
2. See the following texts on questions of truth and creative nonfiction: D'Agata, "Mer-Mer: An Essay About How I Wish We Wrote Our Nonfictions," 66–76; Gornick, *The Situation and the Story: The Art of Personal Narrative*; Gutkind, *Keep It Real*; Hampl and May, *Tell Me True: Memoir, History, and Writing a Life*; and Mairs, "Trying Truth," 89–92.
3. See Casey, 282.
4. See Yagoda, 109–10.
5. See Couser, 107.
6. *The Smoking Gun*'s 2006 essay, "A Million Little Lies," revealed that Frey's memoir (initially heralded by Oprah) may have exaggerated his crimes and other experiences. The tremendous

firestorm surrounding Frey's book foregrounds the privileged nature of certain definitions of truth and reality for the genre. Interestingly, at the precise historical moment when authors are contending that they ought to have more freedom to rhetorically resist these strictures for artistic and philosophical reasons, other authors—especially those whose traumas have had a large hand in shaping their memories themselves—are finding that in order to tell the real truths of our stories, we too must challenge these imposed limits and acknowledge the extent to which they are unattainable.

7. See Shields's *Reality Hunger*. Shields's text (a remix of his thoughts and those of other writers—without any quotation marks around them) calls upon us to read memoirs not as embodiments of authentic truth but rather as moments for examining the very nature of what constitutes fact and truth. While such an interrogation is absolutely essential for the future development of the memoir genre, authorial ethos nevertheless remains paramount within it, a material reality that, as Shields himself notes, makes it problematic if not impossible for memoir authors to enact aspects of what he proposes.

8. See these texts for some crucial examples as well as analyses of the ways in which sexual assault survivors' narratives reshape traditional storytelling modes: Brison, *Aftermath: Violence and the Remaking of a Self*; Francisco, *Telling: A Memoir of Rape and Recovery*; Hesford and Kozo, *Haunting Violations: Feminist Criticism and the Crisis of the "Real"*; Kaplan, *Trauma Culture: The Politics of Terror and Loss in Media and Literature*; Leo, *Rape New York*; Payne, *Bodily Discourses: When Students Write About Abuse and Eating Disorders*; Raine, *After Silence: Rape and My Journey Back*; Sebold, *Lucky: A Memoir*; Tal, *Worlds of Hurt: Reading the Literatures of Trauma*; and Thompson-Cannino, Cotton and Torneo, *Picking Cotton: Our Memoir of Injustice and Redemption*. Brison importantly contends that putting one's experiences into narrative forms (partial though they may be) is what makes the trauma survivor's future possible: "It does this not by reestablishing the illusion of coherence of the past, control over the present, and

predictability of the future, but in making it possible to carry on without these illusions" (104).

9. See Gilmore, 24.

10. Monson's *Vanishing Point* encourages all memoir writers to feature our moments of indecision, when memory and truth fall apart: "The unreliability, the misremembering, the act of telling in starts and stops, the fuckups, the postmarked surface of the I: that's where all the good stuff is, the fair and the foul, that which is rent, that which is whole, that which engages the whole reader. Let us linger there, not rush past it" 17.

11. Neil Genzlinger's essay "The Problem with Memoir" exposes the good, the bad, and the ugly of the memoir genre. Referencing the glut of contemporary memoirs on the market, he offers stark advice: "If you didn't feel you were discovering something as you wrote your memoir, don't publish it." "Salon's Guide to Writing a Memoir" also offers a wealth of suggestions from noted contemporary memoirists. Ta-Nehisi Coates (*The Beautiful Struggle*) reminds the author of memoir that "You are not a bad ass. You are a writer," arguing that "great memoir requires great courage and an appetite for sincere self-skepticism" (3). Lauren Slater (*Lying: A Metaphorical Memoir*) notes that memoir-writing is always about bringing imagination and memory together, that it is a "process of reinvention/revision" during which you "find angles and screws and coils and cogs you missed the first time around" (6). And Avi Steinberg (*Running the Books*) advises the memoir writer to not rest upon her/his own story alone but rather to always "Do research. Bring in other eyes, voices" (8). See http://www.salon.com/2013/01/20/salons_guide_to_writing_a_memoir/.

12. For an excellent analysis of the problems of time in memoir writing, see Birkerts.

13. See Zinsser, 6.

Chapter Fifty-Two

1. See D'Agata and Fingal, 109.

WORKS CITED

1in6 for Men. 2012.Web. 30 May 2012. http://1in6.org/.

Adams, Caren, and Jennifer Fay. *No More Secrets: Protecting Your Child from Sexual Assault.* New York: Impact Publishing, 1981. Print.

Alcoff, Linda Martín, and Laura Gray. "Survivor Discourse: Transgression or Recuperation? " *Signs: A Journal of Women and Culture* 18.2 (Winter 1993): 260–90. Print.

Aristotle. *Poetics.* New York: Penguin Classics, 1997. Print.

Bass, Ellen. *The Courage to Heal: A Guide for Women Survivors of Sexual Abuse.* New York: Harper Collins, 1988. Print.

Baudelaire, Charles. *Les Fleurs du Mal.* Boston: David R. Godine Publisher, 1985. Print.

Birkerts, Sven. *The Art of Time in Memoir: Then, Again.* Minneapolis: Graywolf Press, 2008. Print.

Brison, Susan J. *Aftermath: Violence and the Remaking of a Self.* Princeton: Princeton UP, 2002. Print.

Brownmiller, Susan. *Against Our Will: Men, Women, and Rape.* New York: Ballantine Books, 1993. Print.

Buchwald, Emilie, Pamela Fletcher, and Martha Ross, eds. *Transforming a Rape Culture*. Minneapolis: Milkweed, 2005. Print.

Carroll, Lewis. *Alice's Adventures in Wonderland*. New York: Macmillan Publishers, 1865. Print.

Casey, Edward. *Remembering: A Phenomenological Study*. Indianapolis: Indiana UP, 2000. Print.

Chase, Truddi. *When Rabbit Howls*. New York: Random House, 1989. Print.

Cheever, John. "The Swimmer." *The Stories of John Cheever*. New York: Vintage, 2000. 603–12. Print.

Chu, James A. *Rebuilding Shattered Lives: The Responsible Treatment of Complex Post-Traumatic and Dissociative Disorders*. Hoboken: Wiley, 2011. Print.

"Clery Act Overview." University of California Office of the President. 2012. Web. 15 January 2013. http://www.ucop.edu/ucophome/policies/clery/overview.pdf.

Coates, Ta-Nehisi. *The Beautiful Struggle: A Father, Two Sons, and an Unlikely Road to Manhood*. New York: Spiegel & Grau, 2009. Print.

"Complex PTSD." United States Department of Veteran Affairs. 2007.Web. 23 April 2013. http://www.ptsd.va.gov/professional/pages/complex-ptsd.asp.

Couser, G. Thomas. *Memoir: An Introduction*. New York: Oxford, 2011. Print.

Crane, Hart. "Passage." *The Complete Poems of Hart Crane*. New York: Liveright, 1986. Print.

D'Agata, John, and Jim Fingal. *The Lifespan of a Fact*. New York: W. W. Norton and Company, 2012. Print.

D'Agata, John. "Mer-Mer: An Essay About How I Wish We Wrote Our Nonfictions." Ed. David Lazar. *Truth in Nonfiction: Essays*. Iowa City: U of Iowa P, 2008. 66–76. Print.

Danica, Elly. *Don't: A Woman's Word*. Toronto: Canadian Scholars' Press, 1988. Print.

"Dear Colleague Letter." United States Department of Education Office for Civil Rights. 2011. Web. 15 January 2013. http://www.whitehouse.gov/sites/default/files/dear_colleague_sexual_violence.pdf.

"Dear Colleague Letter: Sexual Violence Background, Summary, and Fast Facts." United States Department of Education. Office for Civil Rights. 2011. Web. 15 January 2013. http://www2. ed.gov/about/offices/list/ocr/docs/dcl-factsheet-201104.html.

Eggers, Dave. *A Heartbreaking Work of Staggering Genius.* New York: Vintage, 2001. Print.

Eliot, T. S. *The Wasteland.* New York: W. W. Norton & Company, 2000. Print.

Erll, Astrid. *Memory in Culture.* New York: Palgrave MacMillan, 2011. Print.

Etherington, Kim, ed. *Trauma, the Body and Transformation: A Narrative Inquiry.* Philadelphia: Jessica Kingsley Publishers, 2003. Print.

Extremities. Dir. Robert M. Young. Perf. Farrah Fawcett. 1986. Film.

Finley, Erin P. *Fields of Combat: Understanding PTSD Among Veterans of Iraq and Afghanistan.* Ithaca: Cornell UP, 2011. Print.

Foucault, Michel. "The Discourse on Language." *The Archaeology of Knowledge and the Discourse on Language.* New York: Pantheon, 1972. 215–37. Print.

———. *The History of Sexuality Volumes I, II, and III.* New York: Vintage, 1982. Print.

Francisco, Patricia Weaver. *Telling: A Memoir of Rape and Recovery.* New York: Cliff Street Books/Harper Perennial, 1999. Print.

Frey, James. *A Million Little Pieces.* New York: Doubleday, 2003. Print.

Frost, Robert. "Birches." *Mountain Interval.* New York: Henry Holt, 1921. 29–30. Print.

Genzlinger, Neil. "The Problem with Memoirs." *New York Times,* 28 January 2011. Web. 20 October 2011. http://www.nytimes.com/2011/01/30/books/review/Genzlinger-t.html?pagewanted=all.

Gilmore, Leigh. *The Limits of Autobiography: Trauma and Testimony.* Ithaca: Cornell UP, 2001. Print.

Gornick, Vivian. *The Situation and the Story: The Art of Personal Narrative.* New York: Farrar, Straus, and Giroux, 2001. Print.

Gutkind, Lee. *Keep It Real.* New York: W. W. Norton & Company, 2008. Print.

Hampl, Patricia. *I Could Tell You Stories: Sojourns in the Land of Memory.* New York: W. W. Norton & Company, 1999. Print.

———— and Elaine Tyler May eds. *Tell Me True: Memoir, History, and Writing a Life.* St. Paul: Borealis, 2008. Print.

Hanson, R. Karl, and Kelly E. Morton-Bourgon. "The Accuracy of Recidivism Risk Assessments for Sexual Predators: A Meta-Analysis of 118 Prediction Studies." *Psychological Assessment* (2009): 1–21. Print.

Herman, Judith. *Trauma and Recovery.* New York: Basic Books, 1997. Print.

Hesford, Wendy, and Wendy Kozo, eds. *Haunting Violations: Feminist Criticism and the Crisis of the "Real."* Champagne: University of Illinois Press, 2000. Print.

Jacob Wetterling Resource Center. 2010. Web. 15 October 2012. http://www.jwrc.org/KeepKidsSafe/SexualOffenders101/LegislationBackground/tabid/106/Default.aspx.

Jankowski, Kay. "PTSD and Physical Health. United States Department of Veteran Affairs." 2007. Web. 15 April 2013. http://www.ptsd.va.gov/professional/pages/ptsd-physical-health.asp.

Joel, Billy. "Piano Man," in *Piano Man.* Cold Spring Harbor. 1973, 33½ rpm.

Kaplan, E. Ann. *Trauma Culture: The Politics of Terror and Loss in Media and Literature.* New York: Rutgers UP, 2005. Print.

Kelly, Liz. *Surviving Sexual Violence.* Minneapolis: University of Minnesota Press, 1989. Print.

Kristof, Nicholas. "A Veteran's Death, the Nation's Shame." *New York Times,* 14 April 2012. Web. 30 May 2012. http://www.nytimes.com/2012/04/15/opinion/sunday/kristof-a-veterans-death-the-nations-shame.html.

LaCapra, Dominick. *History in Transit: Experience, Identity, Critical Theory.* Ithaca: Cornell UP, 2004. Print.

Langevin, Ron, Suzanne Curnoe, Paul Fedoroff, Renee Bennett, Mara Langevin, Cheryl Peever, Rick Pettica, and Shameen Sandhu. "Lifetime Sex Offender Recidivism: A 25-Year

Follow-Up Study." *Canadian Journal of Criminology and Criminal Justice* (2004): 531–552. Print.

Lapierre, Coady B., Andrea F. Schwegler, and Bill J. LaBauve. "Post-Traumatic Stress and Depression Symptoms in Soldiers Returning from Combat Operations in Iraq and Afghanistan." *Journal of Traumatic Stress* (2007): 933–43. Print.

"Legislative History." Kids Live Safe. 2011. Web. 30 June 2013. http://www.kidslivesafe.com/learning-center/legislative-history.

Leo, Jana. *Rape New York*. New York: The Feminist Press at CUNY, 2011. Print.

Mairs, Nancy. "Trying Truth." *Truth in Nonfiction: Essays.* Ed. David Lazar. Iowa City: U of Iowa P, 2008. 89–92. Print.

MaleSurvivor. 2007. Web. 30 May 2012. http://www.malesurvivor.org/.

Masson, Jeffrey Moussaieff. *Dark Science: Women, Sexuality and Psychiatry in the Nineteenth Century.* New York: Farrar Straus & Giroux, 1986. Print.

Mastrosimone, William. *Extremities: A Play in Two Acts.* New York: Samuel French, (1978) 1985. Print.

"Megan's Law: Keeping Children Safe From Sexual Offenders." 2013. Web. 30 March 2013. https://www.meganslaw.com/.

"Midcontinent University Annual Campus Safety and Security Report." 2011. Web. 25 February 2013. https://www.midcontinent.edu/pdfs/annual-security-report-2011.pdf.

Milliken, Charles S., Jennifer L. Auchterlonie, and Charles W. Hoge. "Longitudinal Assessment of Mental Health Problems Among Active and Reserve Component Soldiers Returning from the Iraq War." *Journal of the American Medical Association* (2007): 2141–48. Print.

"A Million Little Lies: Exposing James Frey's Fiction Addiction." *The Smoking Gun*, 8 January. 2006. Web. 15 October 2012. http://www.thesmokinggun.com/documents/celebrity/million-little-lies.

Monson, Ander. *Vanishing Point: Not a Memoir.* Minneapolis: Graywolf Press, 2010. Print.

Moore, Marianne. "A Grave." *Complete Poems*. New York: Penguin Classics, 1994. 49–50. Print.

Moushey, Bill, and Robert Dvorchak. *Game Over: Jerry Sandusky, Penn State, and the Culture of Silence*. New York: William Morrow, 2012. Print.

Murdock, Maureen. *Unreliable Truth: On Memoir and Memory*. New York: Seal Press, 2003. Print.

Murray, Rheana. "Republican Senate Candidates Akin and Mourdock, Both Damaged by Rape Remarks, Lose Their Respective Senate Races in Missouri and Indiana." *The New York Daily News*, November 7, 2012. Web. 30 February, 2013. http://www.nydailynews.com/news/politics/rape-remarks-sink-gop-senate-hopefuls-article-1.1198170.>

National Center for PTSD. 29 May 2012. Web. 15 October 2012. http://www.ptsd.va.gov/public/pages/what-is-ptsd.asp.

National Institute of Mental Health. 21 January 2009. Web. 15 October 2012. http://nimh.nih.gov/health/publications/post-traumatic-stress-disorder-ptsd/what-are-the-symptoms-of-ptsd.shtml.

National Sexual Violence Resource Center. 2012. Web. 30 May 2012. http://www.nsvrc.org/.

One in Four. May 2012. Web. 30 May 2012. http://www.oneinfourusa.org/statistics.php.

"Open: New York Senate Government." 4 January 2012. Web. 30 May 2012. http://open.nysenate.gov/legislation/bill/S2000-2011.

The Oprah Winfrey Show. 14 April, 1988. Television.

The Oprah Winfrey Show. "James Frey Interview." 16 May 2011. Television.

Ousley, Jeff. "Soldier's Continue to Struggle with Public Perception of PTSD." Veterans United Network. 2011. Web. 30 January 2013. http://www.veteransunited.com/network/soldiers-continue-to-struggle-with-public-perception-of-ptsd/.

Ovid. *Metamorphoses*. Bloomington and London: Indiana UP, 1973. Print.

Payne, Michelle. *Bodily Discourses: When Students Write About*

Abuse and Eating Disorders. Portsmouth: Boynton/Cook Publishers, 2000. Print.

Pirandello, Luigi. *Six Characters in Search of an Author.* Lanham: Ivan R. Dee Publisher, 1998. Print.

"Post-traumatic Stress Disorder (PTSD)." The Mayo Clinic. 2012. Web. 30 March, 2013. http://www.mayoclinic.com/health/post-traumatic-stress-disorder/DS00246/DSECTION=symptoms.

Radstone, Susannah and Bill Schwarz, eds. *Memory: Histories, Theories, Debates.* New York: Fordham UP, 2010. Print.

Raine, Nancy Venable. *After Silence: Rape and My Journey Back.* New York: Three Rivers Press, 1998.

RAINN. 2009. Web. 30 May 2012. http://rainn.org/.

The Rolling Stones. "(I Can't Get No) Satisfaction," in *Out of Our Heads.* By Mick Jagger and Keith Richards. London Records. 1965, 33½ rpm.

Rossington, Michael, and Anne Whitehead, eds. *Theories of Memory: A Reader.* Baltimore: Johns Hopkins, 2007. Print.

"Salon's Guide to Writing a Memoir." *Salon*, 20 January, 2013. Web. 30 March, 2013. http://www.salon.com/2013/01/20/salons_guide_to_writing_a_memoir/.

Scott, Charles E. *The Time of Memory.* Albany: SUNY Press, 1999. Print.

Sebold, Alice. *Lucky: A Memoir.* New York: Back Bay Books, 2002. Print.

Sendak, Maurice. *Where the Wild Things Are.* New York: Harper Collins, 1963. Print.

Shakespeare, William. *The Complete Works.* London: Oxford UP, 1988. Print.

Shields, David. *Reality Hunger: A Manifesto.* New York: Vintage Books, 2011. Print.

Slater, Lauren. *Lying: A Metaphorical Memoir.* New York: Penguin, 2001. Print.

SMART. 2012. Web. 15 October 2012. http://www.ojp.usdoj.gov/smart/legislation.htm.

Smith, Sidonie, and Kay Schaffer. *Human Rights and Narrative*

Lives: The Ethics of Recognition. New York: Palgrave MacMillan, 2004. Print.

Smith, Sidonie and Julia Watson. Reading Autobiography: A Guide for Interpreting Life Narratives. (Minneapolis: Minnesota UP, 2001). Print.

SNAP. 2012. Web. 30 May 2012. http://www.snapnetwork.org/.

Steinberg, Avi. Running the Books: The Adventures of an Accidental Prison Librarian. New York: Anchor, 2011. Print.

Tal, Kali. Worlds of Hurt: Reading the Literatures of Trauma. London: Cambridge UP, 1995. Print.

Tanielian, Terri and Lisa H. Jaycox, eds. Invisible Wounds of War: Psychological and Cognitive Injuries, Their Consequences, and Services to Assist Recovery. Santa Monica: RAND Center for Military Health Policy Research, 2008.

Thompson-Cannino, Jennifer, Ronald Cotton, and Erin Torneo. Picking Cotton: Our Memoir of Injustice and Redemption. New York: St. Martin's, 2009. Print.

"Title IX Enforcement." 2 June 2012. Web. 15 October 2012. http://www2.ed.gov/documents/press-releases/title-ix-enforcement.pdf.

United States Department of Veterans Affairs: National Center for PTSD. 11 May 2012. Web. 30 May 2012. http://www.ptsd.va.gov/index.asp.

Van Der Kolk, Bessel A., Alexander C. McFarlane, and Lars Weisaeth Eds. Traumatic Stress: The Effects of Overwhelming Experience on Mind, Body, and Society. New York: The Guilford Press, 1996. Print.

Van Der Kolk, Bessel A., and Rita Fisler. "Dissociation and the Fragmentary Nature of Traumatic Memories." Journal of Traumatic Stress (1995): 505–25. Print.

Vasterling, Jennifer J., Susan P. Proctor, Paul Amoroso, Robert Kane, Timothy Heeren, and Roberta F. White. "Neuropsychological Outcomes of Army Personnel Following Deployment to the Iraq War." Journal of the American Medical Association (2006): 519–29. Print.

Vonnegut, Kurt. Slaughterhouse-Five. New York: Dell, 1969. Print.

Whitehead, Anne. *Memory: The New Critical Idiom*. New York: Routledge, 2008. Print.

Wilder, Thornton. *The Long Christmas Dinner: A Play in One Act*. New York: Samuel French, 1960. Print.

Woolf, Virginia. *To the Lighthouse*. London: Oxford, 2008. Print.

Yagoda, Ben. *Memoir: A History*. New York: Riverhead Books, 2009. Print.

Zielinski, Nancy. "Facts and Figures of PTSD in the Military." *Examiner*. http://www.examiner.com/article/facts-and-figures-of-ptsd-the-military. 2010. Web. 30 January 2013.

Zinssner, William. "Introduction." *Inventing the Truth: The Art and Craft of Memoir*. New York: Houghton Mifflin Company, 1998. 3–22. Print.